THE
GERMAN SHEPHERD DOG
'A PASSION FOR LIFE'

KATHLEEN POWELL

BULLRUSH
Publications

First published in 2011 by
Bullrush Publications

Front Cover Image – Maleeze Axel at Bellacana GSDs & Blueskyday Rudi
© Paula Randall / Pat Doughty
Back Cover Image – Zakasia Frankie at Krisannrio with friends
© Chris and Ann Ridyard
Page ii – V1(GB) Ch Nikonis Yago
© Magicon / Nikki Farley
Page iii – Gayvilles Sammo at Kazeti
© Martin Gale / Karen & Doug Amos

ISBN 978-0-9569441-0-8

Produced by
The Choir Press, Gloucester

Acknowledgements

Many voices speak out across the pages of this book. I am eternally grateful to the many people who have advised and guided me, and who have checked specific sections for omissions and inaccuracies. They have generously given their expertise, time and encouragement, and I am forever in their debt. I hope that I have reflected all comments and suggestions correctly – any errors are entirely my own, for which I can only apologise.

Animal Health Trust, Newmarket – www.aht.org.uk
Ruth Dennis MA VetMB DVR DipECVDI MRCVS – Senior clinician in diagnostic imaging
Isabelle Cattin DVM DACVIM MRCVS – Senior clinician in internal medicine
Richard Elder MVB CertSAM DACVIM MSc (Clin Onc) PhD DVM MRCVS – Senior clinician in internal medicine
Daniela Murgia DVM DipECVS MRCVS – Senior clinician in soft tissue surgery
Alberta de Stefani-Llabrés DVM PhD DipECVN MRCVS – Senior clinician in neurology/neuro-surgery

Dick White Referrals, Suffolk – www.dickwhitereferrals.com
Professor Dick White BVetMed PhD DSAS DVR FRCVS

Centre for Artificial Insemination and Embryo Transfer. University of Veterinary Medicine, Vienna – www.vetmeduni.ac.at
A.Prof. Dr. Sabine Schäfer-Soni DVM DipECAR

Crown Pet Foods Ltd – www.crownpetfoods.co.uk
Dr Pauline Devlin. Director of scientific communications and external affairs

Four Seasons Holistic Veterinary Care, Ninfield, East Sussex – www.holisticvetsussex.co.uk
V.L. Payne BVetMed MRCVS

The Byre Veterinary Centre, Peterborough – www.byrevets.co.uk
A.R. Gillespie BSc BVM&S MRCVS – Practice Manager

Professor W. Phillip T. James CBE, FRSE, MD, DSc Hon – Professor of Nutrition, London School of Hygiene and Tropical Medicine; President, International Association for the Study of Obesity (IASO)
Laura J Sanborn MS – Rutgers University, New Jersey. www.rutgers.edu
Gwen Bailey BSc (Hons) – Behaviourist and author. www.dogbehaviour.com

Alison Bush BSc (Hons) – Behaviourist. www.happierhoundsdogtraining.com

Pat Sears – APDT accredited / BIPDT advanced trainer

Mischa McDonald-Lynch DVM – PennHIP Research Fellow, Veterinary School of the University of Pennsylvania, Philadelphia.

Nikki Morgan RVN MBVNA – Veterinary Support Officer, Intervet / Schering Plough Animal Health, Milton Keynes, UK

Chris Hazell (archive photos and material)

Dan White – Product Manager, Bayer Animal Health

Matthew Bottomley – Breeding Centre Manager, Guide Dogs for the Blind Association

Nikki Farley – Nikonis German Shepherds

PC Andy Brumby – Home Office Approved Police Dog Trainer / PC Geoff Powell / PC Adrian Sheargold / PO Tyler Edgecombe

Angeline McCarthy and James Symington – The Team Trakr Foundation

Ciara Farrell and Debbie Deuchar – The Kennel Club of Great Britain / Bob Burns – The American Kennel Club

June Bass – British Agility Association / Ron Harris – Schutzhund Village

Heather Smith – United States Dog Agility Association / Becky Woodruff – North American Dog Agility Association

Gail Gwesyn-Pryce BIPDT / APDT accredited trainer

Stef Watts BSc (Hons) www.your4legs.co.uk

Roxanne Brown – www.animalholistichealer.co.uk

Fiona Campbell BSc (Hons) Head Nutritionist, Burns Petfoods / David Hussey – Herbal Manager, Dodson and Horrell / Dena Plaice BSc (Hons) – www.kinesiologybydenaplaice.co.uk

Geoff Johnson VetMB MA MRCVS VetMFHom RSHom PCH – www.vethomeopath.co.uk

Tomlinsons Hydrotherapy – www.tomlinsonskennels.com

Maria Day RVN MBVNA – '63 days' – www.63days.co.uk

Keith O'Shea – 'Fitnfertile'

Joanne Chanyi – Hoofprint GSDs

Richard James – GSDL, WDG and SV approved judge

Jillie Wheeler

With thanks to the following for kind permission to use their work / website as a source:

Dr M.B. Willis, *The German Shepherd Dog – A Genetic History of the Breed*, H.F. & G. Witherby Ltd.

Brian H. Wootton, *The German Shepherd Dog*, Howell Book House Inc.

Ringpress Publications, *The Ultimate German Shepherd Dog*, Sheila Rankin, editor

Mike Guilliard MA VetMB CertSAO MRCVS, 'Hip dysplasia breeding schemes and PennHIP' – www.mikeguilliard.co.uk

Laura J Sanborn MS, 'Long-Term Health Risks and Benefits Associated With Spay/Neuter in Dogs'

Fiona Campbell Bsc (Hons), 'Dietary Concerns in the German Shepherd Dog'

The Kennel Club – www.thekennelclub.org.uk

The American Kennel Club – www.akc.org

PennHIP. Veterinary School of the University of Pennsylvania – www.pennhip.org

North American Dog Agility Council – www.nadac.com

British Agility Association – www.baa.uk.net

United States Dog Agility Association – www.usdaa.com

Fédération Cynologique Internationale – www.fci.be

Orthopedic Foundation for Animals – www.offa.org

Francie Stull – www.animalstamps.com

Artwork:

Julie Rhodes – www.julieandpatrhodes.co.uk   xi Police Dog 'Oscar' / 105 Police Dog 'Frank' / 261 Police Dog 'Magnum'

Alison Ingram – www.alisoningram.co.uk   47 'Dax'

Robert Shirt – www.portraitsinpencilbybobby.com   81 'Nikonis Quincie' / 205 'Shoula'

E.C. Watson 145 'George'

Photograph Copyright: Photograph / Owner

Amanda Winborne: 85a

Anna Bryce: 215/216

Angela Garrick: 104

Animal Health Trust, Newmarket: 248a/249/251/253/257

Bayer Animal Health: 154-158

Cheshire Canine Hydrotherapy Centre: 192

Chris Maskell: 57b/198

Cindy Noland/Ron Harris: 4

Chris Ridyard/Ann Ridyard: x/65/139/150/187/189/214/Rear Cover

Chris Ridyard/Gemma & Matty Sheldon: 2

Chris Ridyard/Jeanette Newton: 93

D.A.Degener DVM DAVCS: 199

Dodson and Horrell: 190 191

Emma Jeffery/Martin Gale: 40

Emma Jeffery/Phillipa Tuck: 5/56/61/82/83/87/89/144/145/146/148/149/168/176/180/185/209/233/239/242/248b

Emma Jeffery/Nikki Farley: 43/51a& b/54/56b/67a/70/97/103/112/117/123/134/200/234

Emma Jeffery/Sue Ketland: 118/120/121

Esther Chai; 64/122/130/131/188

Fardogart/David Payne: 211

Fardogart/Nikki Farley: 30/34/159

Fardogart/Jeanette Kirby: 60b

Francie Stull: 3a, b& c

Gavin and Val Thompson: 50a/106/126/132/137/237b

Geoff Powell: 11a,b&c/109/269/274

Gramat Police kennels: 270

Guide Dogs for the Blind Association: 14/15

James Lloyd/Claire Townsend: 124

Jayne Murphy: 92

Jeanette Kirby: 60a

Jillie Wheeler: 267
Julie Pett: 259
June Boorman: 57c
Karen and Doug Amos: 37
Karen Park: 107
Kate Hearne: 46
Kate Powell: 52/55/57a/98/113a/141/165/170/202/207/227/237a/272/279
Lesley Steans: 100/247
Linda Barclay: 59
Magicon/Nikki Farley: ii
Magicon/Wendy Stephens: 45
Martin Gale/Karen & Doug Amos: iii
Michelle Ansaroglu: 85b/91/113b/143/167/181
Nikki Farley: 39/72/159/186/206a&b
Paul Cassidy: 219
Paula Randall/Pat Doughty: Front Cover
Paula Randall/Pat Doughty /Sue and Olivia Atlas: 275
Paula Randall/Ann Ridyard: 88
P.C. Adrian Sheargold: 262
P.C. Andy Dean: 6
PennHIP: 55 a, b& c
Ray Bradshaw: 174
Rhian Stanley: 79
Richard Brown: 50/73/74/76/95
Ron Harris: 129
Sarah Richardson: 67b/71/84a&b/115/185/166
St Louis Police K9 Department: 8/9/13
Sue Williams: 58/162
Tarah and Ian Sullivan: 18
TeamTrakr Foundation: 264/265
The Ministry of Defence: 17
The Peterborough Evening Telegraph/P.C. Geoff Powell: 268
Tim Rose – Dog's Today Magazine/Jillie Wheeler: 266
T.J.Dunn DVM: 194
Urma/Sharon & David Bowen: 28
Vetmeduni: 230

This book would not have been possible without friends and family who have read (and re-read!) the sections as they have progressed, and who have encouraged me along the way.

Special thanks go to Emma Jeffery, Field Officer at Wood Green Animal Shelter, Huntingdon, who has worked tirelessly to collate photographs.

And last, but not least, can I express my gratitude to everyone at The Choir Press. Your support, guidance and attention to detail have enabled a dream to become a reality.

Contents

Part One

The German Shepherd Dog

• Introducing the German Shepherd • Versatile Beyond Compare •
• The Origins of the Breed • Breed Standards •

Introducing the German Shepherd

The well-bred and thoughtfully reared German Shepherd is a dog to rival all others. Visually, he is a picture of power and grace. Mentally, he harnesses extraordinary intelligence with a deep sense of loyalty. The Shepherd is a superb family companion, and his desire to connect with his owner is legendary and undisputable. He truly is the ultimate embodiment of the term 'man's best friend'.

The Shepherd is noble and undeniably handsome to behold, but he is far more than merely a striking and trustworthy companion. His capacity to learn, to think for himself, and to remain committed to the task in hand, has earned him an unrivalled reputation amongst emergency service workers worldwide. He is a tracker, a sentry, and a defender of the peace. He can be a team player, yet he also possesses the capacity to work unaided. He becomes the eyes and ears of those who are vulnerable, and is a courageous protector of human lives.

Depicted in artwork across the past century, his image has been promoted on stamps and on posters, in bronze and in china. He has become a popular icon for children's toys, games and books, and his arresting looks have also earned him a place in television and film. As the heroes of their day, 'Strongheart' and 'Rin Tin Tin' courted favour amongst the public from the 1920s until well after the Second World War. But there have since been many other stars of television and the silver screen: 'London', the elusive star of *The Littlest Hobo*, captured our hearts as he solved the problems of people he encountered on his travels. 'Rebel', the Shepherd depicted in *Champion the Wonder Horse,* had his devoted followers, and more recently, 'Jerry Lee' blazed a trail as a rebellious police dog in the movie *K9*.

Bulgaria

Karakalpakia

Monaco

Rin Tin Tin in particular earned the Shepherd huge popularity. However, at times this came at a price, resulting in issues for the breed. Romantic notions of owning a dog with 'epic qualities' contributed to high demand for puppies, prompting unscrupulous breeders to flood the market. Many people bought their Shepherd puppies without fully appreciating the level of commitment required to train their acquisition and the breed's reputation suffered as a result. When his intelligence is *correctly* channelled, the German Shepherd is a phenomenal breed to be involved with. He loves to be active and he excels at all canine sports: supremely represented within Schutzhund (p. 128) and working trials, he also presents a serious challenge to other breeds within obedience, agility and heelwork to music competitions. He is committed, enthusiastic, and eager to please. His capacity for being consistent and accurate makes him a dog to respect within *all* competitive sports.

The Shepherd can also be a wonderful family member. When correctly socialised, he is at ease with the youngest of children and the smallest of family pets. He has an instinctive ability to sense when his strength and drive are inappropriate, and he becomes quiet and gentle in direct response. His love of people also makes him an ideal 'Pets As Therapy' (PAT) dog, and in this role he brings love and affection to the sick, the elderly and the disabled. As a guide dog for the blind and visually impaired, he brings unique and special qualities into a role which requires him to be intuitive and patient, intelligent but undemanding.

As a military dog, the Shepherd has served us across the world. Deployed as service dogs during both World Wars, the breed has also served in Northern Ireland, the Gulf, Afghanistan, Iraq, and throughout many other conflicts. The service dog in these environments is required to give his all, and frequently has to give his life. The Shepherd has been awarded medals for his part in conflict and during acts of terrorism. Following the 9/11

The Shepherd thrives on being active!
V Arnot vom Tiefen Teich. SchH3 FH1 KK1

attacks, Shepherds were one of the breeds deployed amidst chaos and danger, and this unconditional service led to honours and commendations being awarded in recognition of their innate skills and determination.

The German Shepherd remains the ultimate police dog worldwide. Although other breeds have come and gone, the breed's all-round versatility, physical presence and courage make him, quite simply, a force to be reckoned with. The police dog needs all of the attributes which the Shepherd embodies in abundance, and the breed is also notorious for the ability to turn their 'drive' on and off as the situation requires.

It is fair to say that this breed is not for the fainthearted. Nor is he for those who would want him as a status symbol. The Shepherd has an unrivalled sophistication in terms of canine intellect and attitude. Weakness and inexperience in the owner are all too often exposed, because the Shepherd is highly intelligent and will rapidly become aware of handler inconsistencies. The conflict which ensues can lead to heartache, as the Shepherd responds best to boundaries and positive training methods. Without these he can become confused and unbalanced.

So, if you are at the beginning of a quest to find out if this is the right breed for you and your family, please take heed of the fact that the German Shepherd has the capacity to become the very best dog you will ever own, but he will not fulfil this potential if you fail him in his early months. A good breeder will have already set the stage for your puppy to become your greatest companion, but everything from this point forward is in your hands. A Shepherd puppy will never enter your world with a desire to ruin your every waking moment. He will however, have a powerful need to find his niche and purpose. If you are ready to harness this deep-seated desire to belong and to please, he will repay you a thousand fold in ways you have yet to imagine, for the well-trained, much-loved German Shepherd is extraordinary beyond all words.

Versatile Beyond Compare

The German Shepherd is unique. No other breed is utilised so broadly, or demonstrates such a broad spectrum of qualities. The two roles which are perhaps best placed to illustrate this adaptability are those of police and guide dog. This chapter aims to show that the requirements are poles apart, and yet this wonderful breed can excel at both. However, the Shepherd should never fall foul of stereotypes, because he is innately versatile. There are countless varied and complex duties that Shepherds perform on a daily basis, in service to mankind, and we are indebted to each and every one of them.

THE POLICE DOG

Modern-day police dogs are a far cry from the first dogs that accompanied officers on the beat in the late 1800s. Both the dogs and the tasks themselves have changed immeasurably over the past century and a quarter. From a haphazard and undefined concept, the professional role of the police dog and handler has evolved as a result of research into training

The police dog – just one of many roles that the Shepherd performs

methods and into breed capabilities. Dogs are now routinely bred specifically for this work, and the abilities of the fully trained police dog command a deep sense of respect. The position of police dog handler is highly sought after, and invariably becomes a job for life.

In Britain during the latter part of the 19th century, it was common for police officers to take their pet dogs to work. During this time, 'Topper' the fox terrier frequently went on patrol with officers from Hyde Park police station and in 1888, the 'Jack the Ripper' case witnessed the introduction of bloodhounds into British policing, although this was without notable success.

During the early 1900s Metropolitan police officers gained authorisation to take their dogs on patrol and this incorporated a wide range of breeds patrolling the streets with their masters. The tasks required of the police dog were unspecified. There was no formal training available, and no individual breed stood out at this time as being particularly suited to the task, other than the bloodhound whose suitability as a tracking dog was well known. In his book *War, Police and Watch Dogs*, Major E.H. Richardson, supplier of dogs to the British police, wrote that in Germany, criminal tracking by dogs was more commonly resorted to than in France and Belgium in the early 1900s, and that *'many of these dogs are, of course, extremely gifted: but in England there is no doubt that we stand pre-eminent, as having quite the best animal for the purpose – namely the bloodhound'.*

Elsewhere, the story was very different. In Ghent (Belgium), fully trained Belgian Shepherds, Doberman Pinschers and other breeds were already being used as guards, sentries and messengers, and the formal training of a dog which could track and detain criminals was evolving. Van Wesenmael, the Chief of Police in the town, wrote to the local mayor asking for permission for the use of dogs. He stated that *'A dog works a long time on duty cheerfully, and he is able to follow a fugitive much more rapidly than a man. The dog is equipped with qualities of scent and hearing, and can easily get into any place and examine it without his presence being suspected, and thus surprise the criminal.'* The Municipal Council agreed to his proposition and by 1910 almost 70 dogs were being used as police dogs within the town. In Germany at this time, the German Shepherd was rapidly evolving as a breed. This evolution, shaped by the formation of the SV (p. 19) and the development of working dog trials, led to the escalation of the breed as a service dog in Germany, Belgium, France and Hungary.

During the First World War, there was little interest in developing the role of the police dog in Britain, although elsewhere the German Shepherd was already being utilised. In Germany for example, a training school was established at Greenhide for dog training specifically for law enforcement. After the war, general interest by the British Home Office led to the setting up of an experimental training school for service dogs. A range of training methods were examined, but progress was still remarkably slow. In 1934 a committee was set up to examine the value of using dogs, looking at a wide variety of breeds and cross-breeds. The gradual formalising of the training process and the examination of 'all-purpose breeds' meant that the German Shepherd attracted some attention in Britain, predominantly during the 1930s, but the consensus of opinion was that a general purpose dog was not possible. This clearly was not the viewpoint held overseas.

During the Second World War, research into developing the role of the British police dog was abandoned. Following the war there was a general crime surge, and various forces began experimenting more avidly with potential dogs and training schemes. Stories had abounded from service personnel returning from the war regarding German service dogs. These were predominantly German Shepherds. The stories did not go unnoticed. In 1948 the 'Alsatian Wolf Dog' (p.29) was introduced as a British police dog, and it quickly made its mark.

By 1954 a standing committee had formed. Its aim was to co-ordinate the breeding, supply and training of potential police dogs across the UK. By 1959 the Metropolitan police had 90 dogs. Predominantly these were 'Alsatians'; however Labradors and Doberman Pinschers were also used amongst a variety of other breeds. In terms of an all-round working dog, it was rapidly acknowledged that the Shepherd had the clear edge, and to this day it reigns supreme, not only in the UK but across the world.

In the US, the development of the police dog has largely evolved from the endeavours of the St Louis Metropolitan Police Department. In 1958 they sent several officers to England to study training methods used in police dog training. They underwent instruction at Keston Training School, over a three-month period. On their return, interest in the versatility of the German Shepherd as a patrol dog widened, and a canine training facility opened for various police departments throughout the greater St Louis area and beyond. The facility is widely respected across the US, with dog and handler teams from across the country regularly attending courses.

The development of the police K9's role has expanded from patrol duties to dual-certified duties which incorporate patrol/criminal work and also one form of scent detection. All dogs undertake an annual 'proofing' given by agencies such as the North American Police Working Dog Association (NAPWDA) and dogs undergo rigorous and regular training. 'Proofing' is a term used to convey that the dog has proven himself in certain scenarios, such as canine apprehension. Trials are at local, regional and national level with dogs competing for police working dog titles including IPO (p. 128). There are thought to be around 18,000 dogs involved in police work across the United States at this time. The expansion and demand of the use of the police K9 across the United States has expanded the number of training facilities across the States. It has also increased the numbers of dealers providing dogs for the service. This increase has occurred because of the proven benefits of the working police K9, and has driven up the price of a well-trained K9.

The value of the police K9 remains high in the eyes of the police departments across the United States, and there is an ever watchful eye on correct deployment. The usage of a well-trained canine is held in check by the United States Courts, and by their review of the everyday deployments, training and certification for the disciplines they were originally trained for. Continued respect for the skills provided by the police K9 will ensure that the value of this role can remain high. This is one of the reasons that departments invariably provide a gracious amount of time to train the police service K9 and their handlers.

The German Shepherd is still the most widely utilised breed within for the role of police K9. The Malinois is growing in popularity, but most police K9s in the US are German Shepherds, increasingly from highly prized working lines brought in from Europe.

Characteristics

The police dog is required to be of sound temperament. He needs to be confident, bold and fearless, with no sign of nervousness or unreliability. He must exhibit a strong prey drive, and the ability to track. He must be intelligent and independent, but with a powerful desire to please his handler. A working dog needs to be of sound construction, in order that he can run and jump as required. He needs to be fit, healthy and strong.

In terms of other attributes required for the role, the Shepherd has it all. He appears vigilant, attentive and alert. He is resilient and agile, and he possesses an exceptional turn of speed. The German Shepherd possesses fearlessness, but retains a fundamentally suspicious nature, which means that he does not automatically want to be everyone's best friend. Such noble demeanour and strong presence make this a breed to take seriously. The Shepherd's reputation precedes him within the criminal world across the globe, and such respect is well justified.

Predominantly utilised as a 'General Purpose' dog in the UK, the breed also lends itself to specialist roles such as within the Firearms Units, where specific and comprehensive training harness the sophisticated mind and nature of the breed. Specialist roles are examined later in the chapter.

Required Tasks

The dog and handler are required to:

- provide support at firearms incidents, to provide a non-lethal option and search capacity to assist firearms officers;
- assist at possible public order incidents such as football matches and illegal raves, by being able to contain or disperse a large crowd where officers are unable to control the situation;
- support divisional officers with back-up at violent incidents, and where persons are armed with a weapon;
- assist in the search for wanted persons and missing persons;
- search for persons who have fled crime scenes;
- search for property that may have been discarded by criminals.

Training day. In pursuit of a 'suspect'

Acquisition

Many police dogs are acquired from members of the public, from private agencies, and from rescue centres, with the ideal age being around 12–18 months. This age is not exclusive however, and will depend on the timeframe of when the dog will be required: younger dogs can be run on until they are a suitable age to attend a course. Exceptional older dogs are also used, although this is less common. The working life of most police dogs ends at around 8 years of age, and the costs of training the dog are high, so in some instances age becomes prohibitive *despite* the dog's potential. Some larger forces have their own breeding programme, and successfully produce and train dogs 'in-house'. Smaller forces may not have the facilities and manpower to pursue this.

Assessment

Initial assessments of dogs will look to determine if the dog has a sound temperament, as nervous dogs will be of no use in the role whatsoever. Unpredictable traits will be viewed with negativity by the team assessing the dog. If the dog is to pass his initial assessment he will need to show clear signs of being ball or toy motivated, as possessiveness over toys forms a key foundation of training. The dog will need to show confidence in strange surroundings, and when being approached by an unknown person. A variety of scenarios will be set up to specifically examine the dog's reaction to the unexpected.

Training

In the UK the initial training course usually takes place over 13 weeks, with exceptional dogs 'passing out' (becoming licensed) earlier in some cases. Promising dogs may also be given a little longer if the need arises.

The handler is introduced to the essentials of dog care, such as grooming, feeding, cleanliness of dog and kennel, rudiments of first aid, and all aspects of policy and procedure regarding deployment of the dog. The course consists of a gradual introduction to those elements which the dog and handler are likely to face on a practical level once they complete the course. At the end of the course the dog and handler will be tested on the following exercises:

Obedience
- Heeling on and off leash
- Speak on command
- Sit/down stays
- Recall to handler

Agility
- 3ft clear jump / 9ft long jump / 6ft scale or A frame

Searching
- The dog must search in a building or in the open for a hidden (accessible or non-accessible) person. The dog must give voice on locating the person, stay with them

and make no aggressive contact. The dog must remain under the control of the handler at all times.

- The dog is taught to search for property. The dog learns to search for items bearing human scent (which are mostly articles that are alien to their surroundings) and to passively indicate the item to the handler.

Criminal work

The dog is instructed to chase and detain a running man, holding onto the sleeved arm until instructed to release by his handler. The dog is placed in a strategic position whilst the handler searches the 'criminal'. The dog and handler escort the criminal to a directed place. If the criminal attempts to attack the handler, the dog is trained to defend the handler, and detain the criminal. Police dogs are trained as 'right arm true' and throughout the basic initial course and continuation training, any protective sleeve is therefore worn on the right arm of the 'criminal', whether visible or covert.

The dog is required to perform a 'stand out'. During the pursuit of a running man, the person stops running. The dog is required not to bite, but is required to bark in a surveillance manner, preventing the person from escaping.

The dog is also trained to pursue a running man and to be recalled mid-pursuit by the handler. This is called the 'emergency recall' which simulates the dog chasing a fleeing suspect. An innocent person then gets in between the dog's chase line and the original suspect. If the handler feels that the innocent person might be in danger, he gives the recall command whereby the dog returns to the handler.

As a test of courage, the dog is required to take hold of the criminal during a stick or gun attack. The handler will instruct the criminal to drop the weapon, and once this item is recovered by the handler, he will instruct the dog to release the criminal.

Trials Day: The gun attack   The scale   Speak on command

Tracking

This forms a vital component. A dog who is proficient in all other aspects of training but which shows no desire or aptitude for tracking will ultimately be discarded from the training programme. Like all other elements, this is gradually built up during training to encourage the dog's motivation and to develop his skills. In truth, some dogs are born trackers and appear to have read the manual from day one! This kind of dog is a joy to his handler, as having confidence in the dog's capacity and desire to track is central to the partnership.

The dog will be expected to follow a trail (scent patterns) laid by a helper. The trail consists predominantly of ground disturbance but will also have some human scent left by the person laying the trail. The dog must follow this trail to its conclusion, over a variety of terrain, with various changes in direction.

Licensing / Further Training / Trials

On successful conclusion of the course, the dog and handler will be licensed as a team. They will be required to attend training days each month, in between patrol duties, and they will be re-assessed and licensed each year. Dog and handler will usually attend force trials each year. The next level is to compete in the Regional trials, with the ultimate goal being to compete in the National trials. These are also held yearly. Achieving trials titles takes immense hard work and dedication, especially given that dogs and handlers are also working on patrol throughout the year.

Additional Tasks / Specialist Roles

As mentioned, 'General Purpose' dogs are required to provide support as needed, in a wide variety of situations. Some GP dogs will also serve within a specialist role as an addition to their duties. Others will *only* perform duties as a specialist dog and are therefore not available for general patrol duties.

Riot training

This forms an additional part of the GP role. Once the dog has become fully operational he will attend training which is designed to recreate riot situations. The dogs are taught to work alongside police support units, in preparation for intense and volatile incidents and the dogs are issued with body armour and footpads for protection.

Firearms

The dogs are trained to search for and locate a suspect, and to be recalled from this person back to the handler if required to do so. In some instances the dog is also required to escort the suspect back to the firearms officers, and will have to be able to work away from the handler under his instruction. Firearms dogs have to be at ease with being physically handled by other officers. They have to accept that the handler and other officers will need to step over them, and carry them up ladders. Compliance about being handled by other officers is not for every GP dog, as there are those dogs who will only accept such personal contact from their handler.

Explosives and drugs

These are two key specialist roles, and are rarely performed by the German Shepherd. It is more common to find Labradors and Spaniels in these roles. The dogs are generally smaller than Shepherds, have a superb work rate, and can work in very confined and cramped spaces.

Explosives and drugs dogs invariably do not perform GP duties, as the constant conflict and contrast between the roles would serve to confuse the dogs. Explosives and drugs dogs are taught to recognise particular scents, and to indicate to the handler that they have made a find. With drugs dogs, this indication can be 'passive' or 'active', but where explosives are concerned, the indication is always 'passive' for obvious reasons! The dog is rewarded with a ball or toy on finding the item.

A successful narcotics seizure

Bodies

Searching for human remains presents another specialist role. The dogs are taught to search for remains, using varying stages of rotting meat and bones. This is buried for differing lengths of time, and at different depths in the ground. The whole process is highly disciplined and measured. The dog is taught to dig at the site to indicate the presence of remains, and will be rewarded for his efforts by his handler.

Retirement

The average GP dog's working life ends at about 8 years of age. The physical and mental demands made on these dogs are extremely high, and a well-earned rest awaits them. Some dogs are found homes with the public, but many dogs remain with their handler. The bond which will have developed over the years is incredibly strong, and many handlers feel unable to relinquish the care of their dog to someone else. One force in the UK (namely Cambridgeshire Constabulary) has recently initiated a 'pension' scheme for their dogs, and all retiring police dogs are now covered for life for routine vet bills and food, in direct acknowledgement of the service the dogs provide during their working life. Retirement can be a double-edged sword for some dogs. Having had such a demanding, challenging and varied life, some need to be eased into a more sedate existence … very much as we do!

THE GUIDE DOG

At the end of the First World War, the German Shepherd was utilised as a mobility dog for veterans who had been blinded during the conflicts. Although this was a less defined role than that of our modern day guide dog, it was clearly apparent that the dog was able to promote a sense of confidence and independence in their visually impaired owner. Guide dog training schools were therefore established in Germany following the war, and within a decade the United States had begun to follow suit. 'The Seeing Eye' was established in 1928 in Nashville, Tennessee, and one of the founders, Morris Frank, became America's first guide dog owner. He and his German Shepherd 'Buddy' were actually trained in Switzerland. In

Morris Frank and 'Buddy'

the UK, the first guide dogs were all handed to war veterans who had been blinded during the 1914–1918 conflicts. The dog's names were Judy, Meta and Folly and all three were German Shepherds. In 1924 the Guide Dogs for the Blind Association ('Guide Dogs') was formed. The association has grown and developed beyond all recognition over the years. Today, their volunteer numbers exceed ten thousand, and the breeding and training of the guide dog is a highly researched and professional service.

Characteristics

The guide dog needs to be of impeccable temperament. He also needs to be calm, confident, patient, biddable, reliable and responsive. The guide dog needs to be able to adapt to all manner of new situations, and to be sociable but undemanding of attention. He must be intelligent, in order to learn all that is asked of him, but must also be intuitive and able to make judgements that will benefit his owner.

The Breeds

The Labrador Retriever and the Golden Retriever have proven themselves to be well suited to the role of guide dog. However, a cross between the two breeds has also become a notable addition to breed programmes. The German Shepherd remains a popular choice of breed, valued in particular for their intuition and their ability to bond tightly with their visually impaired owner. Such sensitivity does mean that the 'fall out' is higher than in other breeds, partly because when sensitivity borders on insecurity or possessiveness, these of course are seen as negative traits. This has meant that not all guide dog organisations across the world view the German Shepherd as a 'cost-effective' breed. In recent years, the Guide Dogs for the Blind Inc, San Rafael California, has removed the Shepherd from its breeding and training programmes. In the UK, 'Guide Dogs' has a different viewpoint, driven in no small part by the fact that the Shepherd remains in demand from its clients, especially where the potential client has an active lifestyle, and a love of the breed. The Shepherd is also deeply respected for its capabilities in this role. As is the case regarding other roles that this breed performs across the world, the Shepherd offers unique qualities. In very recent times, the Shepherd has been crossed with the Golden Retriever as part of Guide Dogs' breeding programme. This is still in its formative stages but the results at this point are highly promising.

Acquisition

In the early days, potential older dogs were sourced from members of the public, and puppies were sourced from breeders across the country. Whilst this still occurs, it is now on a much a smaller scale. Guide Dogs has its own highly successful breeding programme. Brood bitches and stud dogs of all utilised breeds, are fully assessed and given necessary health checks. The majority of these dogs then go to live with members of the public (volunteers) for life. Stud dogs will be called for periodically when a suitable mate is determined for him. Brood bitches will have litters at their family home, and the puppies are reared indoors where their socialisation will begin in earnest. Guide Dogs' network of staff offer expertise, guidance and assistance during the pregnancy, throughout whelping and beyond, to ensure that the best of care and advice is always available. It is imperative that the puppies get the very best of care and social education during these impressionable first few weeks of life.

Puppy Rearing

At approximately six to seven weeks of age, the puppies will be inoculated and checked by a vet, and they are then ready to go to their new family. Guide Dogs has a vast network of volunteer puppy walkers, who are given the important task of ensuring that all puppies are widely socialised and given basic education regarding obedience and general manners. Each puppy is assessed continuously throughout the year that they are with the walker, and valuable information is fed back to the team and duly assessed. Breed traits, individual traits, and patterns of behaviour from within the litter are all processed and assessed. If a promising puppy is a little behind, extra time is given for the puppy to catch up. All puppies develop at differing rates, and breed traits may mean that a puppy might excel in one area but struggle with another. This is particularly true of the German Shepherd who may learn tasks extremely quickly but can take a little longer than other breeds to develop full stability of character.

The Shepherd's trustworthy nature makes it ideal as a guide dog

Assessment

At a little over a year of age, puppies are assessed to see which may go into the breeding programme. All others will go on to train to be a guide dog. If he is to be a guide dog, a professional Guide Dog Trainer will begin teaching him all of the skills and tasks that he will be required to perform, in order that he is able to guide a visually impaired person. This can take between three and six months depending on the individual dog's progress.

But his training does not end here. At the end of this stage of training, his education is handed over to a Guide Dog Mobility Instructor. The instructor's task is to further enhance the dog's training, to educate and enable the visually impaired owner's understanding of the dog's role and capabilities, and to correctly match dog to owner, based on a wide range of needs and qualities required.

Some of the facets which make up the matching process include the new owner's lifestyle, environment, likely workload, height, and length of stride. If the owner has a particular desire for breed this is taken into account, as will their previous experience of handling a dog.

Retirement

Throughout their lives, all dogs are assessed regularly by the Guide Dogs' teams, and most dogs will work until they are around ten years of age. It is sometimes impractical for the owner to keep the older dog whilst working with a new one, and in these instances the dog will be rehomed, either to another family member or friend, or to a fully screened member of the public. However, many retired guide dogs remain with their owner for life. Just as it is with police dogs, the owner will have developed a deep bond with the dog during their years together, and will feel unable to part with their faithful companion.

A VARIETY OF SKILLS

As a therapy dog, the German Shepherd has proven himself to be invaluable. Therapy dogs have increased in numbers across the world in recent decades, and there are numerous health benefits attributed to the comfort that they bring to people. Certainly, it is well documented that the presence of pets can bring about a reduction in stress levels and blood pressure, but they can also bring cheer and good spirits in the patient too. Therapy dogs are utilised in homes for the elderly, special needs homes and schools, hospitals and hospices and many other establishments. In the UK, dogs are registered with the organisation Pets As Therapy and are duly known as 'PAT' dogs. The German Shepherd is one of many breeds represented. This much-loved breed is known for his ability to be patient, gentle and friendly, without being demanding of attention. These are key qualities for this role. The therapy dog must be at ease with being handled, stroked and hugged by unfamiliar people, whether they are children or elderly, able-bodied or disabled. He may be faced with people who behave erratically or who are afraid, and he must be at ease with wheelchairs, walking sticks and frames. The therapy dog will encounter all manner of strange situations which he must not react to, and he must pervade a sense of calmness and confidence.

The German Shepherd has a long history as a military dog, going back to the First World War. His special characteristics make him an obvious choice for the armed services, where his extraordinary qualities are deployed with consummate skill. Military dogs need to be self-assured and extremely adaptable, especially given that they are required to deal with the demands of being posted overseas. They also have to be able to form a very close bond with their handler, but able to transfer this to another handler should the need arise. The Shepherd is used as a guard dog in a variety of ways to protect military installations. He is also utilised as a patrol and tracking dog, and his nosework skills are employed in the detection of landmines or in the

The military dog performs many important functions

search for people, explosives and weapons. The Shepherd is also used for crowd control and scouting. His courage and presence are employed for 'attack duties', whereby he is required to deal with threatening people in situations where firearms usage is inappropriate.

Another valuable role that the Shepherd performs is that of search and rescue dog. His keen ability to use his nose lends itself readily to the role, and search and rescue dogs are trained to locate missing persons following avalanches, earthquakes, flood and fire. The SAR dog is required to find lost individuals and to locate those buried alive after man-made disasters such as the 9/11 attacks. He must be able therefore to work in all conditions and terrains. The nature of this work requires mental and physical stamina and a committed, determined approach.

The Shepherd's skill and enthusiasm is harnessed in a wealth of other duties that he performs, but although his name is synonymous with being immensely adaptable, it is important to say that this has not come about simply by chance. For over a hundred years, the Shepherd has been specifically bred as a working dog, and it has long been realised that certain bloodlines lend themselves to producing dogs of excellent physical and mental prowess. The following chapters examine the development of the breed since the late 1800s, and the importance placed on the anatomical construction, stamina and mental supe-riority needed to produce such outstanding canine versatility.

The Origins of the Breed

The German Shepherd is without doubt, one of the most popular and recognisable breeds in the world. It is, however, a relatively new breed (having been developed over the past one hundred years or so), and is now a much more refined animal than the rugged German sheepdog from which the breed originated.

The Shepherd's origins should never be forgotten

Dogs have been utilised to drive and guard sheep, goats and cattle for thousands of years, and dogs that were selected had to demonstrate the correct drive and intelligence to perform their duties. A century ago, the working sheepdog in Germany had no uniformity of appearance, but in terms of their characteristics they were required to be physically tough and hardy, with excellent stamina. They were also required to be intelligent and reliable, and able to work in all conditions. Above everything, the sheepdog had to have a natural instinct and aptitude for work, and their appearance was of little relevance.

Within the confines of regional accessibility, the best dogs were bred from and this led to certain regional characteristics. The German sheepdog was therefore described as a 'type' rather than a breed. It certainly would not have been described as a 'Luxushund' (fancy dog) such as the likes of the English Rough Collie. However, largely influenced by the refining of breeds in England, interest was growing in terms of the standardisation of the German sheepdog, and the 'Phylax Society' was formed in 1892 with this aim in mind. Internal disagreements led to the society disbanding in 1894, and the conflicts are said to be largely the result of members having different visions for the breed – especially in terms of whether the dog should be bred for its appearance or its working potential.

Although the Phylax Society did not achieve their goal, they did set the seeds for future development of the breed, and one member, cavalry Captain Max von Stephanitz, was to take his vision forward within only a few years. In January 1898, von Stephanitz attended a show in Western Germany, where he noticed a medium-sized, yellow and grey wolf-like dog. The dog was of Thüringian origin (see below). He was strong and supple, with stamina, intelligence and a sound character. The dog embodied everything which von Stephanitz felt

18

that a true working dog should be, and the captain was so impressed that he purchased the dog there and then for the princely sum of 200 Marks. The dog was originally named Hektor Linksrhein, but von Stephanitz changed his name to Horand von Grafrath (Grafrath being the name of von Stephanitz' kennels).

Max von Stephanitz and his friend Arthur Meyer subsequently formed the founding club, the 'Verein für Deutsche Schäferhunde' (SV), the Society for German Shepherd Dogs, on 22 April 1899. The first German Shepherd Breed Standard was written during that summer and was published in the magazine *Hundesport* in August 1899. A stud book (*Zuchtbuch*) was established in order to record all dogs and known details on parentage. Horand von Grafrath (SZ1), bred by Herr Sparwasser, and born on 1 January 1895, was duly registered as the first ever German Shepherd Dog.

The SV rapidly became the largest and most influential breed club in the world, and it remains so to this date. Arthur Meyer became its first president, and Max von Stephanitz replaced him in 1901, remaining in post until his death on 22 April, 1936, thirty-seven years to the day since the formation of the SV. Von Stephanitz believed strongly in the promotion of the working attributes of the breed, and said that the true mark of beauty was utility. He had a clear idea about the anatomical and bio-mechanical characteristics required of the working dog. By determining those dogs which could be used to develop the breed, he and the club maintained a tight control of the breed's progression and development. Von Stephanitz' motto was 'Utility and Intelligence', and he saw beauty as a secondary consideration. He strongly believed that a dog with no working potential was worthless.

REGIONAL INFLUENCES

The crossing of various regional 'types' of German sheepdog led to the development of the German Shepherd that we know and love today. This had already taken place before the formation of the SV (for example Hektor von Schwaben SZ 13, was born in 1898), but selective breeding practices under the watchful eye of von Stephanitz and his associates began to finely hone those qualities which it was felt would further enhance the breed's working capabilities and appearance. Regional influences continued to bring many variations in type to the table, and these included large and small dogs, inconsistency of ear and tail carriage, steep shoulders and a wide diversity in temperament. Dogs from the Thüringian region of Central Germany were noted for their erect ear carriage and their capacity for endurance and stocky stature. They were small, with curled tails and wolf-grey colouration, and their coats were either short or shaggy. In Southern Germany, dogs from the Württemberg region were generally of larger stature, heavier boned and with a good gait. Their tails were carried lower, and they came in a variety of colours, although the predominance was wolf-grey. They were described as being calm and steady of character. They had either short or shaggy coats, and sometimes had poor ear carriage. Other influences included dogs from Swabia that had renowned herding abilities and the capacity to navigate complex and difficult terrain. The dogs were noted for their strength, intelligence and endurance. Wiry, course, hardy sheepdogs from Frankonia also contributed to the breeding programme.

Breeding took place at two levels, namely 'Hochzucht' which comprised the high bred lines of Horand and his descendents, and 'Gebrauchzucht', which concentrated on working lines. Later on these lines were blended to bring working and show lines together to keep the intrinsic nature of this developing breed from becoming merely a showpiece, incapable of performing a day's work. This also prevented Hochzucht breeding from becoming too inbred.

THE 'ADAM' OF THE BREED

Horand von Grafrath

Horand von Grafrath was to have a profound influence on the breed's development. Imparting quality to his own offspring in the first instance, he also became a 'blueprint' and was used as the model for the Breed Standard. He was inbred to, and this inbreeding (combined with the SV's tight selection process) contributed to the Shepherd's early development. Horand sired 53 litters with a registered progeny of 140.

Horand was by Kastor SZ 153, out of Lene Sparwasser SZ 156. Around 60–61 cm in height, he was described by von Stephanitz as being of medium strength with good bone. He was of good character, 'marvellous in his obedient faithfulness to his master'. Horand's son, Hektor von Schwaben SZ 13 was awarded the coveted title of Sieger in 1900/01. Another son, the notable working dog Peter von Pritschen SZ 148, won the title in 1902. Out of a Württemberg herding bitch (Mores Plieningen SZ 159 HGH), Hektor is said to be a better dog than either his brother or his father, and this quality was passed down to his sons Roland vom Park SZ 245 and to the litter brothers Beowulf SZ 10, and Pilot SZ 111. The latter's mother was Thekla I von der Krone, a half sister to Hektor – being herself a Horand daughter.

Beowful sired the 1905 Sieger, VA Beowulf vom Nahegau SZ 733, and was noted as an exceptional sire of females, leading to the Siegerinen for 1902–1906. The Pilot line led to Siegers for 1908 and 1910: the 1908 Sieger was a Pilot great-grandson, the grey dog Luchs vom Kalsmunt-Wetzlar SZ 3371, who was widely used. Luchs sired the 1910 Sieger Tell von der Kriminalpolizei SZ 8770.

Hektor also sired an unregistered dog, Heinz von Starkenburg, who went on to produce the highly influential Roland von Starkenburg SZ 1537. Roland was an all black dog, and he won Sieger titles in 1906 and 1907. His own son, Hettel Uckermark SZ 3897 HGH, made Sieger in 1909.

Horand's great grandson Siegfried von Jena-Paradies SZ 1339 KrH, PDH, SH was awarded the first ever performance Sieger title (Leistungssieger) in 1906.

Hektor von Schwaben

Beowulf

Pilot

Roland von Starkenberg

TITLES

As the age of industrialisation progressed, livestock was increasingly transported by road and rail, and the need for the sheepdog diminished to a notable extent. The development of the breed progressed regardless, as von Stephanitz not only promoted the breed as a first class sheepdog – his vision for the breed was far wider. He promoted the Shepherd as an all-round working dog, embracing both the breed's ability to guard and protect livestock and families, and its wider potential to perform duties for the police and armed forces.

Working titles were available from the very early days of the SV. Von Stephanitz placed great importance on evidencing these working attributes during the breed's early development. The following titles were used until the early 1920s:

- Kriegshund. War dog. (KrH)
- Sanitätshund. Red Cross dog. (SH)
- Polizeihund. Police dog. (PH) – Developed as the civilian equivalent of the service dog title PDH – Polizeidienshund
- Herdengebrauchshund. Dog in use with flocks. (HGH). This is a title still used today, and dogs with this qualification can still compete in their own classes at Sieger shows.

The first SV-Bundessieger Zuchtshau (SV Championship Breed Show or 'Sieger Show') was staged in Germany in 1899, and the first Sieger title was awarded to Jörg vd Krone. There have been Sieger and Siegerinen titles since that date, with the exception of 1938–54 inclusive and 1974–77 inclusive. These titles are as coveted today as they were a century ago. Dogs can now attain the titles at Sieger shows across the world; however the most coveted are those awarded in Germany. All adults shown have to have obtained Schutzhund titles and Körungs (Breed Surveys) in order to be able to compete. Progeny are also evaluated, as winners of the VA titles also have to show that they can transmit their qualities to their offspring. Dogs are graded as follows:

- VA. Vorzüglich Auslese. (Excellent Select – Awarded from 1938 onwards)
- V. Vorzüglich. (Excellent)
- SG. Sehr Gut. (Very Good)
- G. Gut. (Good)

'Schutzhund' (SchH/VPG) was developed to examine each dog's courage, athleticism and obedience (p. 128). Only those dogs that performed well in shows and trials were included in the breed programme, setting the stage for the ethos of the SV which remains today, in that dogs have to achieve Schutzhund titles before being permitted to breed. The Bundessieger Prüfung (working trials championship) was an innovation of the SV, and was first held in Germany at the turn of the century. Schutzhund is a breed test, and is also a popular sport worldwide. In addition to a temperament test known as the BH, there are three levels of Schutzhund titles:

- SchH 1/ VPG 1
- SchH 2/ VPG 2
- SchH 3/ VPG 3

THE BREED DEVELOPS

Germany

In early 1922, the SV produced the first breed survey (Körung), providing assessment in terms of anatomical construction and temperament. The first surveys took place with over 200 dogs from Germany, Austria and Czechoslovakia being assessed in the first three months alone.

At the time, German Shepherds were generally of rather large build, and von Stephanitz had become unhappy with the developing trend for square and oversized dogs. But things were about to change. In 1925 Klodo von Boxberg SZ 135239, a Hettel Uckermark great grandson, was awarded the Sieger title at the Frankfurt Championship show by von Stephanitz. Klodo was noticeably different than those Siegers who preceded him, and controversy arose as a result of his achievement. He was a smaller dog, lower to the ground, and longer in the body. He had a level-headed nature, and his bloodline brought about improvements in temperament, construction and working capacity. Klodo was later exported to the United States. He was a potent sire, and greatly shaped the progress of breed type in the US. But he also left a legacy which was strongly felt in Europe.

Hettel Uckermark   Klodo von Boxberg   Utz vom Haus Schütting   Odin von Stolzenfels

One of his sons, Utz vom Haus Schütting SZ 331999 (Sieger 1929), was also highly influential in terms of the development of the breed across the world. A prepotent stud, he sired around 20 American Champions and also 2 Grand Victors. Another Klodo son, Curt von Herzog Hedan SZ 348365 was also significant, and was especially notable for imparting good character, size and confirmation to his progeny. One of his own sons, the grey sable Odin von Stolzenfels, was one of the finest Shepherds of his era but sadly, his influence was scarcely felt in Britain. Odin gained the Sieger title in 1933 and was exported to Japan, becoming Japanese Sieger in 1935.

During the late 1930s and early 1940s the breed continued to evolve into a longer bodied animal than had been seen during the early 1920s, largely influenced by Klodo and his descendents. In 1938 the inclusion of the Vorzüglich Auslese (Excellent select) group, at Sieger shows, allowed for multiple winners of the VA title, with the thought in mind that this would widen the focus on bloodlines, and avoid bottlenecking on one line only.

German and American paths diverged after the war, and in Germany the breed was in a bad way. Many dogs had been killed during the conflicts; others had been abandoned. Line-breeding and in-breeding in Germany re-established the breed. VA Onyx von Forellenbach and Odin von Stolzenfels in particular brought Klodo's presence forward. But arguably the most significant dog to emerge in the latter years of the war was Lex von Pressenblut who was VA3 in 1946. A descendent of Klodo, through Curt von Herzog-Hedan, Lex played a vital role in rebuilding the breed after the ravages of the war, particularly through the famous 'R' von Osnabrücker Land litter. Three of this litter were to gain VA: 'Rolf' became the most dominant influence on type during this period.

During the late 1960s three German dogs had a huge impact on the breed, at a time when it was evolving into a refined and more uniform animal than had been seen over the previous decades. These three dogs were hailed as 'pillars of the breed'. These dogs and their bloodlines dominated breeding throughout the late 1960s and 1970s, and continue to affect breeding today. They were as follows:

Canto von der Wienerau SZ 1176588

Born in 1968, Canto was a medium-sized well-constructed dog of excellent proportions and angulations. He lacked a little masculinity in head and was slightly cow-hocked, but he was a superbly dominant sire, producing top quality sons and daughters, including six VA progeny, the French Sieger for 1974–7 and two American Champions. As well as passing on superb qualities to his progeny, he is also noted for imparting character failings and is implicated in the inheritance of haemophilia. Canto remains one of the most important sires in German Shepherd history.

VA2 Quanto von der Wienerau SZ 1133695

Born in 1967, Quanto was a noble dog with excellent proportions. He was VA in 1969-72, Italian VA 1971–2 and Italian Sieger 1972. Quanto had a masculine head, and a very good front assembly. He lacked a little in terms of length of croup and his pasterns were rather weak. He imparted good type and proportions to his progeny, and occasionally soft ears and long coats. Fears that he might pass on his weakness in his pasterns proved to be unfounded. Quanto produced hundreds of top quality, surveyed stock and 6 VAs.

VA2 Mutz von der Pelztierfarm SZ 1122617

Born in 1966, Mutz was a medium sized, strong male with a good strength of character. He had excellent movement, a firm, strong topline and a good front assembly. VA in 1970, and Italian Sieger 1970-71, he imparted good overall proportions to his progeny, good movement and tough character. His progeny also show improved upper arm and croup. He also produced certain failings such as loose elbows and colour paling. Mutz was an excellent sire for hips. He produced 7 VA progeny and also produced 2 American Champions. He also sired 92 class 1 and 73 class 2 stock.

A fourth dog, VA1 Marko vom Cellerland, born in 1968, was well known during this time, but his influence has not been felt widely as is with the other three males mentioned above. Marko was an over-medium sized dog with good proportions and excellent character. He produced very good quality progeny, evidenced through nearly 200 Class 1 surveyed dogs. He also produced 5 VA stock. However, he also produced a divergence of type, and judges at the time favoured the type produced through Canto lines. Although Marko's influence is perpetuated through daughters or granddaughters, there is sadly no male line of any importance.

| Canto v d Wienerau | Quanto v d Wienerau | Mutz v Pelztierfarm | Marko v Cellerland |

In the late 1970s the world famous bitch V Palme v Wildsteigerland SZ 1478659 (a Canto and Mutz descendent) was born. She was to be highly important to the breed's development, not particularly in the show ring, but in terms of her progeny. Two of Palme's sons (double Sieger VA1 Uran v Wildsteigerland SZ 1526684 and double Sieger VA1 Quando v Arminius SZ 1547134), and a grandson (VA6 Odin von Tannenmeise SZ 1655056), have all exerted influence on German lines to this day. Uran is cited as the greatest sire of the post-war era, and his influence on modern day breeding is immeasurable (see below).

| Palme v Wildstieger-Land | Uran v Wildstieger-Land | Quando v Arminius | Odin v Tannenmeise |

The United States

During the 1920s the demand for the breed in America reached fever pitch, and this was largely attributed to the fame of two dogs. The first was the star of silent movies, 'Strongheart', who had previously trained as a police dog in Germany. Strongheart's movies paved the way for another Shepherd who became known as 'Rin Tin Tin'. Brought back to America at the end of the Second World War, 'Rinty' had been rescued by American soldier Les Duncan, from a bunker where the puppy had been found with his mother and littermates. Sadly, Rinty was the sole survivor. Rin Tin Tin became a canine superstar, appearing in films during the 1920s and 1930s. Such was his popularity that he is credited with saving Warner Brothers from bankruptcy. The public's love for the heroic dog and his exploits led to optimistic ideas of owning such a canine hero. This catapulted the demand sky-high, a demand which could not, and would not, be met by dedicated German breeders. Many American breeders mass produced puppies for the market with some dire consequences for the breed.

Pfeffer v Bern

Odin v Busecker Schloss

Lance of Fran-Jo

Conversely, conscientious development of the breed continued in the late 1920s and early 1930s, with the importation of successful dogs from Germany, including Klodo and Utz: The Utz descendents, Pfeffer von Bern, (Sieger 1937) and his half brother Odin vom Busecker Schloss, exerted the greatest influence over the breed from the mid 1930s. Imported from Germany before the war, Pfeffer in particular dominated bloodlines during the 1940s. He had won the Sieger title in Germany in 1937, and he made Grand Victor in the US in the same year, and also in 1938. He produced over forty American champions, and dominated US bloodlines during the 1940s.

Following the war, new blood came through importation of further German lines, notably through Bernd v Kellengarten, Troll v Richterback (who made Grand Victor in 1957) and Falk von Eningsfeld ROM, SchH 3 (sire of 15 champions including the Grand Victrix, Ch Belvista's Solid Sender).

In the 1960s successes were achieved by Lance of Fran-Jo (a Troll grandson) and Yoncalla's Mike (a Bernd von Kellengarten grandson): Lance of Fran-Jo became American and Canadian Grand Victor in the late 1960s. He was a hugely popular, glamorous dog, who was widely used across the US. Important offspring include Lakesides Harrigan and Cobert's Remo of Lakeside. Lance dominated bloodlines in the US and the concentration on Lance blood was exceptional, leading to exaggerations in type seen today. Yoncalla's Mike was a potent sire and produced rich colouration, good bone and a balanced structure. Mike's son, Hollamor's Judd became Grand Victor.

A significant dog emerged in the late 1980s. Covy-Tucker Hill's Manhattan (or 'Hatter' as he was known) was a flashy, close-coupled showman, who greatly enhanced the popularity of the breed in the States at that time. He went Best in Show at Westminster in 1987 and was the first German Shepherd to be awarded the title since it was first presented in 1907. Westminster is the most prestigious all-breeds show in the US. Hatter won 201 BIS during his career, and produced many champion offspring.

The type of dog currently seen in the US clearly shows that many breeders have established their own direction in more recent years. The general preference is for a Shepherd which differs from International type, in that the dog is longer bodied, the upper arm is longer, the withers higher and the shoulder steeper. The dog is presented with the stance over-stretched, with more extreme hind leg angulation, and the head held erect.

The Shepherd continues to be hugely popular in both the US show and sports arena, and there is a growing following of breeders and owners who follow the rules of the WUSV (World Union of German Shepherd Dog Associations) and who compete for Schutzhund titles. Dogs bred solely for the sport of Schutzhund add a third dimension to the German Shepherd scene in America, with the development of a dog that is unrepresentative of either show faction within the country. These dogs have a reputation for high energy and drive, and for their speed of reaction. They are highly prized within the sport, and have also become a source for police K9s and other working dogs.

The United Kingdom

Primarily owned by the upper classes during the 1920s, the Shepherd rapidly became one of the 'top ten' breeds in the country numerically speaking. Many dogs were imported from Germany during the twenties and early thirties, frequently going on to become British champions. This progression faltered for a while during the late thirties, and came to a halt during the Second World War. However, following the war things began to change for the breed, and there was a significant surge in demand, in no small part due to the rise in fame of Rin Tin Tin.

As happened in America, poor breeding practices by those who were keen to cash in on the Shepherd's rapid rise in popularity led to the perpetuation of inferior stock. As a direct result, temperament and type became an afterthought in the hands of unscrupulous breeders. The breed became subject to reputation about poor temperament, which was enhanced after the war by the increase of the breed within the police force, armed forces and prison service. This led to opinion amongst the general public that this meant that the breed was aggressive. A crime wave following the war added to the demand for a dog which would 'protect home and property', and many dogs were purchased without an understanding of their needs. This was a difficult time for the breed.

As a contrast, conscientious breeders and owners revelled in the dog's potential for canine sports, and over time the breed's versatility became better understood. In terms of developments during this period, the breed had developed into a longer-bodied dog, which was lower to the ground than was seen in the early 1920s. Shows were not held during the war, but re-emerged in the mid 1940s. There were attempts made by certain kennels at this time to return the breed to squarer, taller dogs, but this failed and the breed remained so until the mid 1970s.

The Shepherd 'type' initially echoed that of the breed on German soil. Klodo in particular had a significant impact on the development in the British Isles. Klodo's line, through Utz, led to Ch Danko vom Menkenmoor of Harwick. A dominant sire, Danko became one of the most influential dogs in post-war Britain. Born in 1946, he was imported into the country in 1947 and collected his title two years later. He gained 10 CCs, and became the most used sire of the 1940s. He produced 14 CC winners, winning 58 CCs between them.

Klodo's importance continued through his grandson Odin von Stolzenfels, through to another very important British dog, Ch Avon Prince of Alumvale. Avon Prince was to set the prototype which characterised the breed during the 1950s and 1960s. Born in 1948, he was a long- bodied dog, with a significant length of neck which was carried erectly. He introduced a fashion for length of stifle in the show ring, and was a dominant sire for his own type, giving long bodies, steep upper arms and colour paling. Avon Prince is also considered to be a principal source of epilepsy in English bloodlines. (His great grandson, Hendrawen's Quadrille of Eveley (1964-8), also was a source for this condition.) Winner of 28 CCs, Avon Prince had 20 CC winning progeny of which 17 made champion. He continued to dominate through his descendents during the sixties and seventies, notably through the influence of his grandsons, Ch and Irish Ch Asoka Cherusker, (who won 32 CCs) and Ch Ludwig of Charavigne. Significant dogs include Ch Archer of Brinton / Ch Spartacist of Hendrawen / Ch Ramacon Swashbuckler (BIS Crufts 1971) and Ch Eclipse of Eveley.

Kennels which were influential from the 1930's onwards included Brittas, who produced many outstanding dogs including several International champions. Brittas kept away from Avon Prince, Ludwig and Danko blood and brought new blood in from Germany. Other important kennels included Kentwood whose Asoka Cherusker son, Ch Fenton of Kentwood, won BIS at Crufts in 1965. The kennels of Vikkas av Hvitsand, Southavon and Letton were all of key significance during this time.

There was an increasing bottleneck of lines going back to Avon Prince at that time, and certain breeders cast their net wider, in order to bring fresh blood into the country. The Vikkas v Hvitsand kennels, for example, imported several males including Ilk v d Eschbacher Klippen and Dux vom Braunschweiger Land. Ilk's grandson, Ch Rossfort Premonition, and the Dux great grandson Ch Delridge Erhard, typified the move towards the type of dog favoured in Germany at this time, and bloodlines were more and more frequently blended to move the breed towards the German (International) type. Ch Delridge Erhard was respected by British and foreign judges. He gained 23 CCs and sired 9 champions. He was one of the best sires of his day. Premonition took Best of Breed at Crufts in 1974, and was awarded 26 CCs whilst in Britain He was also the sire of 14 English champions. His progeny dominated during the late 1970s and 1980s, and his influence continued in New Zealand and Australia, where he gained Ch titles after he was exported in 1975.

The influence of the 'pillars of the breed' spread to Britain. In particular, during the 1980s, VA1 Uran von Wildsteigerland (son of Palme) greatly influenced breeding in the UK, just as he did abroad. Born in 1981, Uran was a beautifully constructed male of excellent character. Not only was he of excellent type, he passed this to his progeny, imparting correct proportions, balance and movement. He was not an ideal croup producer, and also produced other failings such as blues, dwarfism and narrow chests. Uran himself had the three 'pillars' within his pedigree. Sire of nearly two hundred V-rated progeny, he also sired Ch Rosehurst Chris, Ch Bedwins Pirol and Ch Exl von Batu. His grandsons Ch Moonwinds Golden Mahdi and Ch Moonwinds Golden Emir continued his influence in the UK. Palme's half brother, Ch Cito vom Königsbruch, became the most widely used male in the breed's history. Purchased by the Vornlante kennels, Cito sired no less than 17 UK champions, and he dominated the 1980s.

During this period a high demand for German bloodlines, regardless of quality, resulted in some poor stock being imported and bred from. This period was hallmarked with an increase in true 'roach' backed dogs, and a propensity for smaller, slighter dogs than was desirable. Cito brought about a consistent and improved type. His progeny exemplified the International type which was increasingly sought after.

However, not all breed clubs favoured the changes. Clear divergence of the breed came about during the 1970s, and opinion polarised during the 1980s. Changes made to the Breed Standard in the 1980s would not justify extremes of either type, yet dogs that would gain titles under either faction are clearly worlds apart. In the late 1980s a referendum was held regarding the splitting of the breed. It was rejected, and the issue has remained in the ensuing years. With the recent rejection of the Kennel Club of the term 'Alsatian' from the breed name and Standard (p. 33), the International type of German Shepherd looks set to ultimately dominate the scene in the UK in the same way that it has made its influence felt elsewhere in the world.

Across the globe, dedicated breeders strive to improve the breed and produce influential dogs which, in time, may leave their legacy upon the breed in the manner of great dogs of the past. In the UK, top winning kennels such as Gayvilles, Nikonis and Lararth have made their mark in recent years. Significant dogs include Ch Gayvilles Nilo (son of the great Ch Rosehurst Chris). Nilo is currently the breed record holder with an extraordinary 52 CCs to his name. The outstanding half-brothers Nikonis Colin and Nikonis Yago took the British Sieger and Vice Sieger respectively in Great Britain in 2008, with Yago also doing much to improve the popularity of the sable dog in the show ring. The excellent male, Ch Lararth Houdini, son of the German import Apollo vom Dakota (a descendent of Uran) and winner of 16 CCs, has also earned an exceptional reputation. Excellent dogs continue to be produced by breeders in the UK who are dedicated to improving the breed, and therefore bright stars of the future will unquestionably be produced from these shores.

Champion Lararth Houdini

OTHER SIGNIFICANT EVENTS

The breed had been given the name 'Deutsche Schäferhund' by Max von Stephanitz, and the name literally translates to 'German Shepherd Dog'. This was because of the breed's original purpose of herding and protecting sheep. This name was adopted by all other countries in the early part of the 1900s.

In the United States, the first German Shepherd was exhibited in 1906 (Mira von Offingen). Mira was a Beowulf daughter, out of a litter sister to Hektor. She made little impact on the breed. The breed was first registered in 1911, with the first registration being given to a bitch called 'Queen of Switzerland'. The German Shepherd Dog Club of America (GSDCA) was formed two years later by Benjamin Throop and Anne Tracy. In the same year, the first Championship was held. By 1914, the German army were using the Shepherd as sentinels, guard dogs, search and rescue dogs, and messengers. During the First World War, the Shepherd proved itself to be versatile and willing, and American and English soldiers returned home from the war with incredible stories about the German dogs. Following the war, the breed club became the Shepherd Dog Club of America due to anti-German sentiment. It was renamed once more in 1931.

The first German Shepherd to be exported to Britain arrived in 1908, but the Kennel Club did not accept registrations for the breed until 1919. (Prior to this, German Shepherds were registered under Foreign Sheepdogs in the UK.) In 1920 the breed gained CC status, and 308 Shepherds were registered that year. By 1926 this had risen to over eight thousand. At the end of the First World War, concerns regarding anti-German sentiment had resulted in the breed being renamed 'Alsatian Wolf Dog' by the UK Kennel Club.' Fortunately the term 'wolf dog' was removed in 1931. The breed was renamed as the 'Alsatian' and remained so until 1936, at which point the breed became known as the 'Alsatian (German Shepherd Dog).' The term originated from a region on the Western front known as Alsace-Lorraine, which is where army officers came into contact with the breed during the war. It is erroneously said that the name was derived from the fact that this is where the breed originated from.

In 1977, the Kennel Club renamed the breed 'German Shepherd Dog (Alsatian)' and it remained so until October 2010 when, finally, the term 'Alsatian' was completely removed from the Breed Standard and from the name itself. The breed is now the German Shepherd Dog. *The Deutsche Schäferhund.*

The German Shepherd Dog Breed Council of Great Britain was established in 1986, and made up of German Shepherd clubs from across the British Isles. It is an advisory body to the Kennel Club of Great Britain.

The GSD League, the UK's largest breed club, was established in 1919. It is a specialist breed club. The League is affiliated to the Kennel Club and shares the WUSV vote with BAGSD.

The British Association for German Shepherd Dogs (BAGSD) is also a specialist breed club, a member of the WUSV and is affiliated to the Kennel Club. It was established in 1933.

Breed Standards

Every dog breed has its own unique characteristics and physical qualities which make it stand apart from other breeds. Each of the recognised breeds has a 'Breed Standard,' laid down by Kennel Clubs and other governing bodies across the world, and in essence these provide a blueprint that denotes the desired qualities which make up the perfect specimen. However, Breed Standards are open to divisions in terms of the way they are interpreted by breeders and judges alike, and this leads to differing opinions within the show world and beyond.

The Breed Standard for the German Shepherd has altered little over the past one hundred years, yet despite this, the breed has undergone a gradual development in construction and in resulting movement. The Shepherd of today is eminently more 'glamorous' than dogs of yesteryear, but the breed's working ability is always at the fore, as the first Breed Standard (laid down by the SV in 1899), was drawn from an understanding and appreciation of the characteristics required of the working dog.

Time marches forwards, and as conscientious breeders strive to improve the breed with every generation, revered dogs of yesteryear would simply not be used in current day breeding programmes. The original foundations of the breed were made up of dogs that would certainly not have made Champion during the 1950s. And by the same admission, Champions of the 1950s would be overlooked by International judges today, although the influence of key dogs throughout history should *never* be underestimated.

FARDOGART FOTO

Some see 'change' in the context of absolute, inevitable and welcome progress, whilst others view certain developments with scepticism and resistance. Breed Standards are open to interpretation, therefore this issue inevitably brings staunch advocates of opposing ends of the spectrum to the table. Beauty can be argued to be in the 'eye of the beholder', but Max von Stephanitz said that the true mark of beauty was utility. Therefore the concept of 'beauty' remained a secondary consideration to the anatomical and mental characteristics which enable the breed to perform his duties. It is these characteristics which founded the breed that we know and love today.

As we have seen, the German Shepherd is

VA1 (GB) Ch Nikonis Colin
SchH3 Kkl1 Lbz

first and foremost a working dog. His physical construction and depth of character have evolved over the past one hundred years or so, but the vision which led to his existence should always be cherished. He may well have evolved from the working sheepdog in Germany, but the aim was to develop an all round, versatile breed that could excel in service to mankind. And so he became what he is today.

The Shepherd is ideally a medium-sized dog, slightly longer than he is high. (The ideal ratio is 10 : 9, ranging to 10 : 8.5 in terms of length to height at the withers.) His head is wedge-shaped with a slightly arched forehead. His eye should be warm and preferably dark, but keen of expression. The Shepherd presents as athletic and well muscled, with a double coat which provides protection against the elements. He should be agile, and alert, portraying a picture of nobility and vigilance. His construction should enable him to exhibit a far-reaching effortless gait. His ancestors needed to possess an enduring trotting gait when working, and this influence continues to this day.

Males should ideally be 62.5 cm in height, and females 57.5 cm. A deviation of 2.5 cm either way is permissible. The ideal weight for a male is between 30 and 40kg, and for the female, between 22 and 32kg. Males should be distinctly masculine in comparison to the female. In terms of character, the Shepherd should be intelligent and biddable, courageous but not aggressive. He should be level-headed and able to adapt to change. He should present as dignified, watchful and confident.

BREED SOCIETIES/STANDARDS AND SURVEYS

IN GERMANY, regulation of breeding is overseen by the SV (p. 19). Only those dogs which are deemed to be quality examples of the breed are permitted to reproduce. In order to achieve this, the dog must hold a SchH qualification, a minimum show grading of 'Good', and dog must also have an acceptable hip and elbow score. Through a process called a breed survey (Körung) an extremely detailed description of the dog's anatomy is given and the dog's temperament is assessed. The progeny of breed surveyed parents are issued with 'pink papers', denoting the quality of the parents. For a dog to gain top honours in Germany, its parents and grandparents must have passed a breed survey. The SV remains the largest and most powerful breed club worldwide. It is a single breed registry, and its pedigrees are arguably the most accurate and informative in the world. The breed itself is tightly regulated, and as a result there is a cohesive aim for the future of the breed. As mentioned, breed surveys tightly regulate the quality of dogs that are permitted to reproduce, and judging of the Shepherd is overseen by trained judges. The SV also promotes working dog activities, therefore its role is dual purpose. The SV is bound by the rules of the VDH (Verband für das Deutsche Hundewesen). This is the German 'Kennel Club' and is itself bound by the rules and regulations of a powerful organisation called the Fédération Cynologique Internationale (FCI).

The FCI is an international federation of Kennel Clubs, formed to link dog clubs from around the world together, and to provide uniformity of Breed Standards. It aims to:

encourage and promote the breeding and use of purebred dogs whose functional health and physical features meet the standard set for each respective breed and which are capable of working and accomplishing functions in accordance with the specific characteristics of the breed; to protect the use, keeping and breeding of dogs in their member countries; to support free exchange of dogs and cynological information between member countries and initiate the organisation of exhibitions and tests.

Across the world, the FCI is hugely important and influential. National clubs from most countries are members of the FCI with the exception of the UK, Canada and America. However, all three are influenced to some degree by the FCI, and their national Kennel Clubs have what is termed a 'reciprocal' relationship. All FCI member clubs are duty bound to promote those Breed Standards endorsed by the organisation, and it is the SV that writes and revises the Breed Standard used by the FCI,

The SV is also a member of the WUSV (World Union of German Shepherd Associations), which was established in the mid 1970s. This organisation aims to bring worldwide German Shepherd clubs together through a direct link with the SV. Across the world during the past four decades, the Shepherd world has gradually become more uniform in its standard requirements, due in large part to the influence of the WUSV. International experts from are brought together and this promotes greater uniformity of approach and interpretation of the Standard. The WUSV is itself, a member of the FCI, providing a further link for clubs with this influential organisation.

Importation of top quality dogs has taken place for decades, but prized bloodlines are now much more readily accessible than ever, due to the introduction of pet passports and developments in artificial insemination processes. High quality dogs of 'International type' are therefore even more readily able to influence the development of the breed worldwide.

IN THE UNITED KINGDOM there are many breed clubs and training clubs which has led to differing opinions in terms of the breed's direction since the 1970's. Certain clubs and breeders remain resistant to the influence of German bloodlines, and dogs of 'English type' are still commonplace. Otherwise referred to as the 'English Alsatian', dogs of this type are steeper in the shoulder, longer bodied, deeper chested and shorter in the foreleg than the dog recognised elsewhere across the globe. The following for this type is not insignificant,

Ch Avon Prince of Alumvale

and is likely to remain so for the foreseeable future, although the term 'Alsatian' was recently dropped from usage by the Kennel Club, and pressures to split the breed have proven unsuccessful.

The Kennel Club is a multiple breed registry, and it is not governed by FCI regulations although they have a 'reciprocal relationship'. The Kennel Club does not place restrictions on the quality or type of German Shepherd which is bred from, and there is limited regulation of breeding practices in general, although the 'assured breeders' scheme may, in time, serve to address certain practices of breeders in the UK (p. 63). By contrast, breed surveys offered by WUSV member organisations such as the GSD League of Great Britain, enable breeders to have their dogs assessed in a comprehensive manner, against the Breed Standard enabling direct comparisons with dogs worldwide.

The impact of International dogs has progressed in the UK at a significant pace. There is an ever growing appreciation for International type, and this is reflected by top-quality, highly respected dogs from the UK competing at Sieger shows both here and abroad. There is also an ever-growing appreciation of Schutzhund across the country, both in terms of a breed test and as a sport.

IN THE UNITED STATES the national Kennel Club does not put constraints on breeders, just as is the case in the UK. The German Shepherd Club of America writes and revises the Breed Standard for the AKC, and the latter is not governed by FCI regulations, although they have a 'working relationship'.

The breed has diverged away from International type, and the resulting development of the breed in the US has led to a dog that is presented as a much more upright and angulated dog. Dogs shown under AKC rulings are generally considered to be more extreme than the International type, brought about by a belief by enthusiasts that the construction of the 'American' Shepherd is better able to exhibit a powerful, flowing, enduring gait. As is the case with the 'English Alsatian', The 'American Shepherd' is met with derision by purists, who feel that this type is physically and mentally far removed from the working breed it should be. Just as is the case in the UK, there is an increasing following for International type within the United States. Clubs such as the WDA (Working Dog Association) and the USA (United

Schutzhund of America) hold Sieger shows where a more International type is exhibited and where Schutzhund titles may be obtained. The USA is a member of the WUSV, and it also promotes an SV/USA registry. The WDA is the Working Dog Association affiliated to the GSDCA (German Shepherd Dog Club of America) which in turn is a member of the WUSV.

In summary, it can be seen that from country to country that there are differences in interpretation of the Breed Standards and levels of control on the quality of dogs produced. Even within individual countries there are different 'fashions' and preferences. However, one of the founding principles which Max von

Covy-Tucker Hills Manhattan

Stephanitz and his associates deemed imperative to the development of the breed, was its potential to work. As such, the required attributes comprise the physical strength, stamina and construction which enable the dog to perform his tasks, and the mental versatility which makes his potential unique amongst the canine species. The German Shepherd that we know today evolved from foundation stock with a working heritage, and this should never be lost. In the 'fatherland' of the breed, tight regulation of all stock aims to ensure the continuation of working drive in the national breed, yet this potential is overlooked in certain other countries in terms of its relevance to the Standard. However, this balance is gradually being redressed by societies and clubs which strive tirelessly to maintain the Shepherd's heritage, as well as promoting internationally recognised examples of the breed.

THE STANDARDS

Fédération Cynologique Internationale

General appearance

The German Shepherd Dog is medium-size, slightly elongated, powerful and well-muscled, with dry bone and firm overall structure.

Important dimensional ratios

The height at the withers amounts to 60 cm to 65 cm for male dogs and 55 cm to 60 cm for female dogs. The trunk length exceeds the dimension at the height at the withers by about 10–17 %.

The show stance ('stack') for the Shepherd is highly distinctive

Character

The German Shepherd Dog must be well-balanced (with strong nerves) in terms of character, self-assured, absolutely natural and (except for a stimulated situation) good-natured as well as attentive and willing to please. He must possess instinctive behaviour, resilience and self-assurance in order to be suitable as a companion, guard, protection, service and herding dog.

Head

The head is wedge-shaped, and in proportion to the body size (length about 40% at the height at the withers), without being plump or too elongated, dry in the overall appearance and moderately broad between the ears.

Seen from the front and side, the forehead is only slightly arched and without any or with only a slightly indicated middle furrow.

The ratio from the cranial region to the facial region is 50% to 50%. The width of the cranial region more or less corresponds to the length of the cranial region. The cranial region (seen from above) tapers evenly towards the nasal bridge with gradually sloping, not sharply depicted stop in the wedge-shaped facial region (foreface) of the head. Upper and lower jaws are powerfully developed.

The nasal dorsum is straight, any dip or bulge is undesirable. The lips are taut, close well and are of dark colouring.

The nose must be black.

The teeth must be strong, healthy and complete (42 teeth according to the dental formula). The German Shepherd Dog has a scissor bite, i.e. the incisors must interlock like scissors, whereby the incisors of the upper jaw overlap those of the lower jaw. Occlusal overlay, overbite and retrusive occlusion as well as larger spaces between the teeth (gaps) are faulty. The straight dental ridge of the incisors is also faulty. The jaw bones must be strongly developed so that the teeth can be deeply embedded in the dental ridge.

The eyes are of medium size, almond-shaped, slightly slanted and not protruding. The colour of the eyes should be as dark as possible. Light, piercing eyes are undesirable since they impair the dog's impression.

Ears

The German Shepherd Dog has erect ears of medium size, which are carried upright and aligned (not drawn-in laterally); they are pointed and with the auricle facing forward.

Tipped ears and drooping ears are faulty. Ears carried rearward when moving or in relaxed position are not faulty.

Neck

The neck should be strong, well-muscled and without loose neck skin (dewlap). The angulation towards the trunk (horizontal) amounts to approx. 45%.

Body

The upper line runs from the base of the neck via the high, long withers and via the straight back towards the slightly sloping croup, without visible interruption. The back is moderately long, firm, strong and well-muscled. The loin is broad, short, strongly developed and well-muscled. The croup should be long and slightly sloping (approx 23° to the horizontal) and the upper line should merge into the base of the tail without interruption.

The chest should be moderately broad, the lower chest as long and pronounced as possible. The depth of the chest should amount to approx. 45 % to 48 % of the height at the withers.

The ribs should feature a moderate curvature; a barrel-shaped chest is just as faulty as flat ribs.

The tail extends at least to the hock, but not beyond the middle of the hind pastern. It has slightly longer hair on the underside and is carried hanging downward in a gentle curve, whereby in a state of excitement and in motion it is raised and carried higher, but not beyond the horizontal. Operative corrections are forbidden.

Limbs

Forequarters:
The forelimbs are straight when seen from all sides, and absolutely parallel when seen from the front.

Shoulder blade and upper arm are of equal length, and firmly attached to the trunk by means of powerful musculature. The angulation from shoulder blade and upper arm is ideally 90°, but generally up to 110°.

The elbows may not be turned out either while standing or moving, and also not pushed in. The forearms are straight when seen from all sides, and absolutely parallel to each other, dry and firmly muscled. The pastern has a length of approx. $^1/_3$ of the forearm, and has an angle of approx. 20° to 22° to the forearm. A slanted pastern (more than 22°) as well as a steep pastern (less than 20°) impairs the suitability for work, particularly the stamina.

The paws are rounded, well-closed and arched; the soles are hard, but not brittle. The nails are strong and of dark colour.

Hindquarters:
The position of hind legs is slightly backwards, whereby the hind limbs are parallel to each other when seen from the rear. Upper leg and lower leg are of approximately the same length and form an angle of approx. 120°; the legs are strong and well-muscled.

The hocks are strongly developed and firm; the hind pastern stands vertically under the hock.

The paws are closed, slightly arched; the pads are hard and of dark colour; the nails are strong, arched and also of dark colour.

Gait

The German Shepherd Dog is a trotter. The limbs must be coordinated in length and angulations so that the dog can shift the hindquarters towards the trunk without any essential change of the top line and can reach just as far with the forelimbs. Any tendency towards over-angulation of the hindquarters reduces the stability and the stamina, and thereby the working ability. Correct body proportions and angulations results in a gait that is far-reaching and flat over the ground which conveys the impression of effortless forward movements. The head pushed forward and the slightly raised tail result in a consistent, smooth trot showing a gently curved, uninterrupted upper line from the ear tips over the neck and back to the end of the tail.

Skin

The skin is (loosely) fitting, but without forming any folds.

Coat

Hair texture
Hair:
The German Shepherd Dog is bred in the hair varieties double coat and long and harsh outer coat – both with undercoat.

Double coat:
The guard hair should be as dense as possible, particularly harsh and close fitting: short on the head, including the inside of the ears, short on the front side of the legs, paws and toes, some-what longer and more strongly covered in hair on the neck. On the back side of the legs the hair extends to the carpal joint or the hock; it forms moderate 'trousers' on the back side of the haunches.

The long coated Shepherd is very popular

Long and harsh outer coat:
The guard hair should be long, soft and not close fitting, with tufts on the ears and legs, bushy trousers and bushy tail with downward formation of tuft. Short on the head, including the inside of the ears, on the front side of the legs, on the paws and toes, somewhat longer and more strongly covered in hair on the neck, almost forming a mane. On the back side of the legs the hair extends to the carpal joint or the hock and forms clear trousers on the back side of the haunches.

Colours

Colours are black with reddish-brown, brown and yellow to light grey markings; single-coloured black, grey with darker shading, black saddle and mask. Unobtrusive, small white marks on chest as well as very light colour on insides are permissible, but not desirable. The tip of the nose must be black in all colours. Dogs with lack of mask, light to piercing eye colour, as well as with light to whitish markings on the chest and the insides, pale nails and red tip of tail are considered to be lacking in pigmentation. The undercoat shows a light greyish tone. The colour white is not allowed.

Size/weight

Male dogs:
Height at the withers: 60 cm to 65 cm
Weight: 30 kg to 40 kg

Female dogs:
Height at the withers: 55 cm to 60 cm
Weight: 22 kg to 32 kg

Testicles

Male dogs should have two obviously normally developed testicles which are completely in the scrotum.

Faults

Any deviation from the aforementioned points should be considered as a fault whose evaluation should be in exact proportion to the degree of deviation.

Serious faults:
Deviations from the above-described breed characteristics which impair the working capability.
Faulty ears: ears set too low laterally, tipped ears, inward constricted ears, ears not firm
Considerable pigment deficiencies.
Severely impaired overall stability.

Dental faults:
All deviations from scissor bite and dental formula insofar as it does not involve eliminating faults (see the following).

Eliminating faults:
a) Dogs with weak character and weak nerves which bite
b) Dogs with proven 'severe hip dysplasia'
c) Monorchid or cryptorchid dogs as well as dogs with clearly dissimilar or atrophied testicles
d) Dogs with disfiguring ears or tail faults
e) Dogs with malformations
f) Dogs with dental faults, with lack of:
    1 premolar 3 and another tooth, or
    1 canine tooth, or
    1 premolar 4, or
    1 molar 1 or molar 2, or
    a total of 3 teeth or more
g) Dogs with jaw deficiencies:
    Overshot by 2 mm and more,
    undershot,
    level bite in the entire incisor region
h) Dogs with oversize or undersize by more than 1 cm
i) Albinism
j) White hair colour (also with dark eyes and nails)
k) Long Straight Topcoat without undercoat
l) Long-haired (long, soft guard hair without undercoat, mostly parted in the middle of the back, tufts on the ears and legs and on the tail)

Breed Standard reproduced with kind permission of the FCI.

Beautiful movement comes from correct construction

The American Kennel Club

General Appearance

The first impression of a good German Shepherd Dog is that of a strong, agile, well muscled animal, alert and full of life. It is well balanced, with harmonious development of the forequarter and hindquarter. The dog is longer than tall, deep-bodied, and presents an outline of smooth curves rather than angles. It looks substantial and not spindly, giving the impression, both at rest and in motion, of muscular fitness and nimbleness without any look of clumsiness or soft living. The ideal dog is stamped with a look of quality and nobility – difficult to define, but unmistakable when present. Secondary sex characteristics are strongly marked, and every animal gives a definite impression of masculinity or femininity, according to its sex.

Temperament

The breed has a distinct personality marked by direct and fearless, but not hostile, expression, self-confidence and a certain aloofness that does not lend itself to immediate and indiscriminate friendships. The dog must be approachable, quietly standing its ground and showing confidence and willingness to meet overtures without itself making them. It is poised, but when the occasion demands, eager and alert; both fit and willing to serve in its capacity as companion, watchdog, blind leader, herding dog, or guardian, whichever the circumstances may demand. The dog must not be timid, shrinking behind its master or handler; it should not be nervous, looking about or upward with anxious expression or showing nervous reactions, such as tucking of tail, to strange sounds or sights. Lack of confidence under any surroundings is not typical of good character. Any of the above deficiencies in character which indicate shyness must be penalized as very serious faults and any dog exhibiting pronounced indications of these must be excused from the ring. It must be possible for the judge to observe the teeth and to determine that both testicles are descended. Any dog that attempts to bite the judge must be disqualified. The ideal dog is a working animal with an incorruptible character combined with body and gait suitable for the arduous work that constitutes its primary purpose.

Size, Proportion, Substance

The desired height for males at the top of the highest point of the shoulder blade is 24 to 26 inches; and for bitches, 22 to 24 inches. The German Shepherd Dog is longer than tall, with the most desirable proportion as 10 to 8?. The length is measured from the point of the prosternum or breastbone to the rear edge of the pelvis, the ischial tuberosity. The desirable long proportion is not derived from a long back, but from overall length with relation to height, which is achieved by length of forequarter and length of withers and hindquarter, viewed from the side.

Head

The head is noble, cleanly chiseled, strong without coarseness, but above all not fine, and in proportion to the body. The head of the male is distinctly masculine, and that of the bitch distinctly feminine. The expression keen, intelligent and composed.

Eyes

Eyes of medium size, almond shaped, set a little obliquely and not protruding. The color is as dark as possible.

Ears should be erect, giving an impression of alert intelligence

Ears

The ears are moderately pointed, in proportion to the skull, open toward the front, and carried erect when at attention, the ideal carriage being one in which the center lines of the ears, viewed from the front, are parallel to each other and perpendicular to the ground. A dog with cropped or hanging ears must be disqualified.

Muzzle

Seen from the front the forehead is only moderately arched, and the skull slopes into the long, wedge-shaped muzzle without abrupt stop. The muzzle is long and strong, and its topline is parallel to the topline of the skull.

Nose

The nose is black. A dog with a nose that is not predominantly black must be disqualified.

Mouth

The lips are firmly fitted. Jaws are strongly developed. Teeth – 42 in number – 20 upper and 22 lower – are strongly developed and meet in a scissors bite in which part of the inner surface of the upper incisors meet and engage part of the outer surface of the lower incisors. An overshot jaw or a level bite is undesirable. An undershot jaw is a disqualifying fault. Complete dentition is to be preferred. Any missing teeth other than first premolars is a serious fault.

Neck, Topline, Body

The neck is strong and muscular, clean-cut and relatively long, proportionate in size to the head and without loose folds of skin. When the dog is at attention or excited, the head is raised and the neck carried high; otherwise typical carriage of the head is forward rather than up and but little higher than the top of the shoulders, particularly in motion.

Topline – The withers are higher than and sloping into the level back. The back is straight, very strongly developed without sag or roach, and relatively short.

The whole structure of the body gives an impression of depth and solidity without bulkiness.

Chest

Commencing at the prosternum, it is well filled and carried well down between the legs. It is deep and capacious, never shallow, with ample room for lungs and heart, carried well forward, with the prosternum showing ahead of the shoulder in profile.

Ribs – well sprung and long, neither barrel-shaped nor too flat, and carried down to a sternum which reaches to the elbows. Correct ribbing allows the elbows to move back freely when the dog is at a trot. Too round causes interference and throws the elbows out; too flat or short causes pinched elbows. Ribbing is carried well back so that the loin is relatively short. Abdomen – firmly held and not paunchy. The bottom line is only moderately tucked up in the loin.

Loin – Viewed from the top, broad and strong. Undue length between the last rib and the thigh, when viewed from the side, is undesirable. Croup – long and gradually sloping.

Tail – bushy, with the last vertebra extended at least to the hock joint. It is set smoothly into the croup and low rather than high. At rest, the tail hangs in a slight curve like a saber. A slight hook – sometimes carried to one side – is faulty only to the extent that it mars general appearance. When the dog is excited or in motion, the curve is accentuated and the tail raised, but it should never be curled forward beyond a vertical line. Tails too short, or with clumpy ends due to ankylosis, are serious faults. A dog with a docked tail must be disqualified.

Forequarters

The shoulder blades are long and obliquely angled, laid on flat and not placed forward. The upper arm joins the shoulder blade at about a right angle. Both the upper arm and the shoulder blade are well muscled. The forelegs, viewed from all sides, are straight and the bone oval rather than round. The pasterns are strong and springy and angulated at approximately a 25-degree angle from the vertical. Dewclaws on the forelegs may be removed, but are normally left on. The feet are short, compact with toes well arched, pads thick and firm, nails short and dark.

Hindquarters

The whole assembly of the thigh, viewed from the side, is broad, with both upper and lower thigh well muscled, forming as nearly as possible a right angle. The upper thigh bone parallels the shoulder blade while the lower thigh bone parallels the upper arm. The metatarsus (the unit between the hock joint and the foot) is short, strong and tightly articulated. The dewclaws, if any, should be removed from the hind legs. Feet as in front.

Coat

The ideal dog has a double coat of medium length. The outer coat should be as dense as possible, hair straight, harsh and lying close to the body. A slightly wavy outer coat, often of wiry texture, is permissible. The head, including the inner ear and foreface, and the legs and paws are covered with short hair, and the neck with longer and thicker hair. The rear of the forelegs and hind legs has somewhat longer hair extending to the pastern and hock, respectively. Faults in coat include soft, silky, too long outer coat, woolly, curly, and open coat.

Color

The German Shepherd Dog varies in color, and most colors are permissible. Strong rich colors are preferred. Pale, washed-out colors and blues or livers are serious faults. A white dog must be disqualified.

Gait

A German Shepherd Dog is a trotting dog, and its structure has been developed to meet the requirements of its work.

General Impression – The gait is outreaching, elastic, seemingly without effort, smooth and rhythmic, covering the maximum amount of ground with the minimum number of steps. At a walk it covers a great deal of ground, with long stride of both hind legs and forelegs. At a trot the dog covers still more ground with even longer stride, and moves powerfully but easily, with coordination and balance so that the gait appears to be the steady motion of a well-lubricated machine.

The feet travel close to the ground on both forward reach and backward push. In order to achieve ideal movement of this kind, there must be good muscular development and ligamentation. The hindquarters deliver, through the back, a powerful forward thrust which slightly lifts the whole animal and drives the body forward. Reaching far under, and passing the imprint left by the front foot, the hind foot takes hold of the ground; then hock, stifle and upper thigh come into play and sweep back, the stroke of the hind leg finishing with the foot still close to the ground in a smooth follow-through.

The overreach of the hindquarter usually necessitates one hind foot passing outside and the other hind foot passing inside the track of the forefeet, and such action is not faulty unless the locomotion is crabwise with the dog's body sideways out of the normal straight line.

Transmission – The typical smooth, flowing gait is maintained with great strength and firmness of back. The whole effort of the hindquarter is transmitted to the forequarter through the loin, back and withers. At full trot, the back must remain firm and level without sway, roll, whip or roach. Unlevel topline with withers lower than the hip is a fault. To compensate for the forward motion imparted by the hindquarters, the shoulder should open to its full extent. The forelegs should reach out close to the ground in a long stride in harmony with that of the hindquarters.

The dog does not track on widely separated parallel lines, but brings the feet inward toward the middle line of the body when trotting, in order to maintain balance. The feet track closely but do not strike or cross over. Viewed from the front, the front legs function from the shoulder joint to the pad in a straight line. Viewed from the rear, the hind legs function from the hip joint to the pad in a straight line. Faults of gait, whether from front, rear or side, are to be considered very serious faults.

Disqualifications

Cropped or hanging ears.

Dogs with noses not predominantly black.

Undershot jaw.

Docked tail.

White dogs.

Any dog that attempts to bite the judge.

Text Copyright The American Kennel Club / The German Shepherd Dog Club of America. Reproduced with their permission.

Kennel Club of Great Britain

The Kennel Club is responsible for writing and revising all UK Breed Standards, taking into consideration the viewpoints of breed councils and clubs. The Breed Standard for the German Shepherd has scarcely altered from its original version.

In October 2009 the standard was altered. The Standard now incorporates a 'fit for purpose' clause, and now reads as follows:

> *A Breed Standard is the guideline which describes the ideal characteristics, temperament and appearance of a breed and ensures that the breed is fit for function. Absolute soundness is essential. Breeders and judges should at all times be careful to avoid obvious conditions or exaggerations which would be detrimental in any way to the health, welfare or soundness of this breed. From time to time certain conditions or exaggerations may be considered to have the potential to affect dogs in some breeds adversely, and judges and breeders are requested to refer to the Kennel Club website for details of any such current issues. If a feature or quality is desirable it should only be present in the right measure.*

In October 2010 the Kennel Club finally removed the word 'Alsatian' from the breed's official name, and Standard.

General Appearance

Slightly long in comparison to height; of powerful, well muscled build with weather-resistant coat. Relation between height, length, position and structure of fore and hindquarters (angulation) producing far-reaching, enduring gait. Clear definition of masculinity and femin-inity essential, and working ability never sacrificed for mere beauty.

Characteristics

Versatile working dog, balanced and free from exaggeration. Attentive, alert, resilient and tireless with keen scenting ability.

The male is larger and more heavily built than the female

Temperament

Steady of nerve, loyal, self-assured, courageous and tractable. Never nervous, over-aggressive or shy.

Head and Skull

Proportionate in size to body, never coarse, too fine or long. Clean cut; fairly broad between ears. Forehead slightly domed; little or no trace of central furrow. Cheeks forming softly rounded curve, never protruding. Skull from ears to bridge of nose tapering gradually and evenly, blending without too pronounced stop into wedge-shaped powerful muzzle. Skull approximately 50 per cent of overall length of head. Width of skull corresponding approximately to length, in males slightly greater, in females slightly less. Muzzle strong, lips firm, clean and closing tightly. Top of muzzle straight, almost parallel to forehead. Short, blunt, weak, pointed, overlong muzzle undesirable.

Eyes

Medium-sized, almond-shaped, never protruding. Dark brown preferred, lighter shade permissible, provided expression good and general harmony of head not destroyed. Expression lively, intelligent and self-assured.

Ears

Medium-sized, firm in texture, broad at base, set high, carried erect, almost parallel, never pulled inwards or tipped, tapering to a point, open at front. Never hanging. Folding back during movement permissible.

Mouth

Jaws strongly developed. With a perfect, regular and complete scissor bite, i.e. upper teeth closely overlapping lower teeth and set square to the jaws. Teeth healthy and strong. Full dentition desirable.

Neck

Fairly long, strong, with well developed muscles, free from throatiness. Carried at 45 degrees angle to horizontal, raised when excited, lowered at fast trot.

Forequarters

Shoulder blade and upper arms are equal in length, well muscled and firmly attached to the body. Shoulder blades set obliquely (approximately 45 degrees) laid flat to body. Upper arm strong, well muscled, joining shoulder blade at approximately 90 degrees. Seen from all sides, the forearms are straight and, seen from the front, absolutely parallel. Bone oval rather than round. The elbows must turn neither in nor out while standing or moving. Pasterns firm, supple, with a slight forward slope. An over long, weak pastern, which would affect a dog's working ability is to be heavily penalised. Length of foreleg slightly exceeds the depth of chest.

Body

Length measured from point of shoulder to point of buttock, slightly exceeding height at withers. Correct ratio 10 to 9 or 8 and a half. Undersized dogs, stunted growth, high-legged dogs, those too heavy or too light in build, over-loaded fronts, too short overall appearance, any feature detracting from reach or endurance of gait, undesirable. Chest deep (45–48 per cent) of height at shoulder, not too broad, brisket long, well developed. Ribs well formed and long; neither barrel-

V1 Nick vom Moorbeck SchH3 Kkl1

shaped nor too flat; allowing free movement of elbows when gaiting. Relatively short loin. Belly firm, only slightly drawn up. Back between withers and croup, straight, strongly developed, not too long. Overall length achieved by correct angle of well laid shoulders, correct length of croup and hindquarters. The topline runs without any visible break from the set on of the neck, over the well defined withers, falling away slightly in a straight line to the gently sloping croup. The back is firm, strong and well muscled. Loin broad, strong, well muscled. Weak, soft and roach backs undesirable and should be heavily penalised. Croup slightly sloping and without any break in the topline, merges imperceptibly with the set on of the tail. Short, steep or flat croups highly undesirable.

Hindquarters

Overall strong, broad and well muscled, enabling effortless forward propulsion. Upper and lower thigh are approximately of equal length. Hind angulation sufficient if imaginary line dropped from point of buttocks cuts through lower thigh just in front of hock, continuing down slightly in front of hindfeet. Angulations corresponding approximately with front angulation, without over-angulation. Seen from rear, the hind legs are straight and parallel to each other. The hocks are strong and firm. The rear pasterns are vertical. Any tendency towards over-angulation of hindquarters, weak hocks, cow hocks or sickle hooks, is to be heavily penalised as this reduces firmness and endurance in movement.

Feet

Rounded toes well closed and arched. Pads well cushioned and durable. Nails short, strong and dark in colour.

Tail

Bushy-haired, reaches at least to hock – ideal length reaching to middle of metatarsus. At rest tail hangs in slight sabre-like curve; when moving raised and curve increased, ideally never above level of back. Short, rolled, curled, generally carried badly or stumpy from birth, undesirable.

Gait/Movement

Sequence of step follows diagonal pattern, moving foreleg and opposite hindleg forward simultaneously; hindfoot thrust forward to midpoint of body and having equally long reach with forefeet without any noticeable change in backline. Absolute soundness of movement essential.

Coat

Outer coat consisting of straight, hard, close-lying hair as dense as possible; thick undercoat. Hair on head, ears, front of legs, paws and toes short; on back, longer and thicker; in some males forming slight ruff. Hair longer on back of legs as far down as pasterns and stifles and forming fairly thick trousers on hindquarters. No hard and fast rule for length of hair; mole-type coats undesirable.

Colour

Black or black saddle with tan, or gold to light grey markings. All black, all grey, with lighter or brown markings referred to as Sables. Nose black. Light markings on chest or very pale colour on inside of legs permissible but undesirable, as are whitish nails, red-tipped tails or wishy-washy faded colours defined as lacking in pigmentation.

Blues, livers, albinos, whites (i.e. almost pure white dogs with black noses) and near whites highly undesirable. Undercoat, except in all black dogs, usually grey or fawn. Colour in itself is of secondary importance having no effect on character or fitness for work. Final colour of a young dog only ascertained when outer coat has developed.

Size

Ideal height (from withers and just touching elbows): dogs: 63 cms (25 ins); bitches: 58 cms (23 ins). 2.5 cms (1 in) either above or below ideal permissible.

Faults

Any departure from the foregoing points should be considered a fault and the seriousness with which the fault should be regarded should be in exact proportion to its degree and its effect upon the health and welfare of the dog.

Note: Male animals should have two apparently normal testicles fully descended into the scrotum.

Part Two

The Journey Begins

• Important Choices • The Search for Your Puppy • Preparations •
• Collecting Your Puppy •

Important Choices

If you are beginning to think about sharing your life with a canine companion, then there are inevitably questions you will want answered. The decision you are about to make will hopefully bring great joy into your life, but dog ownership is likely to require commitment from you for over a decade and should not be entered into lightly. Owning a dog can bring great pleasure and benefits to all your family, but if it is not fully considered problems and heartache may well follow, so here are some of the issues that you might like to consider before bringing your new family member home.

DO YOU REALLY WANT A DOG?

There is no doubt that owning a dog will change your life. In the right circumstances this will be a change for the better, as living with a dog brings a wide range of benefits and pleasures to most owners. But dogs are demanding of time, space and commitment and they love to live to routines. If you have a busy lifestyle you will firstly need to ask yourself how much time you and your family are able to allocate to the care of a dog or puppy. Regardless of breed, all puppies are very time consuming and will need great patience and understanding. Toilet training, socialisation, training classes and daily exercise will each make demands of you in the months and years to come. If you choose to take on an adult dog rather than buy a puppy, you may find that relocating him from his old home is stressful, and he might require a lot of support before he is able to settle into his new life.

It is important to be realistic about your own attitudes to daily life. If you are very house-proud, for example, think about how you will feel if your new dog causes damage. Your house is likely to be coated with fine dog hair, muddy paw prints and half-chewed dog toys! Puppies are likely to have 'accidents' on your carpet in the early days, and you will possibly need space for a puppy crate in your home for several months until your new acquisition is fully settled. Most puppies are likely to chew an item of value at some stage in their development, and adult dogs may have already developed a destructive tendency in response to boredom or stress. If your dog becomes overly vocal, how will you or your neighbours cope with this?

Inevitable changes in routine will have to take place, in order to accommodate the needs of the new arrival. Are you and your family prepared for these changes? Initially, someone will need to be home for the vast majority of the day, and even when your dog is fully grown, it is unfair to leave him home alone for long periods of time. If you travel a great deal, will you be able to make adjustments to this part of your life? If you cannot, please think carefully about the implications for your new family member. If he will have to regularly attend boarding kennels while you are away, this will have a significant impact on him emotionally.

On a financial level, the initial outlay may seem reasonable. But as a lifetime's commitment it may run into many thousands of pounds. Some of the basic costs to be expected include:

- Vaccinations and yearly boosters
- Good quality nutrition
- Insurance costs
- Crates for travelling and sleeping
- Veterinary bills
- Boarding kennels costs when you are on holiday

You might also need to adapt your home and garden to accommodate your dog as he grows. You will need a secure perimeter fence at the very least, and you may opt for a purpose built day-run too. Will you need to change your vehicle? All dogs love an active and varied lifestyle, and you may find that an estate car is the best way to get him to his favourite haunts!

And finally, will you still be there for him in his twilight years, when specialised diets and high veterinary bills are not uncommon? Most breeds average a lifespan of some 12 years, and many dogs need significant veterinary support through their old age.

If you are certain that you are ready to welcome a dog into your life, but are unsure which breed is right for you, then a great way to familiarise yourself with different breeds is to attend local dog shows. These can be readily sourced through dog magazines and through local papers. You might like to also pay a visit to 'Discover Dogs' which is a large exhibition staged by the Kennel Club each year in the UK. A huge variety of breeds will be there for you to see, and you will have the opportunity to talk to owners about the realities of living alongside these dogs, as they all have their idiosyncrasies!

The American Kennel Club holds a similar exhibition every year called 'Meet the Breeds'. Attendees can interact with a vast number of dog (and cat) breeds, at this show, and can learn about their history, attributes and needs.

LIVING WITH A GERMAN SHEPHERD

The Shepherd is a handsome, powerful and intelligent animal. The breed has been carefully developed for over a hundred years to harness keen senses, high drive and superior intellect. They do not respond well to weak handling, nor to heavy-handed approaches. Weak handling may result in a dog that becomes too arrogant. Overbearing approaches may make the dog resentful, nervous and possibly aggressive. Either approach will result in the dog viewing you with suspicion. The Shepherd, like all dogs, responds well to a calm, confident manner, with clear boundaries and expectations. He responds well to praise, and to firm but fair handling. He is a sophisticated canine, able to process information quickly, and his assessment of you will be constantly under scrutiny. You will need to be fully committed to him in terms of training and exercise, and be even-tempered in your approach to moulding him day after day.

The adolescent Shepherd is likely to assert his independence, and can quickly become ill-mannered. Are you committed to ensuring that he becomes a good member of society? The Shepherd suffered a poor reputation in terms of temperament for many years, and so it is imperative that you help him to become a good citizen. On this note, it pays to

A trio of obedient Shepherds

remember that there is still a level of ingrained fear and intolerance to the breed, so you may find that his keenness to make friends in the park can be met with negativity. Are you prepared for this?

Remember that intolerance to the Shepherd can sometimes be justified. He has a strong personality, and may be reluctant to walk away from confrontation offered up by another dog in the park. The Shepherd has an independent nature and is not given to being overly gregarious, but good socialising with multiple breeds as a puppy will help this enormously. Encourage him to form good relationships with other dogs, and this will pay dividends throughout his life. It will also ensure that he becomes a great ambassador for the breed.

German Shepherds require company and stimulation. They do not fare well (especially in their formative years) if left unattended for long periods of time and they can easily become bored, destructive and vocal. Be sure that your life is compatible with the requirements of the breed, as training and socialisation are vital to his emotional well-being.

The German Shepherd is known to suffer from a condition known as hip dysplasia, and can also suffer from elbow dysplasia. During the first 12 months it is especially important that you are committed to short but regular walks with your growing adolescent. It will take time for vital muscle to form around his hip and elbow joints and therefore it is not advisable to have him jumping, twisting or charging around. This is *not* to suggest that puppy cannot enjoy gentle free exercise as they begin to develop, but a

This breed can be destructive if deprived of company and stimulation

considered approach to exercise is vital for the growing Shepherd, and may not appeal to every owner (p. 102).

You may have aspirations to do agility or obedience trialling? The Shepherd excels at all canine sports but if you hope to become a serious competitor, be aware that most breeds are invariably pipped to the post by the Border Collie (which possesses a phenomenal speed of reaction), so be aware of the Shepherd's limitations! Working trials and Schutzhund will see the Shepherd excelling at a far higher and more consistent level as these sports were created with the breed in mind. Go and visit local training clubs and organisations where you are sure to find enthusiasts who can advise and encourage you. You will also get an opportunity to meet dogs at various stages of development and training.

Once you have decided that a German Shepherd is for you (and vice versa!) take the time to read widely about the breed. There is a wealth of literature available, which includes specialist showing and training books.

 However tempting it might be, it is inadvisable to see litters at this stage. In these early days of decision making, it is far wiser to spend time with adult dogs. Puppies of all breeds are adorable at six to eight weeks, and the last thing you would want to do is impulse buy.

PUP/ADULT/RESCUE?

Puppies

It is easy to see why so many people decide to buy a puppy. Rearing a dog from eight weeks to mature adult can be hugely rewarding. There will be undeniable frustrations along the way and you may well become stressed if he becomes a persistent chewer, or if house training seems an impossible hurdle to overcome. But there is huge satisfaction to be derived at every stage as your puppy learns what you are asking of him.

With their unruly ears, huge feet, and joy of life, German Shepherd puppies are a sight to behold. With personality to burn, and keenness to integrate into your family, they can be hugely responsive and rewarding. In sensible hands, the Shepherd pup becomes a respectful and integral part of the household. His keenness to please and to follow your guidance gives you the opportunity to mould your pup into a truly wonderful dog. Training your

The Shepherd puppy is inquisitive and full of mischief!

Shepherd puppy is invariably a joy. Owning an adult dog that you have educated since eight weeks of age should be a matter of huge pride.

It is has already been stated that in inexperienced or inconsistent hands, the growing Shepherd can easily become bored, confused and destructive. If raised with negative approaches this sensitive breed can become belligerent and unwilling. Shepherd adolescents are seen all too often in free ad papers, and in rescue homes. As they grow rapidly in the early months, the once-appealing puppy becomes a large, and increasingly challenging dog. Many fall by the wayside, needing a new home and often total re-education. This is a situation which could largely be avoided if all new owners attended puppy classes.

Novice owners really *do* need to learn how to 'think dog', in order to get the best from their puppy, and thankfully there is now much on the market in terms of books and DVDs which can further support the advice given at training classes.

 If you are a first-time buyer, do not think that the German Shepherd is beyond your grasp, but do ensure you get plenty of good advice at every stage of training.

Taking on an older dog

If the long hours of puppy education, toilet training and sleepless nights are not for you, then the acquisition of an older dog might be a better option. There are advantages in taking on an older dog but there are also potential difficulties. If you are responding to an advert for an adolescent or adult, always try to find out why he is being rehomed. It is possible to find a healthy, well-adjusted adult dog for sale, however it is also common to find that there is a control or destructiveness issue which has led the owner to part with their dog.

Time brings wisdom and maturity

It is wise to ask to see the dog in as many different environments as possible. For example, you might like to see how he travels in the car. Is he happy to meet new people (especially children) out in the park, and how does he react to other dogs? Seeing him in a variety of situations will give you some idea of how well balanced the dog is, and if there are any potential problems. It may also be possible to take the dog on a home visit to see if you all settle, as a loving owner will only want the best for their canine friend, and may well agree to a trial period.

It is also be a good idea to ask if your local training club would let you take him to a class for an initial assessment. If he has started off with good education and training he may be a joy to take on. If not, he may take a substantial amount of re-training regarding manners at home and in the public eye, and you will want to be prepared for this.

If possible, obtain details on his veterinary history, to be certain that there is not a costly underlying reason for his owners parting with him. You might be happy to take this on board, but it is always best to know what this could entail.

You will have already considered that if the dog is well into maturity, you may have him for a greatly reduced period of time. However, offering a home to a senior dog is both valuable and rewarding. There is always a need for people to take on an elderly dog that is homeless through no fault of his own. A senior Shepherd dog will no doubt bring wisdom and gentle companionship into your lives.

Rescue

There are many reasons why a dog ends up in rescue. Marriage breakdowns, bereavement, and all manner of life changes can lead to dogs needing a new home. Sadly, the Shepherd is highly represented throughout rescue centres, and in many cases this is due to a poor start in life. The Shepherd puppy needs thorough socialising and training, and where this is not taken on board this breed quickly develops behavioural issues.

You may feel ethically that you wish to offer an unwanted dog a new start in life, rather than buying a puppy. This is admirable to say the least. But for your peace of mind, and that of the dog, it is important to know as much as possible about the dog, his background, and also about the rescue centre itself. There are centres of absolute excellence that do astounding work, and some of these centres are breed-specific. There are also those who simply do not have time and resources to obtain a full picture of the dog's history and any behavioural concerns. It is wise to source carefully and ensure that the information you need regarding the dog's attitude to life is forthcoming. A good rescue service will not only undertake compre- hensive assessments of the dogs in their care, they will also be keen to 'vet' you and your circumstances. Careful matching is very important if placement breakdowns are to be avoided.

Providing a home for a rescued dog is of immeasurable value to those individuals that desperately need a new start in life. Rescuing a German Shepherd can be hugely rewarding provided you are well-informed by the rescue centre, and that you are keen to source good training advice in the early months. If you are not open-minded on this issue, you may be setting the dog up to fail. Being open to advice is invariably the key to success for many rescue dogs. The Shepherd invariably wants to please and to be given an outlet for his mental energy. The rescued Shepherd has the capacity to respond well once he is given the right environment in which to blossom.

Be aware that many rescue dogs take time to adapt to a new way of life and therefore you will need to be patient while they adjust. It is also possible that deep-seated problems might take time to become apparent, and the dog will need stability from you as issues emerge.

Dog or bitch?

This is very much a personal choice as both sexes can, and do, make wonderful companions. On a practical level, the male Shepherd is likely to be considerably larger and more physically powerful than the female. Males typically have a strong and independent attitude to life, and may gravitate toward one member of the family. They can also be loving, gentle and controllable in sensible hands.

The dog generally requires firmer handling than the bitch

Males can sometimes be harder to house train, as the instinct to mark territory is strongest in the male. But both sexes can be successfully house trained in a few short weeks if commitment and patience are adhered to. People often ask if dogs are less controllable than bitches. Certainly, males can exhibit more independence, especially as they move through adolescence, and this can lead to a battle of wills. However, if the relationship between dog and handler is established on consistent boundaries, a male Shepherd is likely to become a loyal, responsive companion.

Generally speaking, bitches may be more gentle and biddable, but be mindful that they also have a deeply ingrained maternal element to their nature. Therefore, they may become overly protective, especially towards children, if this is not kept in check. Just as with males, everything comes down to sensible handling, and to ensuring that your Shepherd bitch knows what is expected of her within the family environment. It is just as important that family members know where the boundaries lie too.

 Be aware that this breed has a strong protective instinct. Many Shepherds are placed in rescue centres, following protection of their family. This could be readily avoided.

Bitches sometimes experience hormonal mood swings when in season. The first season usually takes place at around eight to ten months, and will then occur every six months. Seasons last three weeks on average, and may necessitate you keeping your bitch at home as the neighbourhood dog population will probably follow her home en masse! She will need isolating from other male dogs in your household during the middle of her season when she is sexually receptive. She is likely to need her own isolation area with lino or tiled flooring or she might stain furnishings and carpet with blood loss. Bitches are to be kept away from all shows and competitions during their seasons, so this should be taken into account if you hope to show or work your dog.

The intact bitch is at risk of developing conditions such as mammary tumours and 'pyometra' (which is a potentially fatal infection of the uterus). Phantom pregnancies are also a

A picture of nobility

consideration, and these can be distressing for the bitch. She will believe that she is carrying puppies, and will behave like a pregnant bitch from six weeks or so after the season has ended. She may nest, hoard toys, and even produce milk in readiness for her offspring.

When making the decision about which sex to choose, you should also give consideration to other dogs you may have at home, or who might visit regularly. As stated, the German Shepherd is not always a gregarious breed. Large, intact, adult males may not become the best of friends. Two bitches in the same household may also take a dislike to one another, and an intact male living with an intact female brings inevitable complications! If you are planning to introduce a second dog to your family, generally speaking a male–female combination is to be recommended, with the bitch being spayed at the appropriate time.

If you have doubts, it is best to go to shows and trials in order to spend time around well-adjusted examples of both sexes. This will help you make your choice.

Coat colour

Coat colour is a matter of personal preference for the buyer, and if this is important to you, your visits to local shows will hopefully have helped you make your choice.

If you are considering showing your dog, then the puppy will need to be of Breed Standard colouration. The most commonly seen are black and tan, and sable. Bi-colour and solid black are colours rarely seen in the show ring. The latter two colours do not change as the puppy moves into adulthood, but black and tan, or sable puppies change noticeably as they develop. As a young puppy, the black and tan Shepherd does not initially have a black saddle. He will initially be heavily covered with black pigmentation over the muzzle, head, neck and body right to the top of the legs. This will diminish as the pup moves into adolescence and will effectively reduce to a black saddle and mask. Sable puppies are predominantly sandy-coloured or grey, with a black mask and black flecking through the coat. As the weeks progress, this develops into a stripe of black along the spine, which gradually widens to give the appearance of a saddle during adolescence. The sable puppy also has a black ring around the upper part of the tail and a black tail tip.

In essence, the black and tan Shepherd loses much of its black pigment as the dog moves into adulthood, and by contrast the sable Shepherd gains it. Both have a black saddle

Black and Tan

Sable

area as adults, and a black muzzle. The sable dog however, retains a gold or grey undercoat through the saddle area and this is easily seen if a hand is run against the lie of the hair. The coat pattern is also further broken up around the neck, shoulders and chest. Both of these colour patterns are recognised in the Breed Standard, and to newcomers to the breed they can look very similar in the adult dog.

Dilute colourations

Blues and livers should be avoided if you are hoping to show. Blues and livers are, in essence, diluted versions of standard coloured dogs. Blues will have grey markings where they should have been black, and livers will have chocolate markings instead of black. Nose and pad leather is also diluted, and eye colour tends to be pale yellow to amber, rather than the usual deep brown eye. Both colours are represented within the same 'patterns' as standard colours, i.e. solid, bi-colour, saddle-marked and sable. Dilute colours can be striking, and although both are frowned upon by those who breed for the show ring, non-standard colours have a large following, especially across the UK and the United States. The isabella Shepherd is rarely seen. Both parents have to carry the genes for both liver *and* blue in order for this unusual colour to be produced in their offspring. It is a colour also seen in the Doberman Pinscher.

| Blue and Gold | Liver and Gold | Isabella (right) |

Brindle

The brindle Shepherd is now unknown, due to selective breeding practices. Brindle markings consist of streaks of brown and grey intermingled with streaks of black, such as seen in the Boxer or Staffordshire Bull Terrier.

White

If you are looking for a white puppy, you will find that the gene pool is relatively small and that the quality of colour is variable. Whites range from 'champagne' through to pure white. The most highly prized dogs are pure white in colour. White dogs have pigment on the nose and pad leather, and this will range from pure black (which is most desirable) through to pale brown. There should also be good eye pigmentation. White dogs are not albinos. Albinos have an absence of pigment in all of the areas mentioned. Whites have a fervent following, especially in the UK, Canada and in the United States.

In the UK the White and Long Coat Shepherd Society (WALCSS) holds shows throughout the year, which are always well attended. In particular the long coated white is well represented at these shows. In most other European countries the breed is classified as the White Swiss Shepherd Dog (Berger Blanc Suisse) and has been recognised as such by the FCI since 2002. In the United States and Canada, the White Shepherd is represented at shows run by various societies, including the American White Shepherd Association (AWSA) and the White Shepherd Club of Canada (WSCC). Standard coated whites appear to be better represented than long coats. Whites are not able to be shown under AKC rulings, but may be shown at UKC (United Kennel Club) shows, as the UKC created a separate White Shepherd Standard and registry in 1999.

The UK Breed Standard for the German Shepherd states that blues, livers, albinos, whites and near whites are 'highly undesirable'. The Standard also states that colour in its own right 'is of secondary importance having no effect on character or fitness for work'. The American Standard states that blues and livers are serious faults, and that whites must be disqualified.

The White Shepherd can compete in competitive sports, such as agility, obedience and herding trials. They also have the same capacity for work as their standard coloured counterparts, and are therefore utilised by the Police and armed forces, and they also are used as guide dogs and therapy dogs.

Long coat

The long coated Shepherd can look very striking and is popular the world over. Recognised by the FCI, the long coated Shepherd can now be shown, in separate classes, at Champ and Sieger shows. At the British Sieger show in September 2011, history was made with the first ever long coated progeny parade. The long coat itself varies in quality and appearance, from a silky, fine texture (which invariably has little undercoat and forms a distinct parting along the spine), through to a dense coat which consists of a thick undercoat with guard hairs. A long coat with no undercoat is considered a serious fault. The long coat is not generally as weather resistant as the standard coat, and it is fair to say that the long coated German Shepherd will need a little more care in terms of daily brushing, but enthusiasts will feel that a few extra minutes tending to the coat is well worth the extra effort!

The long coat comes about due to a recessive gene, which both parents have to carry in order for long coat to be produced. The long coated puppy will always arise from long coat to long coat matings, but it may also arise where standard coated dogs carry the gene for long coat. So don't be surprised to see mixed litters even if both parents are standard coated show dogs. By five weeks, the long coated puppy will be noticeably fluffier than his littermates, and the coat will feel soft to the touch.

Long coated Shepherds are often said to be 'softer' in nature, and some say that they are less intelligent than standard coated dogs, but this is a fallacy. Long coated Shepherds can, and do, work within the Police and Military. They also compete in trials to the same high levels as standard coated dogs, where courage and intelligence are essential characteristics for success. It is fair to say that most long coated Shepherds live their lives as family pets, but having a 'fluffy coat' should never mean that the owner underestimates the working potential of their family pet!

Winners of the Long Coat Progeny Parade, British Sieger Show 2011

Show or working?

It is important to decide what aspirations you have before you purchase your Shepherd pup. You may simply want a family pet, or you might have a keen interest in showing or working your new companion. Either way it is advisable to spend time with those with experience in each field, so that you get a glimpse of the overall expectations which you will face as you begin to educate your puppy.

If you are hoping to show your puppy then your national Breed Council or local breed club secretary will usually be able to put you in touch with a reputable breeder. You might have a long road ahead before a pick of litter can be reserved for you, but quality puppies are worth the wait. Good breeders may already have puppies booked, or be keeping one for themselves, so be prepared that you might have to wait for a litter at a later stage. If you have no experience of choosing a potential show quality pup, then you will need to feel confident in your breeder's integrity to select for you, or to advise you to wait if they feel that a show quality pup is not forthcoming in the litter. Reputable breeders will want the best puppy in the ring, and will be happy to discuss the attributes of the litter.

As previously mentioned, show quality puppies will obviously be of good conformation and the coat will conform to the Breed Standard. The puppy will also need to be of good health and character. Remember that a beautiful but highly nervous puppy is less likely to succeed in the show ring. You are looking for 'promise' – a happy, healthy, confident pup that is keen to show the world just how breathtaking he or she can be! Expect to pay a higher price for puppies whose parents are top quality show dogs, but be aware that there are no guarantees that a puppy bred from show quality dogs will succeed in the ring. Showing is highly competitive and only a select few will attain the highest awards.

It is wise to visit a ringcraft puppy class for general advice and information. The education of a show German Shepherd is unique in terms of how the dogs are presented in order to show movement and conformation to the full. This will take considerable time and effort to achieve.

If you hope to compete in working trials, obedience or agility, again it is clear that you will need to spend time with people who are passionate about their sport. With generations of selective breeding behind him the Shepherd has innate working instinct and ability. All forms of trialling have become immensely popular across the globe, and there are endless discussions and debates about what constitutes the best working lines: expect real passion to come to the fore when discussing bloodlines! As such, those who have competed to a high and consistent level will be best placed to help you in your search. Remember that there will be high demand for puppies from such sources, and if you do not have experience of training high drive dogs, you will undoubtedly require a great deal of support and advice.

Champion Draycore Chili. It takes time and patience to teach a dog to stand and move correctly

Companion

Buying a German Shepherd solely as a companion requires no less attention to detail, but your prime consideration will be focused on the sire and dam's attitude to life as a family dog. As always you should be able to see the dam, and also the sire if possible, and gain a picture of their temperament and character. Check to see what health tests have been undertaken (p. 69) and if the puppies have been reared indoors – you will want the litter to have been well socialised. This is very important, as puppies should be given the opportunity to build relationships with people as early as possible.

One puppy or two?

As a general rule it is a mistake to buy two puppies at the same time. Far from 'keeping each other company' they are likely to become competitive or fractious, and socialising them both effectively will need a lot of dedication. Puppies invariably develop the tightest bond to their human family when they are reared individually. Siblings (or same-age puppies from different litters) may bond tightly to each other, and trying to train *either* of them can become fraught with issues. Conversely, sibling rivalry may also lead to damaged ears and legs as they wrestle and play-bite to establish the pecking order. Life can become a daily battle when sibling rivalry gets out of hand, and you may finally decide to part with one or both puppies.

Of course there are ways of making the best of this situation, but both puppies must be educated and socialised separately, and they will need lots of individual company and stimulation. They need time apart so that they learn to develop their own responses to life, rather than copying one another. It is also a good idea to crate puppies separately when unsupervised so they cannot do damage to each other when left unattended.

There are always exceptions to the rule, but most people find that unless they invest a lot of time in ensuring that both puppies are given broad experiences, friction develops between the two dogs. At the very least one dog will learn to rely on the other, and can experience emotional issues as time progresses: one inevitably becomes the leader, the other becomes the follower. The subsequent development of 'copied behaviour' is undesirable in *any* breed, but with large dogs such as the German Shepherd this is to be avoided, as the resulting responses are less than reliable.

If you want to have a second canine companion, it is generally wise to wait around two years before introducing a second puppy into the family.

The Search for Your Puppy

Now that you have decided that this magnificent breed is the right one for you, the process of finding the right breeder and the right puppy can seem daunting. In truth it is unlikely that you will need a complete and prescriptive diet of information on every aspect, and when you begin to make contacts with breeders, your instincts are likely to guide you. In this chapter you will find answers to common queries, and some general guidance which is aimed to help dispel a few myths.

Registration

If your puppy is Kennel Club registered, this refers to the fact that your breeder holds Kennel Club paperwork for the litter, which the puppies will only be eligible for if both parents are also registered. If this is the case, the relevant Kennel Club will have information pertaining to his ancestry.

Puppy buyers may be of the opinion that Kennel Club papers are in themselves a hallmark of quality, but Kennel Club paperwork can only indicate that the dog is registered, and cannot denote the actual quality of the dog. They also cannot guarantee that the paperwork actually pertains to the puppy itself. However, with the development of DNA profiling, irrefutable details as to parentage will help the compilation of pure and accurate record keeping.

The American, British and Canadian Kennel Clubs are multiple breed registries. Your dog may be registered with a single breed registry. The most notable of these is SV, which is the largest single breed registry in the world. This registry holds detailed information on ancestry going back to the foundations of the breed.

The breeder's affix

Anyone who plans to breed can apply for a 'kennel name' or 'affix'. It is a hallmark name for the kennels, and makes for easy identification of all dogs bred by the named breeder. The affix also simplifies the choosing of registered names for puppies, and can make for easier identification of specific bloodlines when searching for your puppy, as if you know the lines of dogs you admire, you can more readily source related dogs. The affix can be placed on the registered name of any pup that is bred by the affix holder. Some registries also allow breeders to add *their* kennel name to registered puppies which they buy.

Breeder's charters

Across the world, breed clubs, councils and organisations have taken the lead in promoting ethical breeding practices of their breeder-members. Many introduced codes of conduct for their members decades ago. For example, members of the GSD Breed Council of Great Britain agree to abide by certain practices, which are in place to produce improvements in the breed, and which aim to promote ethical practices in terms of the welfare of puppies and adults alike. A similar ethos is upheld by the German Shepherd Dog Club of America (GSDCA) through their 'Breeder's Code', which aims to promote measurable and ethical welfare practices which their members agree to uphold. Other organisations worldwide aim to comprehensively set goals for breeders which will encourage betterment of the breed, and improve welfare practices which impact on the adult dogs and their puppies.

Kennel Club breeder schemes

In the UK, breeders who undertake to observe certain guidelines for their breeding practices can be approved by The Kennel Club as an 'assured breeder'. Their breeding stock has to be health tested for certain conditions and all dogs have to be identified by microchip, tattoo or DNA profile. There is an extensive checklist of points which a breeder agrees to adhere to before being awarded an assured breeder title. The scheme is still in its formative stages, and its aim is to help identify responsible breeders who can be seen to make health and welfare a priority. However, there are concerns about loopholes in the current scheme which unscrupulous breeders attempt to exploit. Therefore at present, assured breeder status does not necessarily guarantee the calibre of the puppies. The American Kennel Club has established a 'Breeder of Merit Program', which honours breeders and exhibitors' dedication and hard work for producing healthy, capable and beautiful dogs. Dogs must have earned at least four Conformation, Performance or Companion awards, and holders certify that relevant health tests as recommended by the parent club (the GSDCA) are performed.

THE SEARCH FOR A BREEDER

There are many ways in which you may find a dedicated and caring breeder. Breed Councils, clubs and societies invariably will be able to provide you with a list of recommended breeders. Kennel Clubs also hold comprehensive lists of litters which are available. In this modern age of technology, the Internet has its part to play, and it can be a huge source of information as many breeders have links from site to site. You can therefore build up a picture in your mind of the individual attributes of different bloodlines, and the attention to detail of the breeders in question. Topical dog magazines and newspapers are an invaluable source of information, and if you have already attended local or national breed shows you might have located breeders this way. If you already know someone with a dog you admire you could talk to them about the dog itself, and more importantly about the advice and support they were offered by the breeder.

Large or small breeding establishment

The Shepherd is an addictive breed, and you will find that many enthusiasts live with multiple dogs! The size of the establishment should not be a defining issue providing that the dogs are well cared for, and that you are able to see the dogs in different environments, not just within their kennel space. 'Kennel-bound' dogs (that is to say those that have had limited social experiences) may well exhibit nervousness outside of the confines of their kennel. Limiting a dog's social experiences should be seen as little short of abusive. You will want to ensure that you are not funding a life of confinement for the breeding stock.

The breeder may show you dogs in training

If you have been using the Internet as a source, you will find breeding kennels which have champion bloodlines and the very best in facilities. Some kennels can seem too big and impersonal for some buyers' liking and you may prefer more of a personal touch, but it is important to state that many are highly specialised and dedicated. Their knowledge of the needs of the breed, and in particular the traits of their own lines, can be truly exceptional. A thorough visit will enable you to see conditions and standards, and to maybe see multiple dogs from the same line. Breeders should be keen to show you around, and if they are trials enthusiasts you may be fortunate enough to watch dogs in training.

If you plan to buy from a show kennels, you may find that the breeder is having a litter so that they can run a puppy on, or let one or two puppies go to show enthusiasts. In this instance you may be able to book a 'pet quality' puppy, who although is of good quality, is not the pick of litter and therefore not being sold to a show home.

You may have decided to buy from a family friend, because you already know and like the dogs? This often seems like an attractive way to bring a puppy into a family home, as the dogs' temperament is already known to you. Getting the opportunity to know adult dogs well is obviously an advantage, but one disadvantage is that bloodline knowledge may be limited, so there might be unknown health or temperament issues in the line. However, a caring hobby breeder will have ensured that certain health tests have been performed, and these are discussed later in the chapter. If possible, it would always be advisable to try to build up a 'family picture'. Ask where the dogs came from and see if you can make a journey to find out a little more regarding their ancestry. If the bloodline is littered with affixes, certain dogs and breeders are easily traceable, and it always pays to do your research.

Puppy farms / pet shops / dealers

You are strongly advised not to buy a puppy from such sources. In particular please do not buy a puppy where offers are made to bring the puppy halfway to 'save you the journey'. With any of these sources, it is likely that little attention to detail has been made in the selection or rearing processes and you will find yourself in the midst of heartache. You are likely to be perpetuating poor breeding. You may also be helping perpetuate lives of abject misery for the adult breeding stock, which are often kept in appalling conditions. It is also possible that the paperwork is not genuine.

 Wherever you choose to visit, you should always be able to see the dam with her puppies. If you are given excuses on a particular day there may be a good reason for this. But arrange to go another day, so that you have peace of mind. If excuses are repeatedly given, you have every right to be suspicious, and to go elsewhere for a more honest service.

You should always expect to meet the dam

First contacts

If you approach a caring breeder your early enquiries into the breed will be well received. Breeders routinely take calls from would-be puppy buyers, only for the buyer to recognise that their timing was entirely wrong, or that they needed to learn more about the breed's requirements. Caring breeders will not see this visit as 'time wasting'. On the contrary, they will know that lengthy conversations about the realities of life with a large, very active and intelligent breed are an essential part of ensuring that puppies end up in good hands. If you are unsure in any way whatsoever, a good breeder will help you arrive at the right decision. They will want you to have a Shepherd for life, not for a disastrous three months which will scar both the puppy and yourselves for ever.

When contacting the breeder, be prepared to ask some basic questions. You will want to find out how they have come into breeding Shepherds, and how often they breed. You will want to know a little about their history in the breed, whether they show or work their dogs, and to find out about their commitment to health screening their breeding stock. Always check that you will be able to see the bitch (and other related dogs if possible). If you are buying a family pet, it is particularly important that you ask whether the puppies are reared within the family home, or if they are being raised in a kennel. Those puppies reared in the family home will have already begun to experience day-to-day living in this environment. Their socialising experience is likely to already be broader than those reared outside in a kennel.

Once you are happy that the breeder has been able to answer your initial queries, do expect that a caring breeder will want to turn the tables! They will always want to determine what kind of owner you will be, and that the home you offer will be a lifelong place of love and safety for the pup they will be parting with.

VISITING A BREEDER

 Please don't make arrangements to visit litter after litter. There is a genuine risk that if you visit multiple litters you may transfer infection from kennel to kennel.

Look for contentment in the adults first and foremost. They should be bright and alert. General 'manners' will indicate that time has been given to help them become well balanced (and that they are not simply kennel-bound breeding machines). Try to get a sense of how many carers there are in relation to the number of dogs. Kennel-bound dogs will be generally less well grounded if the breeders have limited time to devote to training and stimulation.

Always expect adult dogs to bark on your arrival. This is perfectly normal in a breed with such a naturally protective instinct. But once the owners come to let you onto the premises, the dogs should settle quickly and greet you politely. Any signs of aggression or nervousness should be viewed negatively, and the dogs should be relaxed and happy around their owners and yourselves. Look for cleanliness and comfort for the adults. There should be clean water and bedding, and ample evidence that the dogs have access to freedom and play.

Even if you have no plans to show your dog, you will still want a puppy with good conformation. If you are unsure about what you are looking for, talk to enthusiasts at local ringcraft classes or shows as this will help you gain an understanding. If you are really not confident about this, you could opt to take a more experienced person with you; however, if you are buying from a successful and experienced breeder, they will usually be more than happy to explain some of the finer points about the adult's conformation and that of the puppies.

You may have decided on a long coat, or perhaps you are looking for a white or blue, in which case you will find the numbers of breeders with these to be lower than those who conform to the Breed Standard.

 Whatever your choice, being aware of key points of the Breed Standard in terms of physical construction will inform your decision. Being familiar with health tests and documentation will aid you in finding a thoughtfully bred dog.

You will want to know that the adults have plenty of opportunity for exercise and stimulation

As previously stated, remember that regardless of your plans and hopes for your puppy, you should *always* expect to meet the dam. If the stud dog is not owned by the breeder, you could ask to make separate arrangements to visit him. If at all possible, you should be able to see other offspring from the bloodline.

As a golden rule, you should be able to handle the adult dogs, and to have your children move amongst them with ease. These are vital components if you are buying a family pet, as steadiness and manners in your puppy's parents are always the first place to begin. By the same token, a breeder will want your children to be respectful during the visit, and if they are not, you may find that some breeders will understandably refuse to sell you one of their puppies.

Finding out about the litter

- Where are the puppies reared? Ideally they will be in a part of the house where they can experience the hustle and bustle of daily living. Regardless, you will want to know that they have been well socialised with family members and if at all possible with other pets.
- Does the breeder start the toilet training process? Puppies reared with separate bed, toilet and play areas will have already begun to establish good toileting routines.
- What is the bitch fed on during pregnancy and lactation? She should be on a good quality diet in order to give the puppies the best start in life, and to support her during this time.
- What food does the breeder wean puppies on to? It is important that puppies have been given quality food as this is vital to good early growth.
- How has the puppy been wormed to date? Breeders should furnish you with information about the wormers used so that you can discuss future worming with your vet.
- Will puppy have had any of his vaccinations? If the first vaccination is being done prior to leaving the litter, you will need to know, so that you can make appropriate arrangements regarding the second vaccine.
- Will puppy be micro-chipped or tattooed?
- At what age will puppy be able to leave the breeder? Usually this will be between seven and eight weeks. Be wary if breeders are keen to get you to collect any earlier than this.
- What insurance will puppy come with? A good breeder will ensure that you are covered by a good insurance policy. It will be up to you to organise further cover. This is to be strongly recommended! Puppies can do damage to your home in the early months, and are especially prone to illness and injury. There are good policies on the market but you will need to shop around for the right one for you.
- Does the puppy's paperwork carry endorsements? What exactly are they, and what are the implications for the future?

Hip scoring – myths and legends

The German Shepherd is readily associated with having a condition called hip dysplasia (see p. 252). This is a painful condition caused when the hip joint fails to form correctly. In order to determine the presence of osteoarthritis or dysplasia – and therefore the dog's viability for breeding – radiographs (X-rays) can be taken of the dog's hips, and these can be assessed under various schemes:

Under the BVA/KC (British Veterinary Association/Kennel Club) scheme each hip receives a score of 0 to 53. The scores are presented side by side, and added together. The best score available is 0:0 = 0, and the worst score would be 53:53 = 106. The best scores are low and are also evenly distributed, with the left hip score being close in number to that of the right hip (e.g. 5:4 = 9). In the UK, the Kennel Club recommends that breeders should choose to use breeding stock whose *total* score is below the 'breed mean score'. At the time of writing, this is 18 for the German Shepherd.

Similar schemes are offered worldwide, such as the OFA (Orthopedic Foundation for Animals) scheme in the United States, whereby hips are graded from 'excellent' through to 'severe', and the German 'a' stamp scheme, whereby hips are graded from 'normal' through to 'schwere'.

Unfortunately at this moment in time there is no compulsory requirement from certain registries for a dog or bitch to be hip-scored to qualify for breeding status, and unscored dogs can therefore be bred from and their puppies can be registered, providing that the parents are both registered. By contrast, the SV maintain tight controls over potential breeding stock, and only those dogs that achieve a rating of 'normal', 'fast normal' and 'noch zugelassen' ('normal', 'nearly normal' and 'still permissable') are permitted to breed.

A further scheme, more recently developed, is the PennHIP scheme. This incorporates three radiographs being taken, giving a broader viewpoint of arthritic development and movement within the hip. If the dog has been scored under the PennHIP scheme, again you will expect to be shown documentation. (This scheme has limited availability at this moment in time in the UK, but is widely available in Canada and the US.)

It is important to note that myths and legends about hip scoring remain an issue of some considerable vulnerability for the buyer. Unscrupulous breeders might tell you that they 'don't believe in it' and promptly produce a plausible reason to justify their opinion. One commonly held myth states that you can 'tell if a dog has good hips simply by watching him move'. Untested dogs are a complete unknown in terms of hip status. Good movement or conformation alone cannot determine a dog's potential score.

   Please be aware that good hip scores in the parents do not guarantee that your puppy will have sound hips, as environmental factors such as exercise and nutrition also play their part. However, until further research indicates otherwise, hip scoring schemes are the only way of monitoring hip dysplasia in bloodlines and attempting to establish sound stock for breeding.

Documentation

Hip Scores (p. 252)

In terms of paperwork, you should expect to be given the opportunity to see the parents' pedigrees and registration papers. Ask to see all paperwork pertaining to health tests for both parents. Both parents would need to be registered in order for the breeder to hold relevant paperwork for hip scores, as unregistered dogs are simply not eligible for scoring. The breeder should have the certificate with the breakdown of the dog's score written on it. They may also have the radiograph. The radiograph, certificate and KC registration form will all carry the registration number of the dog.

Elbow Scores (p. 249)

Elbow scoring is also now recommended. The BVA/KC scheme for testing elbows is similar to hip scoring schemes offered, and aims to identify the presence of abnormalities in the elbow joint. The dog is radiographed under anaesthetic, and the radiograph is sent to a panel of judges for scoring. The BVA/KC scoring scheme attributes a score for each elbow, with 0 being the best and 3 being the worst. The left and right scores are added together to give a total figure, e.g. 0:1 = 1, and dogs who have a total score of two upwards are deemed unsuitable for breeding.

The OFA provide a similar scheme, and elbows are graded from Grade 1 (minimal change) to Grade 3 (well developed DJD – Degenerative Joint Disease). The SV accepts grades from 'normal' to 'noch zugelassen' for potential breeding stock, but all others are not recommended for breeding.

Haemophilia Test (p. 252)

Haemophilia A is a blood clotting disorder which is known to affect the German Shepherd. It is a hereditary condition. All male Shepherds should be tested for this condition before they are bred from. If the dog has been haemophilia tested clear of the condition, documentation will be available, and a good breeder will willingly present this to you.

Healthy puppies are full of life and enthusiam

VIEWING A LITTER

If a bitch has recently whelped, you should expect that you might not be allowed to see the puppies for several weeks. Most bitches are reluctant to come out and greet visitors in the early weeks, and will want to return quickly to their offspring. This is perfectly normal. A bitch's sense of being protective of her young is at its peak during the first few weeks. However, by the time the puppies are in the middle of weaning (at four to five weeks), it should be possible for you to mix with the puppies and their mother without causing her undue stress.

Even if the breeder does permit you to visit in the very early days you are unlikely to be allowed physical contact with the pups, in order to avoid the risks associated with you bringing disease or viruses into the litter. Some breeders will insist on spraying your shoes with anti-viral sprays such as Virkon® as you enter the premises, and you might be asked to wash your hands, but as this is not a one hundred per cent guarantee you may still not be allowed to handle the puppies at such a vulnerable age.

It is advisable that new owners get a chance to meet 'mum' before pups are born, if at all possible. This gives the buyer an early opportunity to get to know the bitch, and for important questions to be asked. Most puppies are chosen at around six weeks, once they have begun to develop personalities of their own, and then collected at around seven to eight weeks. These visits may involve travelling issues for the owner, and will make for a very busy time for the breeder, but this contact builds a relationship between buyer and breeder, and provides every opportunity for issues to be discussed.

Selecting your puppy

It may be that you feel that you will 'know your puppy when you see it', or that the puppy will 'choose' you. But if you are struggling with how to make a choice, then there are some helpful guidelines you might like to consider when you actually go to make your selection. You will hopefully have already decided on whether you want a dog or bitch pup, and will have made decisions about coat length and colour (p. 56).

Crouch down low with the puppies, and clap gently or call them to you. It would be hoped that in a well socialised litter the pups will be eager and bright and will come happily forward. The boldest and most excitable puppies (who greet you with boundless energy and enthusiasm) are often those who make the best prospects for an experienced owner. It is those puppies that are best described as 'calm but confident' which will suit a newcomer to the breed. This is, in truth, an over-generalisation but is still a useful starting point. A knowledgeable breeder will help you in this process as they will have watched all stages of early learning within the litter, and will have already identified character traits.

How will you choose?

Take heed of how the puppies react to you touching them, and also if they follow you when you move about (as this shows a desire to connect and make a relationship with you). Of particular relevance is 'mouthing' or 'play-biting'. Assertive and excitable puppies will constantly mouth you with their needle sharp teeth, in order to evoke a response from you. Calmer puppies are less likely to persist with this.

Watch the litter playing with toys. You will note how certain pups win the toys and retain possession for longer, often by growling or showing teeth. They will inevitably develop into challenging older dogs that need experienced handlers. If you are buying a puppy with the hope to do working trials, then the puppy would need to exhibit confidence, a keenness to explore and a responsive attitude. A keen desire to play with a wide variety of toys is also paramount. In particular, you would be looking for early signs of prey drive, chasing after articles that you throw, and a keenness to 'rag' with knotted rope toys and with balls on a rope. These puppies invariably have a very confident air about them, and an *insatiable* drive to play and interact. This attitude to life is not for every puppy buyer and such puppies are not generally suitable for novice owners.

Take note of the puppy that does not wish to play or engage in any way with you. Any reluctance or shyness is a quality you should avoid. You may feel a little sorry for him, but the puppy who is reticent and sitting alone is not the ideal family companion, particularly if you are a novice buyer. He will need his confidence building, and will need experienced handling to bring the best out in him.

The puppy that is neither of the above is the most likely to make an ideal family companion. He should be keen to say 'hello' to you and to the family, and will love being fussed and played with. He should show an enthusiasm for playing with toys but will enjoy this being a two-way game, and will not be *overly* possessive. He will sometimes sit and watch proceedings, but he is just as happy to join in.

When you feel you have narrowed down your choice, ask to take puppies individually into a separate room, away from the siblings. It is good to assess their reactions to being away from litter mates, and to see how readily each puppy responds to you in a strange situation. It might take him a moment to adjust, so let him do this at his own pace. He should relax quickly and be interested in connecting with you and exploring his environment. A bit of gentle play and fuss should see if he is relaxed with games and with physical contact.

This is also a good time to run your hands all over the puppy to check that his ears are clean, his eyes are free from discharge or weeping, his anus has no inflammation or discharge, and also to check for umbilical hernias. If you are choosing for pet only, a small hernia should not deter you from choosing your pup as they are rarely of any consequence,

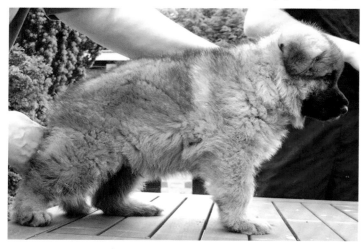

A potential star at 5 weeks

but if you are in any doubt you should consult your vet. A good breeder will have already pointed out minor issues such as small hernias or an incorrect jaw. They will also arrange for puppies to be checked by a vet before they leave. Puppies should be bright eyed and inquisitive, and their frame should be well covered. Puppies should not be thin and pot-bellied (often a sign of a worm burden), but nor should they be fat.

If you see any of the puppies defecating, you should note if the stools are firm. Puppies with an upset stomach might indicate that others in the litter are affected too. It is not uncommon for puppies to have loose motions as they move on to solid foods, but any listlessness in the litter might indicate other concerns. You should check on this again when you collect your puppy. A good breeder will not encourage you to take a puppy home if it has diarrhoea.

Once you have chosen your puppy, the breeder will mark the puppy if necessary. This can be done by cutting a piece of hair from a hind leg, or by marking the puppy with coloured nail varnish somewhere on the coat. Other breeders will 'colour code' the puppies with coloured collars. Puppies change greatly in only a few weeks, and you may not recognise your pup on your return visit!

Preparations

It is important that you make sensible preparations for your puppy's homecoming as you may find that your free time is limited once he arrives!

A VARIETY OF TOYS will be both welcome and necessary if you are to keep your puppy happy and stimulated. It is useful to have a large assortment, but you will only need to give him a few toys to play with at once. You can swap the toys over every few days to maintain his interest. You will need to make sure that playtime becomes a regular part of his daily activities, whilst he is in between periods of sleeping, feeding, or making trips with you into the outside world. You will

Puppy will need a wide assortment of toys (but maybe not all at once!)

want to avoid him focusing on objects you do not want destroyed, such as shoes, chair legs, or corners of your favourite rug! There will be a range of toys available at your local pet stores. Sturdy tug-toys and large balls (which he cannot swallow) will become firm favourites. The Shepherd puppy invariably loves knotted rope toys.

It goes without saying that you should always monitor your puppy while he plays with his toys whilst he is still at the destructive stage. Small objects can easily become lodged in puppy's throat with devastating results, so always be vigilant. Squeaky toys can prove dangerous as puppies have an amazing capacity to remove and swallow the 'squeaker'.

You will need to buy an assortment of CHEWS which he can enjoy when he is left unattended. Nylabone® chews are invaluable. These are almost indestructible and will soothe his gums during his teething stages. Kongs® or buster cubes are also great for puppies in that they can be filled with food or treats, and puppy will have to work hard to empty them. TREATS come in all shapes and sizes, but you will need to be sure that all extras are included within daily rations, and are not in addition to his allowance. Puppies can quickly become overweight if given too many treats.

AN ASSORTMENT OF BOWLS will be needed. Heavy earthenware bowls or stainless steel ones are fine. Plastic bowls are not a good idea as they are readily chewed, and your Shepherd puppy will soon have strong teeth and jaws! A bottom-weighted bowl is ideal for water as he will readily tip over a lightweight one. You may decide to buy a frame which raises the bowls from the floor. This is particularly useful if you have a 'water-baby'. Many puppies simply cannot resist paddling in their water!

A VARIETY OF BRUSHES will be needed throughout his development, but at this stage a soft-bristled brush will suffice. Grooming will need to be introduced gently so that it does not become a battle of wills. Brushing is best limited in the first weeks to times when puppy is resting. You can then groom gently while he is too tired to make a game of it, or protest. He will then learn that being brushed is a pleasurable experience. Later on, you can groom your puppy whilst he is awake and active, and he will begin to learn that you want him to stand still for you during the process.

You will need to add to your grooming kit gradually, to include:

- a slicker brush
- a variety of combs (including a flea comb)
- a grooming rake and mitt
- canine toothpaste and brush
- nail clippers
- ear cleaner / cotton wool balls
- eye drops
- puppy shampoo

A COLLAR AND LEAD are obviously going to form essential training aids, but you will only need to buy an adjustable soft nylon collar at this stage. Keep a close eye on your puppy's neck growth as he will quickly grow out of his first collar. Leads will come in a variety of materials, to

include flat leather, rolled leather, nylon webbing and chainlink. Be careful not to buy a heavy lead at this early stage. The clasp is likely to also be heavy and this may hinder a puppy. You will want a lead which does not put puppy off in these early days of lead training. As well as a lead, you are advised to buy a lightweight training line as this will be useful for achieving puppy recall once you start to offer him more freedom in the park.

There remains continued debate about the use of metal check chains, as some trainers will always advocate the need for them, but this does not fit with current ethical thinking about dog training methods. This particularly applies to the usage of 'prong' or 'pinch' collars. It is not necessary to use punitive collars on dogs or puppies if they are properly socialised and correctly educated.

If you are going to show or to work your dog, it is advisable to talk to enthusiasts for specialist advice on equipment. Some collars can damage the fur round puppy's neck, so bear this in mind when making your choice.

Never leave a puppy unattended wearing a collar as it is remarkably easy for this to lead to injury.

BEDDING is a very personal choice, and pet stores now sell a wide range of beds and blankets to suit all tastes and fashions. You may prefer to stick to the tried and tested oval plastic beds which are still very popular. They are hard wearing and easy to clean, and are virtually indestructible. There are also dog duvets and wicker baskets on offer, but please be aware that these can be dangerous as they can be chewed and pieces swallowed. You will also find a hard-wearing fleecy blanket called 'vet bed'. This is comfortable, warm, and easy to wash and dry, and although it is initially expensive to buy, it should last for years.

Whatever your final choice, remember to 'think puppy'. If you can imagine him destroying his beautiful new bed, then I am sure he can too! It is important to think about where his bed will be situated. He will need somewhere that he can sleep peacefully, but where he can keep half an eye on you in the early days.

CRATES OR PLAY PENS may make this choice easier. These are wonderful if introduced correctly and this is discussed in Part Three. The correct use of a crate will rapidly establish a place where puppy is happy and relaxed. They also help keep puppy contained if he is wet or muddy, or if you have visitors. As an alternative, baby gates provide another invaluable way to keep your puppy confined to areas where you know he will be safe. Be aware that puppies are notoriously good climbers when it comes to stairs, but stair climbing can put strain on developing joints and is not to be advised.

You will find that crates come in two principal designs:

- The wire crate is useful as this allows the crated puppy the opportunity to keep an eye on the world around him. He has an unhindered view from all angles and as a result he will not feel hemmed in. The wire crate affords good air circulation which is clearly important when travelling by car. Wire crates have a removable tray at the bottom which can easily be cleaned if puppy has an 'accident' in the early days. If the puppy appears to like more seclusion, you can simply put a blanket over part of the crate to make it feel more of a den. Wire crates are easy to store as they fold flat when not in use.
- The plastic crate is enclosed on all sides, except for air vents and the wire front door. Certain makes are airline approved, and if you plan to travel with your dog, it is a good idea to start off with this design so that your dog is accustomed to this well in advance. Plastic crates are easy to wipe clean, and although they are lightweight, they are also sturdy and durable. Plastic crates do not fold flat and are therefore not as easy to store when not in use.

It is a good idea to borrow or buy a travel crate in readiness for the journey home. You may eventually remove a travel crate from the rear of the car once puppy moves into adolescence, as crates take up valuable space. For hatchback models there are many varieties of dog guard on the market, and there are tail guards too, which allow you to open the back of the car but still keep the dog contained safely. For saloon cars, an alternative comes in the form of the travel harness, but you will want to be sure that puppy is beyond the chewing stage!

Collect a plentiful supply of NEWSPAPER to help with the toilet training process. Always use ordinary newspaper rather than magazines, as newspaper is more absorbent. Avoid those with staples at their centre as these can be lethal to a puppy if swallowed. They would easily puncture your puppy's paws too, if trodden on.

FOOD: Make sure you have sourced a supplier for the puppy food he is currently eating. If you plan to rear puppy on a different diet, do discuss this with the breeder before taking puppy home. Always make sure you do not make any changes until the puppy has settled in his new home, and then make the change over at least five days. If you attempt to do this any faster, you run the real risk of your puppy developing diarrhoea.

PREPARE YOUR HOME AND GARDEN: It makes sense to prepare your home much in the same way as you would if you had an inquisitive toddler. Electric cables, china ornaments and other valuables should all be made puppy safe, and put out of harm's way. Not only can puppy inflict damage on such items, he could be seriously hurt in the process.

Be sure to make your garden puppy proof

Ensure that all poisons and pesticides are out of reach, and that the garden is free from debris and rubbish. It is essential to ensure that your garden perimeter is secure. Valuable or poisonous plants will need to be fenced off if at all possible, as will ponds.

An outdoor playpen, or covered run, is always a great idea if you can arrange it. Puppy can be introduced to this slowly, and if this is done correctly he will soon learn to relax and enjoy his environment.

PRE-ARRANGING A CHECK UP at your vet is always to be advised. This should ideally take place within the first 48 hours. Make it a pleasant experience by giving puppy fuss and treats and have your vet check him over thoroughly. If you have bought from a reputable breeder there should not be any issues, but if there are, it is far better that they are identified early for all concerned.

IDENTIFICATION: If your breeder has not already made the decision for you, you might like to think about forms of identification for your puppy. You may wish to get him tattooed or microchipped. Tattooing usually takes place at the breeders, and the details of ownership in the UK are held with the National Dog Tattoo Register. Some breeders dislike tattooing the German Shepherd, as the tattoo can be very visible in breeds with erect ear carriage. Microchipping is a relatively painless procedure, and the microchip is inserted into the tissue on the nape of the dog's neck. This holds a unique identification number, and ownership details are held in the UK by schemes run by Petlog and also by idENTICHIP. It is said that there is a very small risk that microchips can migrate into other areas of the body. If you have concerns about either procedure, it is wise to talk to your vet.

WORK ISSUES: Finally, you may be wondering how much time you should take off work. New owners often think that they should take several weeks off to 'settle puppy in', but then they wonder why the puppy stresses once they return to work! It is far better to spend two weeks doing 'separation training' as your primary piece of puppy training (p. 98), than to make yourself initially indispensable to him and then suddenly abandon him for periods of time. Feeling confident about being left alone is one of the most valuable lessons that you will teach your new pup.

A caring breeder will not sell to those people who work full-time, as leaving a puppy unattended all day is nothing short of animal cruelty. However, puppies can learn to cope with short periods alone providing that this is introduced correctly. People who work part-time *can* successfully share their life with a dog. Being left for a few short hours a day should present no problem at all for a puppy, providing that the routine and ground work have been established, and that the puppy is left in a safe environment.

Separation anxiety and boredom are the root causes of puppy becoming frantic, fearful and destructive when left alone. If you are likely at any stage to be away for longer than one or two hours, you will want to make arrangements for a puppy sitter or visitor, in order to break the day for puppy. He will need company and stimulation, and an opportunity to go to the toilet out in the garden.

Collecting Your Puppy

This is always an exciting day, when your plans, preparations and hopes come together. Ideally most breeders will want you to come to collect puppy early in the day, so that he has the maximum opportunity to become familiar with his new environment.

PAPERWORK

You will expect to be given your puppy's registration papers and his five generation pedigree when you collect him.

The registration form will need to be signed by you. Your address details will also be required, along with a specified fee in order for you to transfer puppy's registration to yourself. Be sure that the breeder has signed their part of the document before you leave.

Good breeders will have also drawn up a document which will give you all relevant information and their personal advice. This would include:

- Feeding advice. (What food the puppy is having / How many feeds per day / Quantities etc.)
- Details on wormers used. (Brand names / The dates on which this was administered.)
- Information about vaccinations/microchips/tattoos.
- Advice on early issues such as toilet training/first nights etc.
- The breeder's contact details/Receipt of purchase price.

Amongst this paperwork, you may also find a 'liability clause' which covers the breeder's commitment to you and the puppy should things not go well for any reason. You will want to know what the breeder offers by way of support or finance if something should go wrong. It is best sorted out at this stage so that there is no room for misunderstanding.

You should also have been told about any 'breeding endorsements' or 'export endorsements' which the breeder may have placed on the paperwork. If you hope to breed from the dog at some stage in the future, the breeder will outline in writing what will be required of you in order for that to happen. You will no doubt be expected to hip score the dog at a year of age, and for that score to be acceptable, but there may be further criteria such as elbow scores, and also haemophilia tests (males only). The breeder will have to write to the Kennel Club in order for the endorsement to be lifted. Discuss this with your breeder so that you are fully aware of the implications of any endorsement on your puppy's paperwork.

You will expect to be given details of any insurance policy that the breeder has taken out for the puppy. Be sure to read this carefully so you know what is covered, and when the period of cover ends.

A SENSE OF COMFORT

You may be asked to bring a blanket which is then placed in with the litter for a short while. It is given back to the owner for the puppy's bed at home. This helps puppy relax amongst a familiar smell on the first night. A caring breeder will give you a quantity of the puppy food on which the litter is feeding, and possibly a selection of any treats or chews which the puppies have grown used to. Some breeders will also provide a few puppy toys.

The new owner is usually given time to play with their pup prior to going home, so that puppy has bonded a little and is also tired and ready to travel. Ensure that puppy has also had a chance to relieve himself, so that he is comfortable for the journey ahead.

FIRST JOURNEY

If you are using a travel crate to bring puppy home in, you may find he cries a little at first, but most puppies quickly settle down with motion of the car. Travel crates diminish the possibility of road accidents caused by a stressed puppy, and they also give the puppy a sense of security. Plenty of newspaper for the floor of the crate is to be advised, as are several towels or a blanket for his comfort. Some owners prefer to have a family member hold puppy on their lap during the journey. A caring breeder will have made sure that puppy travels on an empty stomach, but be aware that it is still possible that your pup may be sick, so come prepared!

Take a bowl for water, in case your journey is prolonged and you need to take a break in order for him to have a drink. It is a good idea to fill the bottle with tap water at the breeder's premises, as new water could precipitate a tummy upset on the way home.

Your puppy may be hungry when you get home, but it is best to let him settle for several hours before you offer food.

Regardless of the length of your journey, do not be tempted to get him out of his crate so that he can go to the toilet. He is at high risk of infection until fully vaccinated, and also may be frightened by the experience, given that he does not know you yet.

This journey is a memory he will hold on to tightly, and it is therefore a good idea to reintroduce puppy to the crate and car the following day for a half mile journey on an empty stomach. Repeat this regularly to develop his confidence and 'car legs'. A carsick dog is something which is distressing to dog and owner alike, and this can largely be avoided. These early, short runs in your car will hopefully prevent this from occurring.

Part Three

The New Arrival

• Home at Last • Life's Early Lessons •
• Boundaries, Exercise and Playtime! •

Home at Last

There are often big expectations placed on puppies. Please remember that your new arrival is only a baby, and try to see the world through his eyes. He has been in the same, safe environment for eight weeks and his life has suddenly changed. Do not underestimate his stress, and ensure that your home is a calm, supportive place in the early days while he 'finds his feet' and begins to trust you all.

On the day he comes home he will no doubt need the opportunity to go to the toilet when he first arrives, so sit out on the grass with him for a while, or ensure you lay down plenty of newspaper on the floor for him as soon as you get him home. Remember that this is all new to him, and he will take time to learn the rules of the house!

Let him explore his new world without undue pressure from you all. First impressions count, and you will want him to quickly feel confident in his new environment. He may need a drink of water, but food should not be offered for a few hours at least, as his tummy might be tight with apprehension and this leaves his digestive system vulnerable.

This is an important day for your puppy

CHILDREN AND VISITORS

Any children in the household will inevitably descend and want to make friends with the new arrival! This is an exciting day for everyone, but it is important to ensure that puppy is not made to feel overwhelmed. It is a good idea to encourage children to sit quietly and let puppy come and say 'hello' when he is ready to, but do remember that some puppies will not want to interact immediately. He has a lot to process and he might just want to do things at his own pace. His keenness to play with toys may also be diminished on the first day, so just let him potter around and get to know his environment and new family.

With supervision, puppies and children can develop a lifelong friendship

It is likely that your friends will want to visit as soon as puppy has had a chance to settle in. All of his new experiences teach him a great deal about his family, and how he is allowed to behave in his new home. So think carefully about the way you will want him to greet your friends when he is a large adult dog, and work towards this from day one.

If he is permitted at this early stage to put his feet up on their laps for example, he is likely to become a dog with no respect for personal space, and will probably be keen to greet visitors with his feet on their shoulders! If this is not what you want, then ask your visitors to encourage him to sit quietly and receive a gentle fuss. He needs to also understand that he is not the sole centre of attention, so 'time out' in his play pen or crate will undoubtedly be a good lesson to introduce over the coming weeks (p. 99).

INTRODUCING FAMILY PETS

If puppy is going to be living with another dog, introduce the pair well away from the tensions which can be created by the presence of food or children. The older dog will therefore have an opportunity to meet the pup without feeling the need to be overly territorial or jealous.

Many older dogs are initially quite 'grumpy' with a puppy, regardless of how level-headed they have been throughout their lives! There may be a bit of low grade grumbling, and puppy is likely to respond with 'calming' behaviours, such as presenting his neck and shoulder, putting his ears backward, and by licking at the older dog's lips. If the older dog is not particularly accepting at first, be aware that this is perfectly normal, but the behaviours should never include physical confrontation, and you will need to intervene if stress levels are rising. You will want to keep your older dog calm, and to praise him for any signs of positive response to the puppy. Remember, this is his home. As far as he is concerned the puppy is an intruder, and all good relationships take a little time to evolve. In some instances it is better to ease the pair into a slower introduction by providing puppy with a safe place (for example behind a baby gate), so that the dogs can become accustomed to each other's presence gradually.

Some people believe that they should put the puppy straight in with an adult dog and 'leave them get on with it'. This is not to be recommended, as the puppy's anxious energy is likely to unsettle the older dog, and may lead to serious problems. In the early weeks, always supervise contact between pup and the older dog. Puppies can easily be hurt, even if the adult intends no malice. Even the gentlest dog can unintentionally

Older dogs can offer companionship to a new puppy if introduced carefully

knock a pup over whilst trying to establish 'ground rules'. If you are vigilant and watch for tensions, you will be able to deal with things before they get out of hand. With a thoughtful introduction and some early supervision, your adult dog and puppy will no doubt soon be the best of friends.

Do not allow puppy to have access to the older dog's food. This can obviously cause friction between the pair, and besides, a rapid change in puppy's diet can cause diarrhoea.

With regard to other pets in the household, such as caged birds, cats or pet rabbits, your

puppy will need to learn respect from day one. If he develops early manners with your own pets, he is likely to become very trustworthy and will be a pleasure to take anywhere. It is also a good idea to introduce him to large animals such as horses as soon as you are able to.

FIRST MEALS

Your puppy's first meal, and those to follow in the first 24 hours, might not be a roaring success. As a general rule, this is perfectly normal. Anxiety, excitement and the need to explore may all lessen a puppy's appetite. Don't be tempted to introduce increasingly inventive foods, as he will eat when he is hungry. Trying to cajole him into eating will add to any existing stress, and you will undoubtedly find that this leads to problems. In these early days, just stick to the breeder's advice, and if you are hoping to wean puppy on to a different food, remember that the first few days are not the time to attempt this. If puppy continues not to eat, watch for signs of listlessness or sickness which might accompany this and which would signify that vet advice should be sought promptly. Otherwise, take up any food that he has refused, and offer it again later in the day. A healthy, happy puppy will eat when he is ready to do so.

Your breeder will have explained to you that puppies need small, regular meals which are given at frequent intervals. Most eight-week-old puppies are on four feeds each day. This can be dropped to three feeds at about 12 weeks of age, and down to two feeds by the time he is six months old. If you are feeding your puppy on a 'complete' diet, be sure to read the feed guide on the bag, and to keep a weekly check on his weight so you can ensure you are feeding the correct amount. However, don't assume that because your dog is on the most expensive complete food that he will want to continue to eat it for the rest of his life. All dogs have preferences, and what may be appetising to one dog may simply not suit another.

Fresh water should always be made available. Do not be tempted to offer him milk to drink as this will invariably give him diarrhoea. By eight weeks he would have been fully weaned from his mother, and milk no longer forms an essential part of his diet. At weaning, the pup's digestive system begins to change and the capacity to digest lactose wanes (p. 178).

 Do note that *slightly* loose motions in the early days are not something to be unduly alarmed by. Your puppy will take time to settle, and once he does his tummy will usually return to a less fragile state. Resist the temptation to change puppy's diet at this sensitive stage, and be sure not to overfeed him. Diarrhoea, p. 167), is an *entirely* different matter and should be taken seriously, as it can quickly lead to dehydration.

FIRST NIGHT

One of the most important issues that your puppy will face is learning to sleep on his own. It is very important that his first experiences of being left alone are introduced sensitively, or you may find you set up unwanted behaviours for the future. German Shepherds are well known to suffer from 'separation anxiety'. This is discussed on page 98 and is an important issue for the new owner to consider. Take time to think about the way you wish to approach puppy's first few nights, and be sure that your family is on board with your final decisions.

Above everything else, remember that your puppy has spent every night with the comfort and security of his littermates. This is a stressful moment for him and he may respond in a very vocal manner if he is left feeling unsafe. We would highly recommend that you crate train your puppy from the very first day. It takes a little time and preparation but reaps superb results in only a matter of days, and will set your puppy on the right road for the future in terms of him being left alone for short periods of time.

We personally always sleep near to our puppies in the early nights. Over the years we have found that the very best start in life for our puppies is to crate them at night, and we then sleep beside the crate on a camp bed or similar. If puppy wakes during the night and needs to go to the toilet, we are easily woken and can ensure that he can be taken outside to relieve himself before being put back to bed. Within only a few nights, puppies usually accept this routine readily. If you also reinforce crate training during the daytime, this will build a solid foundation for the future and you will never look back.

IMMUNITY

In the early weeks with your puppy, remember that his capacity for learning is at its peak. This is the time when you need your puppy to see and experience as much of the world as possible, but if he is exposed to certain harmful infectious diseases this could prove fatal. These diseases are generally passed via aerosol droplets during dog-to-dog contact, or through contact with infected faeces. Other methods of infection may occur via a bite from an infected animal, or from infected waterways. Your puppy will need vaccinations to protect him from these diseases, and until he is *fully* vaccinated he is not protected. Be aware that this involves at least two veterinary visits at approximately three week intervals, and after the final vaccination you will still have to wait for at least a week for your puppy to be fully protected. (See 'Vaccinations', p. 149 for fuller details.) However, there is a great deal that you can do in the meantime, to begin his education.

The following chapter discusses the important processes of socialisation and habituation, and the reasons why it is so important that the Shepherd puppy has an early introduction to the outside world.

Once covered by vaccinations, your puppy
can go out in public

Life's Early Lessons

Whilst you are waiting for his vaccinations to be completed, there is a great deal for puppy to learn. This is a crucial time in his emotional and mental development, and if you keep him house-bound until his vaccinations are complete you will have missed a vital stage in his learning process which can never be replicated. It cannot be stressed strongly enough how important this period is, particularly for the German Shepherd puppy. He is destined to become an intelligent, sensitive and powerful animal, and it is imperative that his early life experiences are full and varied so that he grows into a balanced adult dog.

 Until he is fully vaccinated, he cannot be put down on the floor in public places. If you carry him to places of interest, and take him out in the car, he can still learn about the world without being exposed to the risk of infectious diseases. A 'papoose' made from an old rucksack is ideal for this purpose!

SOCIALISATION AND HABITUATION

Puppies process information rapidly at this age

The term 'socialising' is not just about puppies meeting people. This process will also involve your puppy being introduced to other animals, so that he learns how to interpret their intentions and become at ease with their presence. Once he is fully vaccinated he will be able to go to puppy classes and begin the very important process of learning how to behave with other dogs. A Shepherd who has not been widely socialised with other dogs can present real problems later in life.

'Habituation' refers to the animal becoming accustomed to non-threatening stimuli, objects and events, so that he learns to ignore these and accept them as a part of everyday life. It is vitally important that your puppy experiences all manner of life events before he reaches around sixteen weeks of age. After this time, everything becomes increasingly difficult for him to process without reservation.

If you want your dog to have a bombproof attitude to life, he will need to have been broadly and creatively exposed to the world at large and within your home. This process helps introduce, expose and desensitise your puppy to all kinds of sensory experiences that make up the world he will live in. The more varied exposure he receives during this critical time, the better he will cope with the future challenges of life in a calm and confident manner.

All dogs are programmed with a 'fight or flight response', also known as the 'acute stress response', which was first described by Harvard physiologist Walter Canon in 1929. The theory states that an animal's reaction to stress is as a result of the activation of the sympathetic nervous system: chemicals are released into the body, preparing it to protect itself, or flee, from the perceived threat. It is a genetic response designed to protect animals from harm. Blood sugar levels increase to enable the accessibility of a rapid energy source. The stress hormone cortisol rises, and the brain is in a high state of alert. The heart rate, blood pressure and adrenalin increase, whilst digestion is inhibited, as is the blood supply to various parts of the body. This reaction is genetically programmed within your puppy, but the more situations he is exposed to in these crucial weeks, the more confident he will become in facing life's events. He will also build great trust in you, as you face these tasks with him.

Unwanted behaviours are lessened by socialisation and habituation. Guarding, anxiety, aggression, chewing and barking are all heightened by inadequate early experiences. If you make his early exposure to people, animals and the environment varied *and* fun, he will become desensitised to some of his instinctive responses and will be less likely to become stressed and reactive. He will also be better stimulated, and therefore less likely to become a problem dog.

 There is an age-old saying that 'prevention is better than cure'. This is profoundly true in the case of puppy development. If you leave these crucial lessons until it is too late, your puppy's social development could be permanently affected.

To better appreciate why all of this is necessary, it may be helpful to discuss a brief outline of the individual stages of canine development:

CANINE SOCIALISATION (0–7 weeks)

Your puppy's mother and littermates will teach him valuable lessons about 'species-specific behaviours' in the first seven weeks. He will learn how to interpret and utilise these. In the first few weeks, the puppies learn that the dam is a source of warmth, safety and food. They will already be learning about competing for the warmest spot and for the best teat to nurse from. Newborn puppies will also learn about touch from rough licking by the dam.

Siblings learn a great deal from each other

89

As the weeks progress, the pups will become less reliant on their mother, and they will begin to learn about body postures, vocalisation and facial gestures. They will discover what it feels like to be nipped and bitten by their littermates, and what happens when they do the same in return.

Chase games develop early prey drive, and as they rough and tumble around, the puppies' co-ordination will develop. Throughout this period, puppies learn how to greet one another, how to fight and to play, and they will learn about dominance and the signs of submission.

Socialisation period (7–12 weeks)

Your puppy will already have begun to associate the human beings in his life with touch, food and play. This early relationship between puppy and breeder should have set the stage for you and your pup during this very important learning period.

From the time that puppy leaves his littermates and mother, he will look to you to provide him with the experiences which will make him at ease with your world. This is the period during which you will need to be creative! Socialising him will include meeting a wide variety of people of all ages, shapes and sizes, and he will also need to meet a variety of livestock.

As previously mentioned, habituation is also very important at this stage. You will want puppy to become accustomed to prams, bikes and wheelchairs and he will need to experience car travel too. He will need to be exposed to objects, situations, and all manner of environments from supermarket car parks to car boot sales! Always remember that he will need to be carried in public places until his vaccinations are complete.

Take the time to introduce him to items within your home which he might perceive as threatening, such as the vacuum cleaner or hairdryer. He will need to learn that the mower and broom are neither to be played with nor feared, and he will need to be introduced to the wider world: buses, trains, and busy town centres are all things for him to process. If these are introduced carefully and without fuss, they become ingrained in his memory bank as nothing to fear or over-react to.

At this stage, your puppy has a short concentration span, but his actual ability to process information is strong. Rapid learning is a hallmark of this stage, so maximise on this before it is too late. Whatever he learns now will surely make a strong impression on him for life. Obedience training and general manners (discussed later) will also begin at this time, as this is a perfect time to condition your puppy's responses.

Fear imprint period (8–11 weeks)

Clearly this overlaps with the above period. From around eight weeks, your puppy begins to assess situations that frighten him in such a way that means these impressions are long lasting. Everything you expose him to in this period needs to have a positive outcome, and should be introduced with care. Your responses to these stimuli are also crucial in the eventual outcome. If you are positive and calm about each new situation, your dog will no doubt mirror your reaction and become well adjusted to life.

A common mistake is for owners to attempt to 'reassure' a puppy if he shows any fear.

Dogs interpret reassurance in a different manner to humans, and will undoubtedly view any cosseting as 'praise' for being afraid. (He may also pick up on your own heightened state of anxiety and respond negatively to this.) Try to resist this temptation. If you are calm and quiet and allow the puppy time to get over any initial reservations at his own pace, he will learn that there is nothing to fear. You can praise him once his confident state of mind returns.

Seniority period (12–16 weeks)

Once he is fully vaccinated and able to walk freely beside you, previous excursions to train stations, busy car parks and all other early experiences can be re-visited from floor height. This consolidates the lessons learned whilst he was carried in your arms. Your puppy will gradually be relying on your affirmation less and less, as he steadily develops a certain level of independence. He will want to explore more and more, and his concentration span will increase. He may begin to challenge you a little more, and early issues such as 'play-biting' may rear their head again. This needs to be dealt with quickly and firmly so that it doesn't develop into a bad habit. Toilet training often suffers during this period. A puppy who had seemed 'clean' in the first few weeks may now regress, so it is important to continue praising whenever he gets anything right, and being clear about  the behaviours you do not want. Jumping up can become a particular nuisance at this stage.

You may hear this referred to as the 'cutting' stage: the puppy tries to cut the apron strings, and is also cutting teeth!

Second fear imprint period (6–14 months)

This is not as crucial as the first fear imprint stage but you need to be aware of this period's potential to impact on your puppy's development. If he has previously been level-headed, and suddenly starts to have aversions to people he knows or situations he has already been comfortable with, you may worry – often unnecessarily. This is not usually a radical step backwards, and his behaviour is perfectly natural. Tackle this with sensitivity, and let him work out these situations in his own time. Alternatively you can take a toy into the environment to distract him with, so that he completely forgets about his 'issues'. Once he is relaxed and finds his feet again in any situation reward him and move on. This will increase his levels of self-confidence.

A day at the beach! A great place to socialise your puppy

Flight instinct period (during 4–8 months, but may be intermittent)

This is a period in his development when puppy may challenge your recall and head off, 'doing his own thing' instead. It is a period where independence comes to the fore, and consistent and regular training is crucial if you are to prevent him developing a defiance of you whilst out in public. His adult teeth will begin to erupt during this period and his desire to chew will be heightened. Give him plenty to exercise his jaws and teeth on, and also to occupy him mentally.

Adolescence

From around 6–8 months your puppy moves into adolescence, when the body begins to go through hormonal changes. Both dogs and bitches will become sexually mature during adolescence. Sexual maturity in a bitch (the point where she is able to conceive and carry offspring) arises at around 8–10 months in most cases. However, the bitch is unlikely to be physically and mentally mature enough to undertake this task until she is around two years of age, and in some instances much later. Males can produce offspring from around 8 months, but most people would not use a dog at stud at this age. It is also important that he is mentally mature enough for this not to have an adverse effect on his behaviour.

Training continues to be a vital tool in reinforcing boundaries as the dog reaches his adult height, and yet continues to present you with adolescent challenges. This is often a time when owners stop going to classes with their young dog, but it is doubly important that training be reinforced during this period.

Adulthood

Adulthood, in biological terms, is reached somewhere around 18 months in the German Shepherd, but behaviourally, this breed matures gradually, and may exhibit puppy behaviours for some considerable time after! The German Shepherd is known and loved for his desire to play and seek out attention. He has an enquiring mind and will undoubtedly want to challenge boundaries during adolescence.

From the age of two onwards, he should be at his peak in terms of fitness. Lithe, active and healthy, his body will no longer be subjected to the stresses and strains of growth. It is easy for owners to become complacent during this period. But attention to detail now will stand him in good stead for his future old age, so be sure to feed him with a quality diet, maintain his health checks and exercise, and keep him at an appropriate weight for his frame.

Maturity

Your dog will move into maturity at around six years of age. With a dog that has received a solid and consistent foundation in terms of socialising and training, this should be a phase when he takes life in his stride, is at ease with the expectations placed on him, and develops what appears to be a sixth sense in his relationship with his owner. In terms of his physical well-being, this is the stage which precedes old age, when the body begins to change imperceptibly, on a cellular level.

Old age

Clinical old age begins at around eight years of age, although most Shepherd owners will not feel that their dog is old for some time to come! However, from this point forward the dog will experience a gradual decline in fitness and stamina, speed and reaction. Physiologically the changes result in an increase in the dog being more susceptible to ill health, and the immune system declines gradually.

The well socialised Shepherd puppy becomes a confident and happy adult

Boundaries, Exercise and Playtime!

You will probably find that there is a lot of help offered in the early days with your new arrival. This can be a confusing time as viewpoints on every subject differ, and you may worry about which advice to take. You have already placed your confidence in your breeder, by buying one of their puppies. Their advice about rearing one of their puppies will no doubt be a great point of reference. There are also superb books available, which give further insight into dog psychology and early training. Above everything else, remember to keep things simple at the start and be sure to combine any reading material with practical assistance at a good puppy class, once your puppy is old enough to attend.

During the first few weeks, until your puppy is fully vaccinated, much of your time will be spent establishing routines, manners and simple house rules. These establish a world of boundaries by which the puppy learns what it is that pleases you, what is expected of him, and where he fits in the pecking order.

THINK DOG!

Start as you mean to go on! It is far easier to shape a puppy's behaviour at eight weeks of age, than to try to correct arrogance and ill manners in a large, ten-month-old stroppy adolescent. Establish where he can and cannot go within the house. He should learn that he does not climb onto your furniture, that shoes are not for chewing, and that he does not steal from the table. In these early days it can quickly seem as if everything is centred around the word 'No!'. This can be a difficult time for you *and* for puppy. So, remember that your playtimes with him should be based on things he can achieve and be rewarded for. If his day is littered with negativity he will become confused and withdrawn, so keep encouraging him and praising him whenever he gets things right. This will make for a happy relationship between you both. It will also make correcting him a great deal easier for you to enforce, and for him to understand.

Puppies are adept at making us smile when they do the unexpected. But be aware that the cheeky puppy who chews and 'rags' your jacket is less likely to amuse you if this behaviour continues into adulthood. Just keep 'thinking dog'. Your puppy will continue to exhibit behaviours that he is allowed to get away with in his early months, and will not understand, later in life, if you become cross with him about the things that used to make you laugh.

PLAY-BITING

Puppies bite! This is perfectly natural behaviour, as puppies explore both the world *and* relationships with other dogs by using their teeth. But if this is left unchecked, it can escalate and lead to highly inappropriate, unwanted behaviours. Therefore all 'play-biting' should be nipped in the bud at the earliest opportunity.

The Shepherd is well known for his enthusiastic play-biting. It is particularly common in high drive, assertive puppies, as they use their teeth to 'needle' litter mates. The resulting reaction to his behaviour tells a puppy a great deal about his status within the litter. If you have ever noticed how adult dogs react to an unruly puppy, this may help you to realise how important it is that you tackle this problem if and when it emerges. An adult dog will usually grumble in displeasure if a puppy needles them. As a result, the puppy will clearly know that he has overstepped the mark, and that his bite was too hard. Littermates are more likely to squeal than growl, but as the litter develops, expect to hear some grumbling from the more forceful pups. Such reactions encourage the diminishing of play-biting behaviours, and this is known as 'bite inhibition'. The other thing you will notice is that other puppies refuse to engage in play when they are bitten. They end the game by walking away.

Bite inhibition begins in the litter, and is a lesson that the new owner will need to continue once the puppy is in his new home. You will therefore need to learn how to replicate the responses of your puppy's littermates, so that unpleasant biting behaviours do not escalate in the coming months.

 Be aware that this is not something that your puppy will merely 'grow out of'. He actually needs to learn how to inhibit his bite.

If your puppy inflicts play-biting onto hands and legs, this should be dealt with swiftly by all members of the family (especially where small children are concerned). If this is left unchecked it can become a serious habit, and may prove difficult to reverse later on. The puppy needs to understand that his actions do not lead to him getting attention, or this will only add to the problem. If you give a shrill cry or 'yelp' at *any* attempt to bite, this usually has the desired effect. It is also important that you immediately stop any

Teaching your puppy bite inhibition is very important

interaction you were having with the puppy. He needs to understand that the game ends as a consequence of him biting. Teach your children how to replicate this wherever possible, depending on their age and understanding.

Your puppy is likely to be subjected to all kinds of inconsistencies by members of the family, and as such will probably attempt to bite periodically to see if he can reassess his relationship with you all. Any play-biting should always be dealt with *instantly*. A common trigger is when children wave their hand around puppies' noses in a circular motion, as puppies will inevitably want to grab hold. Be sure that children understand that this will make matters worse and will confuse the puppy about what is acceptable.

Children also need to understand that puppy playtime is *not* an opportunity to have the puppy hanging from the seat of their pants or their trouser leg. This only increases puppy's prey drive, and is likely to lead to issues further down the line. It is really important for an adult to supervise playtimes, especially with young children. Shepherd puppies quickly become over-excited, and accidents can quickly happen if pups are left to play with small children unattended. (This is especially true as puppies move into adolescence, as they are usually at least 70 per cent grown physically, but their boundaries are not always clear at this stage!)

Most puppies will have a 'mad half hour' at some stage in the day. By letting your puppy let off steam in a safe environment, with things he can play with, he will learn to channel his excessive energies appropriately. It is advisable that the children in the household do not engage with him when he is in this high energy mode. In the early weeks, if children are around the puppy while he is excitable, he is likely to play-bite or grab clothing and may view the children as littermates. Children can feel powerless at this time, and this can damage the relationship. As time moves forward, and everyone learns how to play well together, it will become less of an issue, and playtime becomes vital to the growing relationship.

Your puppy is likely to keep bringing the play-biting issue to the fore as he goes through various stages of development. Where there are children in the household, expect this challenge to remain for longer, as children invariably bring mixed messages into the equation. If puppy is not sure where the boundaries lie, he will just keep trying to establish what the rules are. This needs dealing with at all times of re-emergence, as it can present serious problems once the dog is fully grown.

PUPPY PLAYTIME!

Playtime should always be creative, varied and fun! Your puppy will thrive on the positive energy which playtime can provide, and he will learn quickly in this environment. You will have a wonderful time too! Remember to keep all games short and focused, and ensure that playtime ends on a positive note. This is a great time to start introducing a variety of games which will develop your relationship with your puppy. These games will help him begin to understand what you want of him, and how he can earn rewards and praise. Playtime can be used for many different purposes:

- To help with the bonding process
- To teach basic commands in a fun environment
- To establish and reinforce your relationship with puppy
- To help puppy develop wider relationships, not just with his key handler
- To promote 'good manners'
- To stimulate and satisfy the dog mentally (especially important whilst exercise is limited in the early months)

'Hide and seek' is a prime example. This will involve two or more people, one of whom will initially stay with puppy whilst the other goes and hides. It will help to show puppy a favourite toy before running off to hide with it. When the person hiding is ready, the puppy is called by name, and he is encouraged to 'go seek'. This will need to be built up slowly so that he is always able to achieve the aim, so don't hide too far away at first. When he finds the hidden person, he should be instantly rewarded with the toy. You can also use praise and treats to keep the game varied. He will enjoy hunting out the person hiding, and this will encourage him to use his nose and his brain. This can gradually be developed to include the command 'come'.

 You may choose to use a whistle to get his attention, and this transfers well into achieving a solid recall to the whistle once you are in the park.

Playing 'piggy in the middle' will develop his understanding that any member of the family might ask him to come to them, *not* just the person who does most of the training. Start by using two people but this can be added to by a ring of family and friends once puppy is familiar with the game. Using a variety of toys and treats he is encouraged to go to the person who calls his name. (Once he has begun to understand the game, you can introduce the word 'come'.) He is always rewarded by the person he has come to, before another person in the ring calls for him. Be sure that no one else interacts with him if he has come to the wrong person by mistake. Make it exciting and happy, and make the rewards varied, and he will surely enjoy the attention he is getting.

'Tug-of-war' with a knotted rope can provide hours of fun! Remember that no one likes to lose all of the time, so if you constantly win the toy, your puppy will lose interest in the game. However, if you let *him* win all the time he will learn nothing from the game. Variety is the key to success. If you are going to let him win, have a little tug on the rope and then simply let go. Next time let him win again, and then it is your turn. With a firm command of 'leave' he will usually quickly learn to let go. Tell him he is a 'good boy' immediately, and return to the game, offering him the toy. If he is reluctant to let go when you ask him, use another toy to distract him, or offer a treat. This is better than having a battle of wills on your hands, or trying to prise his mouth open, which is counterproductive. Keep alternating with who wins and who loses, with a general rule that you win more than he does!

When deciding on toys for your puppy, it is useful to remember that all puppies need a variety of things to play with, but they don't need them all at the same time! Toys are best rotated every few days as they lose their value and interest if they are constantly available: leave three or four toys out at a time, and swap these every so often for another set to keep his interest. It will also encourage him to learn to amuse himself at times.

THE CLINGY PUPPY

The Shepherd is a sensitive breed. His genetic make-up combined with life experiences that come his way will shape his personality. If your puppy is already rather clingy, remember that the first few days will be the blueprint for the future, so try not to feed into insecure or neurotic behaviours as and when they arise. The Shepherd will often gravitate towards one member of the family, but you need to enhance his view of the whole family as people he can trust and bond with. Get everyone involved in socialising, feeding and training, and you will help him attach to everyone in equal measure.

Try not respond to his clingy moments by 'reassuring him'. He will misinterpret this as praise for being that way, and he may sense any heightened state of anxiety in you which could add to the problem. Let him wander around and explore new environments, and resist the temptation to over-fuss him. By letting him simply 'be a puppy' in the first few days and weeks, he will develop a good measure of self reliance.

SEPARATION ANXIETY

Literally translated, separation anxiety means the fear of being abandoned. From a primitive, canine viewpoint, if a pup is left alone in the wild, it instinctively knows its life is threatened. Its mother is probably dead or injured, and as for the rest of the pack ... well who knows? If a pup senses that it is in danger – left unprotected from predators and unable to assuage his thirst and hunger – his fear will be profound and genuine.

In the domestic environment, you become the pup's primary carer and so you become the surrogate family. Your actions are interpreted as such, so keep trying to see the world through his eyes.

You might feel you have left puppy with all he needs while you go to work or go shopping. But toys, ticking clocks or radios will never keep anxiety at bay if your puppy does not trust you to return without him having to scream in distress.

If you do leave puppy for longer than he can cope with, then you will have broken his trust in you. The impact on each pup varies, as does their ability to recover and relearn. Trust *can* be repaired, but it becomes increasingly hard to do this the older the pup gets, and the more times he is put in this position. He will also develop the 'habit' of becoming fearful about being left alone. This issue is integral to all training, as fear and stress will block the capacity to process information. He may mess in his bed area, become vocal, or destroy anything he is left with. These are all symptomatic of great stress, and can easily be avoided if you take some simple steps.

All puppies need 'time out'. But some will become fearful when left

A PLACE TO CALL HIS OWN

Organising a crate for puppy is to be strongly advised. It is *never* used as a place of punishment, and should be introduced from the start as a safe place to sleep. The dog is a natural 'den animal', and in the wild a den would provide a place of comfort and protection. The crate will replicate this for the domesticated dog, and if introduced with sensitivity, it will represent a place of warmth and security for him.

In the early months, you will need to resist the temptation to confine puppy to the crate when he is clearly active. If you use the crate in this negative way, he will develop the view that the crate is a place of isolation. If you build up his tolerance by introducing him to it when he is tired, he will begin to enjoy his 'time out'. This will help your general training enormously, and will also help you establish a great relationship with him. Some people also use a crate in the bedroom at night in the very early days. If puppy wakes during the night and needs the toilet, someone is on hand to quietly take him outside. He can then be settled back into the pen with the minimum of fuss and interaction so that everyone can continue to enjoy a good night's sleep. By using a similar crate for sleep periods during the day, it is easy to move around freely and get on with your daily tasks within earshot of sleeping pup. As an alternative, a play pen or utility room with baby gate will be more than adequate.

Your puppy will sleep through the night once he is secure emotionally about being left alone in your chosen area. We do not advocate ever that pups are 'left to get on with it' in these early weeks. A puppy shouting and wailing in a kitchen is telling you he is distressed. If you allow this to happen, the pup may develop a fear for life of being left alone, which often transpires into destructive, frantic and hyper behaviours so symptomatic of separation anxiety. If your pup learns slowly that when you drop from sight you will be back *before* he gets frantic and starts to scream, then he builds trust that you will always return. He learns that there is no need to panic, and can relax and enjoy his time alone instead. Some owners advocate that pups should be left alone from the very first night. It may work for some dogs, but in many others it begins the development of separation issues, and this is a cause of many dogs being rehomed or put into rescue.

CRATE TRAINING

The keys to success with crate training are consistency and patience. For a few days of hard work, you will be rewarded with a puppy who can be toilet trained with ease, who does not destroy your new oak kitchen, and who is relaxed about you popping out without resorting to tearing up your home or barking incessantly for hours on end. You can enjoy life, so can he, and so can your neighbours!

In the early stages, puppy should only be put in his crate when he is so tired that he can no longer fight sleep. Try not to break this routine in the early months by letting puppy sleep at your feet or letting him curl up on your lap! He may look sweet, but you will put your routine back a large step, and you will miss the opportunity to reaffirm that his pen is the greatest place to be when he is tired.

Initially you may find that you need to quietly close the pen door, wait a few seconds and then reopen without any fuss. This might have to gradually be built up so that puppy does not see being crated as a threat. Be prepared for this to be a slow process with some dogs, although others will lie down, give into sleep and never look back! Resist the temptation to open the door if he whines, just avert eye contact, stay still and calm next to the pen, and open the door when he is quiet once more.

Once he is settled in the pen and ready to sleep, stay around within his sight. If you walk away immediately you will probably trigger an adrenalin rush in your pup, and he might wake fully and fight sleep in a distressed state. He may lose confidence in the process and become unsettled. So take it all at a slow pace and you will reap good rewards.

Once puppy falls asleep, go about your day, but keep a close eye on him for signs that he is waking up. The trick is to be nearby when he wakes, so that you can quietly and calmly reassure him simply with your presence. Resist the urge to speak to him while he is penned. He needs to learn that this is 'time out'. If he receives no stimulation from you he will learn to settle well, and will also learn to amuse himself with available toys, or a favourite chew. He will need comfortable bedding, and an area of newspaper in the early days in case he suddenly needs the toilet.

Gradually you will be able to build up the delay between him waking and you letting him out. This will encourage the development of the muscles which hold his bladder and bowels, little by little. You can also begin to practise dropping in and out of view of puppy in his crate, to develop his tolerance to your absence. If he learns that you ALWAYS return, he will have no need to become stressed, or to call you to him. He will be prevented from developing the habit of chewing on things he shouldn't. Supervise his early playtimes and he will quickly learn what he can't chew before bad habits begin. If he goes to chew on something he shouldn't, give him an alternative item and praise him for chewing on this instead. He will develop an understanding that whenever he has the perfectly natural desire to use his teeth, there are things which he is permitted to destroy and others which are out of bounds.

TOILET TRAINING

When he awakes, calmly let him out and take him straight outside so that he can go to the toilet. Wait patiently for nature to take its course. Your puppy will almost certainly go to the toilet. At this stage, it is best to not pre-empt the situation by commanding him to go, so you will need to wait silently while he decides what to do. Once he begins to go to the toilet you can use your chosen command repeatedly, and praise him once he has finished. This helps him to build up the association between word, deed, place and praise. It is this whole combination which makes this effective. It is no use just shutting him outside and hoping he goes to the toilet. He is likely to become distracted, or confused at being left outside alone, and you will have broken his training routine before it has begun. He might then ask to come in, and urinate in the house.

Once he is familiar with your chosen command, you can begin to prompt him with it. He *will* gradually get to the stage where he is happy to go off to the garden alone, but keep an eye on him, and praise him as often as possible when you see him getting it right. He may at some stage revert to 'accidents' in the home. If this happens, you will need to take things back a step by accompanying him outside again to reinforce early training. Remember, you can establish the principle of toilet training in a few days, but it may take several months before he is totally trustworthy. The key to successful toilet training is establishing good habits. If you lapse and allow him to make mistakes or develop poor habits, it becomes increasingly difficult to re-establish the good ones.

Your puppy will need to be offered the chance to urinate frequently during periods of play, and should be given the opportunity to relieve himself prior to going back in his play pen to sleep. Following a meal or long drink you should be vigilant too. If you catch your puppy beginning to circle or squat in readiness to go to the toilet, you will need to get his immediate attention without frightening him. If you call him and distract his attention, you can then entice him to go with you into the garden. Try to resist the temptation to carry him outside as he needs to learn how to find his toilet area. It may be a good idea to keep newspaper close to the back door in case he gets 'caught short'.

Do not ever punish your puppy if he has an accident whilst unsupervised. It is your fault for leaving him unattended. If you punish him, it will serve no purpose other than to damage the bond between you. The key in the first month or so is to supervise him whilst he is having play time, and to initiate toilet times for him. The German Shepherd puppy is intelligent and willing, and if you give him the opportunity and the guidelines to be clean, he will learn what is required of him at a rapid pace.

SUBMISSIVE URINATION

Some puppies will naturally urinate spontaneously when greeted by their owner or friends. It is important to remember that this is not naughtiness, it is a natural canine behaviour. It evidences the puppy's awareness of their low ranking position, and eagerness to greet you. It is also a response to being stressed or a little over excited. This is a habit best broken by ensuring that people do not greet puppy in an excitable manner. Greet puppy calmly, a few minutes after arriving home, once puppy has settled down a little. Submissive urination is most commonly exhibited by bitch puppies. Please do not react to this negatively, as this will increase the puppy's stress and make matters worse.

THE IMPORTANCE OF ROUTINES

All too often, puppies are on the receiving end of negativity in response to accidents (or chewing indiscriminately) when left. In the early months, do not be tempted to give puppy the run of your home. If he is left unsupervised, and he feels the need to relieve himself, he will! If he finds something he wants to chew on, he will! It is way too late to then correct him, and is wrong to do so. Toileting in the wrong place causes huge problems with the relationship between pup and owner. Indiscriminate chewing of your beloved home will cause similar friction. It is easy to see why puppies are often rehomed rapidly, but with a little forethought about helping your puppy develop good routines, this need not happen. If you establish a world where the expectations are clear and easily achieved you will have a clean, happy, and non destructive puppy.

EXERCISE

Your German Shepherd puppy will eventually become a large energetic adult, that requires plenty of daily exercise. Until he has really begun to mature, however, he only needs a very gradual build-up of walks and gentle playtime. It is very important to restrict *certain* forms of exercise until he is at least a year of age; for example he should not participate in flyball or agility training, as this can cause a damaging strain on the growing puppy's joints.

Exercising the growing Shepherd is a hotly debated subject, and many breeders recommend lead walking only, until the dog is a year of age. There are also varying regimes proposed which recommend 'x' number of minutes of exercise, per month of the puppy's life. Others believe that this is far too restrictive, and that it also impedes sufficient mental stimulation (which is absolutely vital in the developing puppy). What *is* certain is that you will want to find a balance, whereby puppy can develop muscle tone at a gradual pace, but his socialising experiences are not compromised.

Your puppy needs to see the outside world, and he will be too heavy for you to carry once his vaccinations are completed. So if you build in a few short walks in different places each day he will be given the opportunity to learn the rules of lead walking, and to enjoy seeing the outside world.

These short lead walks will of course help him build certain muscle groups. But you will also want to give him some freedom just to 'be a puppy', whilst always taking into consideration his developing frame. This is best achieved by allowing him short periods of time off lead (or on a long lightweight line) to explore. He will particularly enjoy this in your local park. If this is done gradually it is unlikely to harm his natural growth.

If he is just creating his own bit of fun, chasing falling leaves, or trotting around with a toy in his mouth, then this is a great opportunity for good mental and physical development. But jumping, or excessively long walks (especially on hard surfaces) are to be avoided, as they can induce strain. Muscle production takes many months, so whilst the joints are unprotected try not to encourage high-energy 'rough and tumbling').

  Before introducing time off lead in public areas, of course you will want to ensure that your puppy is obedient to the recall, and that you are in a safe area to let him loose.

At around six months, your pup will be going through his 'long and lean stage'. Like all adolescents, his bone growth will far exceed his muscle growth and he may look like a gangly teenager! Some puppies experience growing pains during this stage, more correctly termed panosteitis (p. 258). The length of his daily walks will have increased, but it is important not to get complacent and start exhaustive forms of exercise. This is often the time when owners lose interest in classes, but is more important than ever to attend at this stage. Firstly it will help channel his mind at a time when he is eager to be occupied. Secondly, like all teenagers, he will really be starting to develop a mind of his own, so setting good boundaries is important.

If you reinforce good behaviour, and learn new things together, you will help keep his mind focused on pleasing you, rather than learning how to please himself. If you tackle this period of development with the same enthusiasm you had in his first few weeks you can reap enormous rewards. Puppy classes are readily attended and yet adolescent training often gets by-passed, usually with sad results. German Shepherd adolescents can easily regress and become independent or defiant.

As your dog moves into early adulthood you will at last begin to exercise him more freely, without worrying about his joints. An adult Shepherd will need at least an hour's free running exercise every day, and this need is not met by wandering around your garden, however large it might be. He needs an opportunity for free running, and will also benefit from being introduced to canine sports such as agility or flyball once old enough.

By adopting a sensible, measured approach to your growing dog's exercise, you will have given him a good chance of achieving sound hips and elbows for the future. Unfortunately, this does not mean that he is guaranteed to be problem free, as hip and elbow development have genetic, environmental and dietary components, but this careful approach is all about maximising the *potential* for future health.

Part Four

The Importance of Education

• The Makings of a Partnership • The Joys of Competition •
• 'Troubled Times' •

The Makings of a Partnership

The German Shepherd provides invaluable assistance for us within a vast range of services. This clearly shows the breed's ability to respond to a whole spectrum of tasks. But most German Shepherds will not find themselves as a servant to the public, and are more likely to simply become a much loved member of the family. However, the majority of these dogs will have potential which far exceeds this role, and, with the introduction of basic training as a puppy, and continual consistent training, they will begin to develop into reliable and obedient companions. By taking this training forward once your dog is old enough (see overleaf), and introducing him to the joys of agility, obedience and working trials, you will see this companionship develop further, into a true partnership where trust, loyalty and commitment on both sides reaps rewards for dog and handler alike.

WHY TRAIN?

In terms of the mental welfare of your dog, there is no substitute for regular and enjoyable training. Your dog will benefit greatly from the mental stimulation it provides, and will be given the opportunity to relate to you in a positive and meaningful way. The German Shepherd needs this stimulation so that he does not become vocal, challenging, and destructive: these behaviours are invariably symptomatic of boredom and mental distress. Regular training is therefore a must, especially where individual dogs have an abundance of mental energy.

The dog's physical fitness is also enhanced by regular training. A wide variety of exercises will build stamina and strength in the dog, as he retrieves, tracks, and scales the A' frame (some of the exercises commonly learned). If he is mentally and physically fit he is more likely to perform well. You will need to keep him in tip-top condition if you hope to compete!

Many people rightly worry about 'control' as an issue when owning a German Shepherd, as they can be quick to take advantage of handler inconsistencies! This is a medium-large breed of considerable strength, and this power needs to be managed correctly. Self-control of the handler is of equal importance, as Shepherds respond best to consistent, reliable handling. Regular training will help identify strengths and flaws

The well-trained Shepherd is a joy to own

within the relationship in the crucial formative stages. Signing up for professional training classes with a qualified instructor is therefore vital, especially for the novice Shepherd owner. You and your puppy will learn how to connect with one another, under the watchful eye of a trainer who can guide you through early difficulties. The boundaries are gradually established so that a harmonious relationship can flourish, and the dog's understanding of your expectations of him can be reinforced in a fun environment.

The benefits of training your dog are wide and varied, but the impact on your own life should not be underestimated. Being involved in the education of a German Shepherd puppy is a wonderful experience. Of course you will have frustrations along the way, but the rewards are huge. You will certainly get to know yourself better, because any relationship with a bright and challenging Shepherd will make you examine your own strengths and weaknesses! You will meet like-minded people, some of whom may also make you think long and hard about alternative methods of training. This can only serve to broaden your approach to achieving your goals with your beloved dog. You will shape your Shepherd's behaviour as his life progresses and will no doubt end up with the dog you had always dreamed of. He will not get to this point without your commitment, and your sense of pride will make it all worthwhile.

The German Shepherd has an incredible aptitude for absorbing information. If you take the time to develop this and to channel his enthusiasm, you are likely to develop a close and rewarding bond. The breed has evolved over the past century to be loyal, protective and responsive to training. The stage is therefore set, and it is now down to you.

COMMUNICATING WITH YOUR DOG

Dogs have inherited genetic blueprints for certain behaviours from their distant ancestor – the wolf. Domesticated dogs still have the same innate drives as their ancestors: to eat, to reproduce, and to protect their young, food and territory. This invariably incorporated belonging to a pack with clear rules regarding competition for resources, although evolution of the dog is also believed to include solitary, scavenging and foraging individuals. Domestication of the dog has resulted in us gradually learning how to manipulate many canine drives to suit our needs and lifestyle. In recent decades, this understanding has deepened significantly and as a result, we are able to live in greater harmony with our canine companions.

Learning the basics of formal obedience is a crucial part of educating your puppy, but *everything* you do from day one is being assessed and assimilated by your new charge. Always bear in mind that dog training is not just about formal exercises – it is also about applying these exercises to daily life. Your dog might be happy to sit for a treat, but will he sit patiently while you talk with a friend on the street? He may execute a good recall at classes,

but will he return in the park where distractions might tempt him away from you? Think ahead about what you will want from him in the future, and begin shaping his behaviour from day one. If you reinforce formal exercises in a wide variety of daily situations, this will result in a stronger and far more pleasing relationship.

A mutual understanding of each other's language, both verbal and non-verbal, will be vital in establishing the relationship. This begins from the moment you start interacting with your puppy. As his new world unfolds he learns about the dynamics between you from a variety of sources, so you will need to think carefully about how you communicate with him and take time to understand what he is telling you. The subtleties of intuitive learning may be infinite, yet the signals which will guide your puppy towards becoming a great companion are relatively simple, if you make an effort to understand them.

WHAT ARE YOU TELLING YOUR DOG?

Body language

You will need to be calm and confident in your approach. Are you easily agitated, excitable or forceful, or perhaps you are not of strong character? Whatever your personality type, you can be sure of one thing – that your Shepherd puppy will rapidly assess your body language, so you will need to be consistent, especially in the early days of training. With every exercise, think about how your body language impacts on his response. If you are doing a recall exercise for example, open your arms wide to give him a welcoming space to return to, and crouch down so that you are less intimidating to a small puppy. If you are teaching a 'stay' exercise to your puppy, be calm and steady in your body movements, and try not to raise his energy levels by sudden actions, as he will readily pick up on, and respond excitedly to, high energy movements from you.

Touch

This is a valuable asset. Most dogs love the affection given to them by their owner, and one the great pleasures of owning a dog is the mutual exchange of affection. A fuss on the top of his head or a pat on the shoulder reinforces your verbal praise when your dog has pleased you. But it can be over used. Ask yourself, do you fuss him constantly, or does he have to earn it? If he does not have to do anything to earn this affection, you will have negated a valuable tool for reward: Over-fussing leads to a deadening of response, and physical praise will no longer present as a motivation. Using touch in a negative way (i.e. as punishment) is to be avoided. Smacking your dog merely vents your own anger, and is likely to damage the dog's trust in you.

Emotion

Your puppy assesses your emotion through the tone of your voice, and through chemical changes in your body which indicate to him that you are perhaps stressed or excited. You need to be in a positive state of mind before you embark on a training session. If your voice is welcoming and cheerful, conveying a positive state of mind, your dog will be more inclined to work for you. Clearly there are moments when you will need to be firm, if your

From pet to police dog, he will give more of himself if he is happy

dog needs correction, but this should not be prolonged, and *never* aggressive. If you become overbearing or erratic your relationship will become unstable.

WHAT IS HE TELLING YOU?

If you study your dog's posture when he is greeting other dogs (and people), you will see many signals form throughout his body. Dogs use a wide range of gestures such as a gentle wagging of the tail to show pleasure, but he can incorporate the whole body combined with vocal signals when communicating anxious or aggressive behaviours. Dogs use body language to build friendships and to avoid confrontation. They use it to take control of situations and to show preference for specific resources. The better you understand your dog's signals to you, the better you can interpret their needs.

Confidence

The confident stance is straight and tall. The head is held high but the posture and facial expressions are non-threatening. Ears are forward. The eyes are bright and wide, and will hold your gaze but they do not portray a 'hard stare'. Nothing about the body suggests stiffness or tension. The dog is content with its situation and its status. Confidence is not the same as dominance.

Dominance

Dogs assert dominance over other dogs regarding a variety of resources, for example food, territory, sex or offspring. A dominant dog will make direct eye contact. The ears are forward expressing an alert attitude, and the gait is stiff. The dominant dog will stand straight and tall, with tail held high, and it may attempt to put its head over the other dog's neck and shoulders.

Submissiveness

The dog shows meekness, and an acceptance of low ranking status. The head is held low, the ears are flat against the head, and direct eye contact will be avoided. The tail is held low and may wag between the legs. Typically, a submissive dog will expose the neck and shoulder area to the perceived aggressor, or will roll on the back and expose the belly. The subservient dog may lick around a dominant dog's mouth, and slink their body along the other dog's flanks to display passivity.

Anxiety

The anxious dog is unstable, and may act submissively, but this could unfold into fear aggression if the dog feels put under pressure. The eye contact is likely to be intermittent. The ears will be held back, possibly 'flicking' though partially erect stages and back again to flat. The neck may be outstretched, and the dog will pace and pant with apprehension. The tail is held low or may wag between the legs, to appease the 'foe'. An anxious dog may try to escape its environment.

Fear

All of the above signals may be seen. The fearful dog may also tremble or shudder, may urinate or defecate, and may 'grimace' by bearing teeth in defence. The hackles are raised, as the dog attempts to make itself look bigger. Some low-grade growling is common because the dog feels uneasy and unsure of how to deal with the position it is in. If the dog's fear escalates, this can transfer into aggression.

Aggression

Canine agression is a complex subject as it can have many root causes including fear, pain and the desire to protect certain resources.

With 'nervous aggression', the behaviour is erratic and unpredictable. Eye contact will be intermittent, and the dog may whine and bark, usually in a high pitch. It may lunge erratically in the direction of the perceived threat. Every attempt should be made to lessen the dog's perception of threat, but they should not be 'reassured'.

A dominant dog, protecting his territory or a potential mate, will have a stiff gait, tail upright, and will meet its 'aggressor' with a cold hard stare. Barking, growling and baring of teeth are all carried out with a continuation of the stare, and the dog's chest will be presented square-on to its adversary.

HOW DOGS LEARN

Dogs learn in a similar way to humans, and this gives us a valuable opportunity to understand how to get the very best from our canine companions.

Dogs learn by association, known as 'classical conditioning', which was clearly illustrated by the work of Russian physicist Ivan Pavlov. Pavlov was doing studies on saliva, when he realised that an unidentified stimulus was causing the dogs to salivate before they were fed. He subsequently introduced a bell which he rang every time he fed the dogs. Ultimately they did not merely drool at the smell and sight of food, but they would begin drooling at the sound of the bell. They had begun to associate the bell with the presentation of dinner, just as your dog probably gets excited when you take your coat from the rack, in anticipation of his walk. Classical conditioning denotes the situation whereby a *stimulus acquires the capacity to evoke a response that previously was evoked by another stimulus*.

Dogs also learn through a type of learning known as 'operant conditioning'. This was studied by psychologist B.F. Skinner (1904–1990) who identified three types of operant which can follow a specific behaviour:

- NEUTRAL, which results in no effect on the likelihood of a behaviour being repeated
- REINFORCERS, which increase the probability of a behaviour being repeated (these can be positive or negative)
- PUNISHERS, which decrease the likelihood of behaviours being repeated.

Reinforcers teach the animal that certain behaviours result in certain consequences. Positive reinforcers (where a rewarding stimulus follows the behaviour), give the most reliable response. They also strengthen the desired response. Negative reinforcement describes the situation whereby an aversive stimulus is removed. As positive reinforcement harnesses the individual's ability and willingness to learn, it is widely accepted that positive reinforcement results in behaviours which are long lasting. Punishment on the other hand, harnesses the fear response and blocks the capacity to learn effectively. Punishment results in behaviours occurring temporarily and it may also result in adverse side effects. It produces unreliable responses and in some instances, fear. A fearful frame of mind can result in aggression which, in a large dog such as the German Shepherd, is to be avoided at all costs.

Before you begin to command any action from your puppy you will need to set the stage for him so he learns to associate action and reward. This will progress to him making the connection between *word*, action and reward. Very early training will utilise actions that the puppy does all of his own accord, and you will maximise on his learning potential merely by adding the correct word and praise at the appropriate moment. If you 'condition' a puppy to respond in this way, the groundwork is set and he begins to understand your words for his deeds.

It sounds simple to say it, but too many people think that the dog somehow knows what 'no' means, by some act of magic! Our language means nothing until puppy begins to attach it to his actions. Be consistent and patient and do not give him too many words to think of. Be prompt with your timing of praise or reprimand, as if you do not respond within a few seconds, the association means nothing to him. Resist becoming too repetitive in any one session as boredom kills enthusiasm! 'Think dog' at every stage.

Incentives

Verbal praise is always vital in establishing a good working relationship. You will need to harness his keenness to please, and develop his understanding of what it is that you are asking of him. Always be clear and positive with your voice when praising him. He needs to be sure that he has pleased you enormously, so do not be shy and reticent! Your tone of voice is all important. Be exuberant and warm with your praise, and firm in your tone with any reprimand.

Playtime will help him learn to channel his 'drives'

Toy-reward forms the ideal foundation of training for most dogs. Earning a game with a favourite toy brings fun into the sessions, and increases motivation. Give your dog the opportunity to find, 'rag', or chase after his favourite toy, and you will see increased desire and drive coming to the fore. Using a favourite toy works best when this toy is only used for training, and does not form a part of his group of playthings at home. This helps it become of high value.

Food-reward forms the basis of much debate and dispute amongst trainers. Some feel that its usage produces a dog that will not work for anything else. If you plan to use food rewards as an incentive, keep the portions small and remember that alternating with *other* incentives will help you produce consistent responses from your dog. Make sure that your treats are deducted from the dog's daily food rations, as you can soon find you have a fat dog on your hands! Small pieces of hard, mild cheese or cooked chicken are good motivators for even the pickiest of puppies. You can buy ready-made training treats from your pet stores. 'Pedigree Rewards®' are particularly convenient. Another popular treat is liver cake. Keep the most delicious treats for training out in public areas, especially for recall exercises, along with high value toys as already discussed.

TRAINING AIDS

Chains / collars /devices / face collars

In days of old, training incorporated the use of a check chain. Otherwise termed a 'choke chain', this can be a tool of some considerable cruelty and at the very least it is not appropriate on a puppy. It certainly is dangerous if put on the wrong way around as the chain will not release once 'checked'. Your early training collar is likely to be a soft, flat, nylon collar. You may wish to introduce a 'half-check' at a later stage but these are not suitable for very young puppies. (These are made of nylon with a small chainlink section, and will restrict partially when 'checked'.) Sadly, punitive collars (including prong, pinch or radio-controlled electric collars), are used in a variety of situations, usually when control becomes a serious problem. Their usage creates heated debate across the dog world. If you start your puppy's training correctly, and instil a solid foundation for manners, respect and an eagerness to please, you will hopefully never decide to resort to controversial measures in order to keep your dog 'under control'.

The face collar provokes mixed reaction from dog owners and the wider public, as it loosely resembles a muzzle and can therefore lead the onlooker to the wrong conclusion. Some dogs will persist at rubbing their face when wearing a face collar, so its usage can be

A leather slip lead will suffice if the dog walks well on lead

Face collars can be useful if your dog pulls on lead

viewed with negativity as the dog appears distressed. Face collars do however enable an otherwise unruly dog to be walked with greater ease, and it should be taken in context. If introduced with sensitivity, most dogs learn to accept face collars without undue fuss.

Harnesses

Harnesses are used by some as an alternative to the collar and lead. If you hope to compete with your dog at any stage in the future, such usage of the harness is inadvisable. Firstly, your dog will need to be correctly educated to walk on the lead in all activities, and secondly, some harnesses enable the dog to pull more effectively! This kind of harness is the equipment used when the police or military dog is tracking a suspect. It is also used during working trials. Made of webbing or leather, a well-fitting harness gives the dog a clear signal about the task ahead. It provides a strong frame for the tracking line to be clipped to, and avoids the enthusiastic dog being choked which would happen easily if the line was clipped to its collar. The harness spreads the strain of tensions in the line across the dog's shoulders and chest. It also gives the dog free movement to stretch forward and put his nose to the ground.

The anti-pulling harness is a completely different matter. It is specifically designed to exert pressure under the dog's front legs if it is trying to surge ahead. Dogs usually learn that the discomfort eases when they are calmly walking beside the owner.

Whistles

The whistle can be used to back up (or replace) the word 'come' in certain situations. If you always food reward the dog whenever he returns after hearing the whistle, he will make the association between whistle and reward, and your recall will be all the stronger for it.

Environment

Puppies will benefit enormously from being trained in varied locations. All too often, owners will glumly state that 'he does it perfectly at home' when their dog becomes unwilling at training classes. If you only train at home, your dog will never learn to ignore distractions, and his obedience will become tenuous. If you are creative and train him while other dogs and distractions are present, you will build up his ability to focus on you. You will also help him to develop manners in all situations. Of course you can train in the garden and in the home itself, but there is little substitute for training out in public. Puppy needs to understand that good manners and obedience are part of the requirements of everyday life, *regardless* of location.

WHY ATTEND CLASSES?

Experienced owners are sometimes reluctant to attend classes and may feel that that they have nothing further to learn. But even if you have a wealth of experience behind you, your new puppy has none. All puppies will benefit hugely from an environment where they can meet other dogs. The Shepherd can develop unwanted behaviours such as barking on the lead at other dogs, if not properly socialised with multiple breeds early on.

Puppy can learn how to focus on you in this busy and exciting environment. This can be invaluable, as he will need to develop the skill of keeping his attention on you in busy places later on.

From the owner's point of view, training classes can be great fun, and

Good introductions with other dogs will help your pup to be sociable

thought provoking, as there are always new approaches and new thinking to absorb. Dog training has come many miles from the days of hard discipline methods. Punitive attitudes to dog training have shown that they build unreliable responses from our canine companions. Positive training methods now pave the way for enjoyable and productive training, and they are here to stay.

DIFFERING APPROACHES TO TRAINING

You will possibly anticipate that at your first session you will simply be introduced to obedience basics. However, you may be in for a shock if you have not attended classes for a decade or so. In days of old, puppies would be marched around village halls, to the strident tones of a Barbara Woodhouse convert shouting 'Heel, turn and *sssiiittt!*' You will now find classes are often restricted to smaller numbers. 'Puppy socialising classes' will form the first stage in educating your new addition.

If you attend a mixed breed class, your instructor will usually discuss some of the traits of each breed in the class, and an initial assessment of each puppy will be made. They will talk to you about any early problems, and will want to know how much education your puppy has already received. There will be minimal 'regimented heel work', and owners will be encouraged to reward the puppy for focusing on them. Puppies will be encouraged to 'play nicely' and this will be monitored for any signs of unwanted behaviours. Some classes provide an invaluable opportunity to socialise the puppies with other livestock, and you are likely to be introduced to clicker training.

Clicker training

This is highly effective when taught correctly, but is of no use in the hands of someone who has not done their homework! Clicker training has a huge following worldwide. Pioneered by Karen Pryor whilst working as a dolphin trainer, this has also been used to train dogs, parrots, horses and more besides. It utilises the notion of positive reinforcement discussed earlier. Using a small box with a metal tongue which emits a 'click' when pressed, the animal is conditioned to learn that the click initially signifies a reward. This is then developed so the animal learns that his precise action initiates the click, and subsequent reward. The beauty of it is that there is no anxiety, anger or frustration transmitted by the clicker, so the animal's focus is never distracted by negative emotions.

If you plan to try clicker training, be sure to work with an experienced trainer, as so many mistakes are made by people who simply don't take the time to absorb its potential. Your dog will also learn to think about how to achieve what is required, rather than simply responding to a command. This is called 'shaping'. For hyper or anxious dogs, the removal of verbal responses and the replacement with pinpoint affirmation is liberating to say the least.

Natural training/dog whispering

Fashions change over time, and you would be hard pressed not to know about 'dog whispering', or 'natural' training, which use body language and the application of calm-assertive states of mind in order to achieve results (particularly with dogs that have behavioural issues). But good dog trainers have known since the human–dog relationship began, that being relaxed, consistent and positive throughout the dog's training sessions and daily life, produces reliable and solid results. Weakness, inconsistency, aggression and punishment lead to a relationship which is based on a rocky foundation, and whilst there are always moments which require firmness or correction, respect has to travel both ways and it should never be based on fear. A good leader is always calm and fair, consistent and clear. You are first and foremost the provider of food which makes you respected, but what other signals do you give? Do you allow your dog control over your bed or other furniture? Is he allowed to eat food from your kitchen table and barge past you at the gate? Your dog will respond best to clear guidelines about how you want to co-exist. He will become troubled if you constantly change the 'goal posts', and the relationship is especially tenuous if you are heavy handed, unpredictable or aggressive.

Clicker training and natural training have their critics, as do some traditional methods. When deciding on where to take your puppy to classes, it pays to go and visit several clubs and organisations. You will see dogs trained in a variety of ways, and emphasis may differ especially if the ultimate aim is to be competing in working trials, or obedience. For example, The Association of Pet Dog Trainers (A.P.D.T.) has clubs across the UK, and classes are based on the benefits of positive reinforcement, through praise and clicker-motivation training. These classes are invariably mixed breed classes. If you prefer to be breed-specific, your local German Shepherd breed club will be able to encourage a wide understanding of working positively and effectively with your Shepherd puppy, by harnessing the knowledge of Shepherd trainers whose experience can be invaluable. Many clubs also offer the Good

Citizen Award Scheme (p. 132). These offer the owner an opportunity to think deeply about everyday manners and their relationship with the dog.

Spend time talking to Shepherd owners locally and at shows or competitions. You will hopefully find the right class for you.

 Regardless of the approach you decide on, you will find that the key to all successful training remains the same. It comes from a consistent and positive approach, by never over-doing things, and by being precise and timely with reward.

You may need to reinforce boundaries with young adults

EARLY COMMANDS

In the weeks between collecting puppy and attending your first training class, you will have begun setting boundaries, and will have introduced some of the following words:

- Good boy!
- No!
- In your bed
- Be clean (toilet training)
- Off / Leave
- Take it (encouraging manners when taking treats)

Try not to flood him with multiple new words in a session. Too much information will confuse him. You would never expect a rapid learning curve from your newborn baby in the first weeks of their homecoming. You would want to make them calm, safe, and comfortable, and gently begin to get to know one another. Clearly, puppies develop at a faster rate than babies, but your pup is still a newcomer to the world, and has a long way to go before he becomes the dog of your dreams. Puppies need plenty of sleep and the opportunity to learn things for themselves, so they should be given the chance to build a little self reliance, as well as learning how to interact with you. Enjoy watching your puppy explore without always intervening.

PRACTICAL TRAINING EXERCISES

As well as the general list mentioned above, you will also want to introduce him to formal obedience commands. The exercises below will form the foundation for future training. You will need to practise these at home, and in public places. It is important that once you begin puppy's education that you build it consistently into his daily routine. Below is a standard list of the most basic commands and some thoughts on how they can be introduced.

Heel on lead

The object of the exercise is to have the dog walking beside his handler. In competition, he would be required to walk on the handler's left hand side, but even if you don't plan to compete with your pup, it is important that you adopt this from day one, as he will need to know what is expected of him.

A dog that is walking correctly will be relaxed, and not attempting to pull or gain advantage. The lead should be relaxed and is held in the right hand. The left hand is used at moments when guidance is needed, and also to reward the dog.

In his first few weeks with you, you can introduce puppy to the collar and lead in your garden. Distract puppy with a game or a treat when you first put his collar on, and he will rapidly forget all about it. There may be a bit of initial scratching and 'worrying' at it, but he will soon accept its presence. After a few days, if you wish to introduce his lead, do so with discretion as you would not want him to fear it. It is useful to let him simply wander around the garden trailing the lead behind him at first. You can then gradually take hold of the lead once he seems at ease with its presence.

Have treats in your pocket to entice him to come towards you rather than pull away. It is important in these early days that he does not associate the lead with restriction or he may panic. Begin to build his understanding by showing him a treat or a favourite toy, and entice him to walk beside you. As he moves beside you encourage him with the word 'Heel' and reward him when he is in position.

As training progresses, you may find that puppy attempts to get ahead of you. Do a right about turn, bend down with a treat (or toy) in your outstretched left hand, and give him plenty of verbal encouragement.

As he changes direction and begins to follow you, use the command again to reinforce what you are asking of him. Continue to encourage and reward his behaviour. Keep your tone of voice light and cheerful, as you will want him to be keen to be beside you. Several short sessions of this will usually help puppy realise that any attempt to rush ahead is to no avail, and that he is constantly praised and rewarded when by your side. He will soon develop a willingness to follow your every move.

The recall

This is the most important of all the obedience exercises, and it is something which many owners battle with on a daily basis. From a safety point of view this exercise could save your dog's life, but regardless, a solid recall denotes clear respect for the handler. It is also important to remember that any dog which fails to return when called is a social problem. A German Shepherd that ignores his handler does not enhance the public's perception of the breed, regardless of how friendly he is! The command to 'come' will ultimately form part of the formal recall exercise, whereby your dog will be left sitting until you call him back to you.

You can begin teaching him to enjoy returning to you from day one. As puppy rushes to greet you, you can use the word 'come' excitedly and reward him once he is with you. Use open body language and a welcoming tone to your voice. He will soon associate the word 'come' with his action, and also with the reward which awaits him. Don't ask him to 'come' in these early days whenever he is distracted, or you will simply be teaching him to ignore you. If you do ask him to come but receive no response, don't become over bearing. Distract puppy by clapping your hands and then make yourself irresistible and inviting! When he returns, don't chastise him for his earlier indiscretion, or you will make your recall tenuous.

The recall can be developed in very young puppies by playing games such as 'hide and seek' or 'round robin' at home (p. 96). These will build fun and excitement into the exercise. You can be inventive and use toys to make the exercise varied and interesting. If you use a favourite toy or a treat as the 'lure' to entice him back to you, then the recall is instantly associated with reward.

The exercise can be introduced in other ways too. Whistle training is a fabulous way of developing a reliable recall. Let puppy know that you have a treat or high value toy in your hand, but don't let him have it. Run backwards a little way and blow the whistle. If puppy comes to you, give him his reward. If you repeat this several times each session he will readily associate the whistle with a desirable reward. This will be especially useful out in the park a little later on.

Whatever your preferred method(s), this needs to be practised regularly in the early months, so that the puppy doesn't get into the habit of ignoring you when you call him. A strong recall is paramount, and so you need to reinforce this regularly with praise, treats and games in varying measure.

Once you begin taking puppy out in the park, it is wise to have a lightweight training line attached to him that he can trail about behind him, but that gives you an instant source of connection to him if he fails to respond to your command or whistle. Build up little sessions into your stroll, always make yourself inviting, by running backward, opening your arms to him and encouraging his return with your voice. He must learn early on that failure to respond to 'come' is simply not on the agenda, and that his return to you is always met with praise in abundance. This way you will set the stage for a reliable relationship when out in public, and you will feel at ease with him running free in the park. You will need to reinforce this training as puppy goes through adolescence as this is a time when your youngster will exhibit increasing independence.

'Sit'

If you want to begin introducing the word 'sit', use a toy or a treat and bring this up over puppy's nose as he stands before you. He will naturally bring his head up and put his bottom down. Once his response is reliable, you can begin to add the verbal cue. Always reward him. If you follow this method you will find it takes very little time for him to have made the connection. You can also enhance the his understanding, by introducing the command during the day, at the precise moment your puppy sits for any reason.

It is important that you introduce him to the fact that he will also be required to sit by your side, not just in front of you for a treat. Once he has learned the command, build it into your lead walking exercises. Ask him to sit by your left hand side, and be ready to use your left hand to gently guide his body into position against your leg.

'Down'

With your puppy in the sit position, hold a treat below his nose and bring the treat towards the ground. Your puppy will almost definitely follow the scent and will lay down, as he tries to get the treat. You can also encourage puppy to do this from the 'stand' position, although at the beginning the puppy is likely to pace around your hand rather than lie down. The drop from 'sit' to 'down' is more natural for him. Once he responds readily for his treat, you can begin to add the verbal cue.

'Stay'

Having your dog remain in a static position is important in all kinds of situations, and from a competitive point of view it forms the basis of many exercises. Teaching the 'stay' exercise can be done through a variety of methods. Some people will alternate the use of the word 'wait' for incidences where a recall will follow, and will use 'stay' for situations where the handler returns to the dog's side. Some feel that 'stay' should be used regardless. Other trainers do not use this as a command at all. (The dog is simply educated to remain in any static position, following the basic command of 'sit' etc., until given an appropriate release command, e.g. 'heel,' 'come' or 'go play'.)

To teach the command 'stay', your puppy will initially need to be in a sit or down position, as you will want to develop his response to the word stay before progressing to the stand stay. Using the palm of the hand facing towards the dog, as a visible signal, you will step slightly away from the dog, and return before he goes to break the position. This is gradually increased to build the dog's tolerance to time in the position, and to the increasing distance between you. Again, add the word 'stay' once his response is reliable.

Do not praise instantly on your return. This only encourages the dog to anticipate the release from the position. Step away a second time and return to your dog. Wait a moment before rewarding him and letting him break from position.

SUMMARY

 Keep your sessions simple, short and fun!

Train regularly. It is better to do five minutes every day than half an hour once a week.

Take your time to introduce new words. The family should all use the same word for each command.

Only ever give one command. The more times you repeat a command the more deadened to it he will become. You don't want him thinking he gets told five times to 'come' before he has to!

Make progression logical. Don't rush to do 'sit-stay' until you are certain that he fully understands 'sit' for example.

If he fails to grasp an exercise, go back to basics and slow the process down. Do not become negative or frustrated with him.

Only train when you are in a positive frame of mind.

Always make sure your sessions end on a positive note.

The Joys of Competition

The German Shepherd has the ability to be highly successful in all strains of competitive sport. Although it is fair to say that the Border Collie dominates competitive obedience and agility, the Shepherd produces work of quality, flair and accuracy, and provides the Collie with a very serious competitor! Working trials provides the German Shepherd with a natural opportunity to show off his strengths, and 'Schutzhund' is the pinnacle for many trainers across the world, with tests designed over a hundred years ago to specifically show the innate skills and courage of the breed.

COMPETITIVE OBEDIENCE

Your first introduction to this will hopefully have you hooked from the start! As your puppy progresses through each stage of his training, he is likely to be graded within your club. You will be rightly proud of your pup (and yourself) as he passes each stage with flying colours, and this may just give you the thirst for knowledge you will need in order to take this to a competitive level. Competitive obedience will require great commitment and attention to detail from you, and it is a good idea to go to local shows/trials to begin the task of understanding why every exercise has to be worked through with accuracy and care. Little errors made now might impinge on later successes, and every stage will need to be achieved through fun and plenty of praise. Your dog will need to be sharp and accurate with responses, and driven by a clear desire to please. It will need to be a lot of fun for him too.

Some of the exercises you will gradually aim to perfect include the following:

- Heelwork- on and off lead / changes of pace
- Recall
- Retrieve
- Sit/down and stand stays
- Distance control
- Sendaway

- Scent discrimination
- Temperament test
- Advanced sit/stay and down, performed on the move.

Competitive obedience has existed as a sport in the US since the mid 1930's. It was introduced to the UK in the 1950s. It is a licensed sport offered by Kennel Clubs and governing bodies around the world. If you wish to compete just for fun, you will find that exemption and companion dog shows, run by a wide variety of charities and clubs, will provide you with a great introduction to the sport. If you are hoping to compete under Kennel Club rules and regulations, your dog will need to be registered with your national Kennel Club either on their breed or activity registers.

Puppy games should be varied and fun!

If you enter obedience competitions under British Kennel Club regulations, you will find that the sport is graded as follows:

- Pre-Beginner
- Beginner
- Novice
- A/B/C
- Championship C (winners of this can compete at Crufts).

Obedience certificates of Merit, Excellence, and ultimately that of Obedience Warrant (OW) are the progression of titling offered by the Kennel Club.

The American Kennel Club offers progression through Novice, Open and Utility classes, with the titles CD, CDX and UD being awarded once the dog has qualified at each respective level under 3 different judges. The coveted title of UDX can be achieved after 10 wins in Open B and Utility B. Achieving the further title of Obedience Trials Champion (OTCH) is the ultimate honour and requires that the dog has been awarded 100 points in Open B and Utility B classes. The top OTCH pointed dogs from each breed (and those who qualify through Regional Obedience Championships), receive an invitation to compete in the National Obedience Championships, with the coveted NOC title given to the top dog each year.

AGILITY

Introduced in the late 1970s, agility is a really exciting sport which has become hugely popular and accessible in recent times. You will need a fast-minded, fleet-of-foot Shepherd to tackle this on a competitive level! Dogs should not start agility training until they are at least 12 months of age, due to the potential for impact injuries on their growing frame. If you hope to compete in this sport, be aware that your dog will invariably not be permitted to compete until he reaches 18 months of age. Both you and your dog will need to be fit and healthy, and superb control of the dog is a must. The dog's capacity to respond to split-second commands (verbal and non-verbal) becomes highly developed through this training.

The agility course comprises a number of obstacles which dog and handler may be asked to negotiate in a set order. They are marked for each obstacle and for the speed in which they complete the course. Faults may be incurred at each obstacle, for example a failure to touch 'contact points' on the see-saw, or if they refuse to tackle an obstacle. The test will be performed off lead, and the handler is not permitted to touch either the dog or the obstacles.

Obstacles vary according to country and organisation, but may include:

- Tunnels – Collapsible or Pipe
- Hoop or Tyre
- Rising spread jump, Water jump / Single hurdles
- A-Ramp / Frame
- Weave poles
- Dog walk and See-saw ('Teeter Totter')

There are many permutations of classes worldwide, but may include:

- Standard / Regular or Agility
- Jumpers/ Jumping
- Gamblers / Joker or Jackpot
- Snooker
- Power and Speed
- Teams, Relay and Pairs

Agility in the UK

There are three major agility organisations in the UK today:

- The British Kennel Club offers a grading system from Grade 1 through to Grade 7, and three jump heights are offered. If competing under KC rulings, your dog will need to be registered on the breed or activity register, and he will have to be officially measured.

- The British Agility Association, founded in 2002, offers a grading system from Introductory through to Masters. Four jump heights are offered with a large overlap to comfortably accommodate all breeds and sizes. Registration with BAA is free and automatic with your first entry.
- UK Agility, founded in 2004, provides two progression programmes which lead to titles, namely Performance and Steeplechase, and five jump heights. You will need to pre-register before you can start competing at UKA shows.

Both BAA and UKA do not mark the 'up' contact on the A Frame, Dog Walk and See-Saw. This is especially beneficial to larger dogs as it allows a natural stride onto the obstacle.

Each of the major organisations has their own rules, progression systems, leagues, awards and major finals. There are also many small unaffiliated shows around the UK offering a variety of fun classes.

Agility in the US

- The American Kennel Club (AKC), offers Agility in a variety of classes, including Standard, Jumpers with Weaves, Fifteen and Send Time (FAST) and Preferred. Novice, Open and Excellent form the levels of progression, with the Masters Agility Championship Title (MACH) being highly prized.
- The North American Dog Agility Council (NADAC), established in 1993, is the largest agility only organisation in North America. Over 60,000 dogs are registered and compete in the sport in the US, Canada and also Australia. NADAC strives *to protect and advance the interests of dog agility by encouraging sportsmanlike competition and responsible dog ownership*.
- Established in 1986, the United States Dog Agility Association (USDAA) is a large independent authority for the sport of dog agility, and is a charter member of the Internationale Fédération Cynologique Sports (IFCS). The USDAA has more than 25,000 registered competitors, and events are held across the US, Canada, Mexico and Bermuda, Japan and Puerto Rico. The USDAA produces three international tournament series each year, namely the Grand Prix of Agility World Championships®, the Dog Agility Steeplechase® and the Dog Agility Masters®.

At International level, the Agility World Championships are held yearly by the Fédération Cynologique Internationale (FCI). Only pedigree dogs may compete. Although the UK, America and Canada are not members, teams are able to compete if invited to do so by the FCI.

WORKING TRIALS

The civilian equivalent of police dog training, this sport was developed during the early 1920s – the first trials took place in 1924 and were held by The Associated Sheep, Police and Army Dog Society. It was recognised by the British Kennel Club in 1927. In 1961 the format was changed and has remained largely unaltered until the present day.

Working trials are not confined to the German Shepherd, but the breed is certainly well represented in the sport. Smaller breeds cannot achieve the higher stakes, and all dogs that compete in working trials have to be registered with the British Kennel Club, either on the breed or activity registers. All dogs have to be 18 months old before they are allowed to participate. You and your dog will need to be in tip-top health because the trials will demand a high degree of fitness and stamina from you both.

Breed clubs, training organisations and weekend courses all form part of the wide avenues through which you can access the sport, and you will invariably find that training is done in a positive manner, encouraging the dog to work with enthusiasm and commitment.

Working trials require a high level of obedience and control. Throughout the training you will enhance the bond you have, whilst also encouraging the dog to work with independence and intuition. This is a competitive and enjoyable outdoor sport which takes place across the country throughout the year, in all weathers and across a wide variety of terrain.

It is a sport which certainly suits and develops the natural abilities of the German Shepherd, enabling the dog to have a channel for its innate drives. Training for trials builds a great bond between dog and handler, and helps the dog develop and satisfy its physical and mental needs.

In competition the different levels are termed 'stakes'. In addition to the existing list shown below, the Introductory stake (ID) was added in 2010, to encourage newcomers. Extra commands are permissible, the jumps are lower and 'stays' are in sight. There are also Veteran stakes for retired dogs with no upper age limit which involve just the tracking and searching.

- Companion Dog (CD)
- Utility Dog (UD)
- Working Dog (WD)
- Tracking Dog (TD)
- Patrol Dog (PD) – 'Manwork' is included in this stake (see below)

The top two stakes are interchangeable, in that they can be achieved in either order, or in isolation.

If a dog wins either of the latter two stakes twice, they are awarded the title of Working Trials Champion. NB 70% must be obtained in each section to qualify, and 80% overall must be gained in the Championship stakes in order for the dog to qualify 'Excellent'.

Control

This section requires an increasing degree of control as the levels progress. This incorporates heelwork exercises, recall, stays (2–10 minutes depending on the level), retrieve, sendaway/redirect, steadiness to gunshot, speaking on command.

Agility

The dog's agility skills will be developed as he is introduced to 'clear' and 'long' jumps, and the 'scale' – a 6ft high wooden obstacle which the dog is required to negotiate.

Nosework

This forms a crucial part of the exercises, which can be broken down into two key areas:

Tracking

A patterned track of set length will be laid across country, and the dog will be expected to follow this track to its conclusion, locating several articles of property on route.

The age of the track will increase as the stakes get higher, from half an hour old (UD), to three hours old, in TD stakes.

Searching

You will be introduced to scent work (identification of property). In trials, the dog will be expected to work independently of you, to locate and retrieve items which are within a marked area.

Manwork (PD stake only)

Quartering the Ground

In this exercise, the 'criminal' hides out of sight of the dog and handler, somewhere on the patrol field. The dog is sent to locate the criminal and when he does so, he is required to bark at the person spontaneously and vigorously until his handler joins him.

Courage Test

This incorporates a variety of exercises, none of which should produce a nervous or fearful reaction from the dog. The exercises include: bin lids being banged / large bags being shaken / gunfire or car horns being sounded, and shouting / threatening body language by the aggressor. The dog should challenge the aggressor without hesitation.

Search and Escort Prisoners

The dog is required to watch and guard the criminal, whilst the criminal undergoes a body search by the handler. The dog and handler then escort the criminal towards the judge. During the escort, the criminal attacks the handler and the dog must respond accordingly.

Pursuit and Detention of Criminal

The handler has to engage the criminal in conversation. The criminal flees and the dog is sent to detain him. The dog is required to do this by taking hold of the arm of the criminal which has a protective sleeve on it. He is required to hold on until he is commanded to release by his handler.

Recall from Criminal

This is set up exactly the same as the pursuit and detention. If the dog fails the pursuit and detention then it shall not be tested on the recall.

The criminal flees. The dog must give chase, but abandon this and return to the handler when called.

SCHUTZHUND (VPG)

Schutzhund ('SchH') literally means 'protection dog' and is, in effect, a stylised version of police dog training. As already discussed, the German Shepherd originated from herding dogs, but it was developed as an all-round working breed. As the breed developed in terms of physical appearance, Schutzhund was developed as a test to determine if a dog also possessed the mental and physical attributes which would make it suitable for inclusion within breed programmes. Max von Stephanitz and his associates were determined that the German Shepherd was a working dog first and foremost. Today the same ethos applies in Germany, in that dogs which are permitted to breed must have already been awarded a SchH title. Although this is not compulsory elsewhere, SchH titles are available in many countries. Dedicated breeders, who aim to maintain the Shepherd's working characteristics within their breed programmes, place great emphasis on attaining SchH titles.

Schutzhund has further developed over the past century. As well as being a breed test, it is now a hugely popular sport worldwide, not only for the GSD enthusiast but for owners of a huge variety of breeds, such as the Malinois, the Giant Schnauzer, the Rottweiler and Bouvier des Flandres, to name but a few. But the GSD commands the most consistent place in terms of sheer numbers and success at gaining titles.

Schutzhund is also known as VPG and IPO, although for all practical purposes there is little difference. VPG (Vielseitigkeitsprüfung für Gebrauchshunde) means 'versatility test for working dogs' – a more politically correct description than 'protection dog'. VPG was adopted initially in the mid 2000s in Germany as a response to increasing media sensitivity to aggressive dogs. By 2010 this was being superseded around the world, especially in all-breeds clubs, by IPO, the recognised standard of the FCI ('Fédération Cynologique Internationale'). The SV, however, retain the usage of SchH for its titles.

The titles begin with the BH (Begleithundprüfung) which is a companion dog test. This requires a good level of obedience and sureness around strange people, other dogs, and traffic. It also requires the dog to be sure and confident around strange noises. The dog has to show no signs of nervousness or inappropriate aggression, or it will be disqualified, and will be therefore unable to enter for the higher titles.

The SchH test has three levels: SchH1, SchH2 and SchH3. At each level, the dog is required to show aptitude in the following disciplines: Tracking, Obedience and Protection. The dog has to pass all three phases to gain a SchH title, and must gain 70% in tracking and obedience, and 70% in the protection phase to gain the title. 80% must be obtained in protection in order to move on to the next title. The dog must evidence a strong, steady character, an eagerness to work and a clear obedience to handler, especially throughout the protection phase (where physical restraint of the 'decoy' or 'helper' must be appropriate and under control). The 'decoy is a skilled individual who acts as a criminal.

Tracking

The dog is required to work over a wide variety of terrain and in all weathers. He must follow a pre-laid track, and must locate and indicate articles along the track. The dog is marked on the manner in which he tracks and in which he indicates the articles. Accuracy and commitment are crucial to gaining points, and the track is designed to test the dog's mental and physical endurance. The nature of the track, its length, pattern and age, varies for each title. So, too, do the numbers of articles laid along the track itself. Many people do not realise that tracking is surprisingly tiring for dogs, as it requires intense concentration.

Obedience

The dogs are tested in pairs, on a large open field. One dog is required to remain in the 'down' position for the duration of the other dog's test, and then they swap places.

The dog is marked on a variety of heelwork exercises. All heelwork exercises are performed off lead except for during the BH which also has an on lead exercise. Heelwork exercises are performed in a set pattern in the open field, and also through a group of people. A gun is fired twice during the test. Sit, down and stand stays are interspersed, with the handler required to keep moving whilst the dog remains in position. The dog is required to perform recalls, and his retrieve exercises are performed in three phases – on the flat, over a hurdle and over an A frame. He is required to do a sendaway and an emergency 'down'

Retrieving the dumb bell over jumps.
Guyot von Bachhaus SchH3 IP03

Protection

During the protection phase, a decoy is deployed, with a padded sleeve on which the dog is expected to bite when required to do so. The decoy will initially hide in the last of several 'blinds' which are hideaways located on the field. The dog is expected to locate the decoy and bark. He guards the helper until the handler arrives. In SchH 1 there are two blinds, SchH2 there are four blinds, and in SchH3 there are six blinds.

The dog is required to locate and then guard the 'decoy'

In the SchH2 and 3 protection phase, the dog does a directed search of the blinds until he locates the decoy. He then performs the 'hold and bark', guarding the individual until the handler arrives. On the judge's signal, the dog is called to heel by the handler. The handler then instructs the decoy to move to a predetermined place. He then heels the dog towards the decoy, places the dog in a down and leaves the dog watching the decoy. As the decoy attempts to escape, the dog pursues and detains the individual by biting the sleeve. Once the decoy is motionless, the dog will be commanded to release the sleeve and guard him. The decoy is required to perform two further attacks, including stick hits, one on the dog and then one on the handler/dog during an escort, each time threatening with a padded stick. The dog is expected to prevent these attacks by biting the decoy's sleeve and holding on, until told to leave by the handler or until the decoy is still. The handler then disarms the decoy and with the dog escorts him back to the judge.

During SchH3, a second decoy is also deployed. Despite this individual making threatening gestures the dog must remain sitting and under control until the judge's signal. The handler releases the dog who must go directly to take the sleeve of the decoy without hesitation. During this phase the dog is commanded by the handler to release and guard and in the guarding phase the decoy attacks the dog, threatening and hitting him with the padded stick. The striking with the padded stick is to allow the judge to assess the dog's character and fighting spirit, for which he is given a grade of 'pronounced', 'existing' or not graded. These grades are used by breeders as part of their assessment of breeding stock.

The dog must not bite the decoy unless the dog or handler is under attack or unless the person runs away, and the dog must attack with determination and confidence. He must then release on command, or when the decoy becomes still, without hesitation.

The dog must only react when appropriate. This level of training takes time and commitment

Why Does The German Shepherd Excel At This Sport?

They have a great capacity for nosework, which clearly forms an integral part of the sport. The dog will be required to follow ground disturbance and deposited scents, as he follows the trail of the tracklayer. He will also need to use his nose to identify articles left behind. The Shepherd is invariably a keen tracker, and there is little else which can bring about such a sense of achievement and pride than a successful track.

The Shepherd is eminently responsive in good hands, and the obedience phase challenges this aspect of the breed to the limit. He has a strong desire to trust and to commit to his handler, and the well-trained Shepherd is unlikely to lose focus on his handler even when distractions are put his way. He is an agile and strong breed and enjoys the challenge of the jumps and the 'A' frame, which will test his physical prowess as well as his obedience.

The protection phase provides the handler with the opportunity to learn about his dog's reactions to stress, excitement and aggression. The depth of training leads to a close

The Shepherd excels at nosework

and deep bond between dog and handler, and the dog is taught to control his instinctive drives even when highly stimulated. The German Shepherd is often described as having an 'on-off' switch. This is an integral part of the breed's makeup, and becomes highly developed through Schutzhund training. Far from encouraging inappropriate aggression in the dog, Schutzhund protection training is an exercise in which obedience and control are practiced and honed in the face of extreme levels of excitement.

HEELWORK TO MUSIC (HTM) AND FREESTYLE

By comparison with other competitive canine sports, heelwork to music has only recently developed. The Musical Canine Sports International (MCSI) established the rules and the guidelines for judging the sport in 1992. America followed in 1993, and in 1996 England had its inaugural event at Coventry. It was formally recognised by the Kennel Club in 2002. It originated from heelwork exercises found in competitive obedience, and now incorporates intricate and imaginative routines. HTM is devised from heelwork exercises off lead, with the dog working beside the handler for a minimum of two-thirds of the routine. The heel position is not the same as in obedience. Freestyle has evolved from HTM and incorporates a certain amount of heelwork, but is also interspersed with a wide and creative variety of routines, where the dog can work in many positions, and also away from the handler's side.

These are both demanding disciplines, and have a broad appeal and following. Widely available across the UK, it is now a Kennel Club licensed competitive sport, and if you wish to compete you will need to ensure that your dog is registered on the breed or activity register. At present, dogs need to be a minimum of 12 months old to compete in HTM, and 18 months for Freestyle (due to the potentially more strenuous moves).

GOOD CITIZEN DOG SCHEME (GCDS)

The GCDS has been developed with the aim of promoting responsible dog ownership, and is now the UK's largest dog training scheme. Exercises have been developed to build the dog's confidence and ease with a variety of everyday situations. It also aims to enhance basic obedience requirements, and to develop the owner's sense of responsibility. The levels range from Puppy Foundation Level through to the Gold Award, and training may begin very early, although the trainer is permitted to set a minimum age during the puppy foundation assessment classes.

Puppy foundation assessment

The exercises lay the foundation for education and training, and all of the exercises are designed to build the puppy's confidence. Noises and distractions are introduced, but with care and consideration, and these are always done at a distance.

There are a multitude of exercises that the puppy will be introduced to, and these include the following: The puppy is required to show attentive response to his name, to play sensibly without play fighting, and to be relaxed and at ease with being handled. A basic puppy recall is introduced, as are the basic positions, and the puppy will learn manners around food. He will be introduced to strange people and strange dogs, and this will be done in a calm and non threatening way, so that he develops appropriate responses.

Bronze / silver / gold awards

Heelwork will be assessed, with increasing demands through the levels, until the dog is walking freely off lead in the gold award. The dog will be required to walk to heel amongst other people and dogs / to be well mannered at the kerb / to be well mannered through gates and doors and to remain unresponsive to bikes and prams.

Throughout the levels, the dog will be exposed to distractions during recall, and will be expected to exhibit good manners in terms of being sent to lie on his bed or to behave in a controlled manner inside the car. He will need to perform a reliable emergency stop when required.

The handler will be assessed throughout the level, and will be required to be compliant with cleanliness and identification issues, and with the 'responsibility and care' sections. The handler is not permitted to use toy or food rewards during any of the exercises, as the bond between dog and handler is a key part of the assessment, and additional incentives therefore cannot be used.

AND JUST FOR FUN!

There are a range of other activities which you might like to consider, which will add new experiences and dynamics to the relationship that you have with your Shepherd. 'Rally Obedience' (Rally O) is gaining popularity, and is a more relaxed form of obedience. Dog and handler navigate their way around a course with numbered signs. The signs indicate a specific exercise for the pair to perform, which include both obedience and agility exercises such as 'sit-down-sit', 'send over jump', and 'recall over jump'. It is great fun and offers the participant a great opportunity to become accustomed to the sport arena without the stress of more formal competition!

'Urban Mushing' comprises canine sports derived from winter sports such as skijoring, now made accessible to warmer locations. These sports have a wide following for the range of activities they incorporate. Teams or single dogs pull sleds, bikes and scooters across a variety of terrain such as tracks, roads and beaches. Bikejoring and urban scootering are included, and in these events, a dog or dogs are hitched to a non-motorised vehicle.

'Canicross' is also hugely popular, which is actually cross country running, hitched to a dog on a harness.

'Troubled Times'

Because this is a strong and enquiring breed with limitless energy, there are bound to be times when the relationship encounters difficulties. The Shepherd is bright and sensitive, so the potential for extremes of behaviour is high. Some of the issues which are commonly seen in the breed range from needy, dependent behaviours, through to general ill-manners and aggression.

It is true to say that a dog's capacity to deal with life's challenges is partially influenced by genetics. But by and large, most extreme behaviours can be directly linked to gaps in socialisation and education, particularly in the formative months. What starts out as a minor issue with a German Shepherd can soon develop into an unmanageable one, as this breed has the capacity to process a huge range of information, and quickly develops mannerisms in direct response. The Shepherd is also a medium-large breed of considerable power and strength and this can contribute to already difficult situations.

When facing the prospect of turning your dog's unwanted behaviours around, it is clear that your patience will need to be at a premium and you will need to draw on your ability to be calm and consistent. You may also feel the need to seek advice from a trainer, vet or

Puppies need lots of stimulation and playtime

qualified behaviourist, but do take heart! One of the German Shepherd's strongest desires is to please, and this provides enormous potential for turning things around. The Shepherd is quick to learn, and will usually respond well to clear guidance and boundaries.

Always remember that your efforts to mould your dog's behaviour will be most effective if you use positive, reward-based training. Negativity only compounds difficulties, and will further confuse or distress the dog.

Another thing to bear in mind is the issue of time scales. If a young dog develops an unwanted behaviour, it is more readily reversed if you 'nip things in the bud'. This of course is less easy where you are dealing with a rescue dog, as the behaviour may be well established, and your relationship may be relatively new.

 Unless you are well versed in re-training methods, it is always wise to ask for professional help when dealing with a German Shepherd that exhibits challenging behaviours.

CLINGINESS

If your dog is essentially well balanced, but is very 'connected' to you, his desire for a close relationship is unlikely to be something of concern, and is more likely to be exactly what you had hoped for when buying a German Shepherd. This breed has a strong desire to bond (often with just one member of the family), and providing this does not become controlling or disabling, it is usually accepted as part and parcel of a close relationship. However, where it impacts on the dog's ability to be independent, or on the owner's ability to move about freely from the dog, it becomes a trait which needs modifying.

'Clingy' behaviour is commonly seen in dogs who have had had limited early socialisation, or inappropriate reassurances from the handler at times of stress. If a dog moves beyond the primary socialisation period without being widely exposed to the world, new experiences may seem suspicious to him and he may latch on tightly to his owner for stability. The clingy dog will usually exhibit a range of behaviours. He will attempt to be physically close to his owner, will often try to climb onto the owner's lap (or shoulders), and may control their space and attempts to move around. The clingy dog will invariably exhibit separation anxiety when the owner leaves him (p. 98).

Clinginess usually denotes a lack of independence in the dog, and it will take a patient approach to turn the situation around. The key to diminishing neediness is to rebuild the dog's independence from the person he focuses on. Clingy behaviours will usually have taken time to create, so it will therefore take time and patience to reverse them. When re-training older dogs be aware that some deep-seated mannerisms will still re-emerge periodically, but progress *is* possible. If you can help him become more stable it will make life much more bearable for you both.

It will be important to help the dog establish a sense of ease when you are away from him, and to help him view all members of your family with equal regard and affection. Everyone in the household should be involved with exercising and training the dog. He needs to bond with each of you in order to feel that he can broaden his horizons. Your family is central to his re-education, and it is important for everyone to realise that an insecure dog is likely to seek 'reassurance' from them in situations he is uncomfortable with. It has already been mentioned that 'cosseting' merely feeds neurosis, and is to be avoided at all costs. The dog needs the opportunity to face situations free of any emotional crutch, and to develop trust in you all. He will gradually learn to make his own decisions about life, and each good experience will add to his development. Constant touching and fussing when the dog is in 'needy' mode, will merely serve to reinforce his sense of imbalance and dependency, and may give him signals that you are in a state of anxiety too.

Try to create varied situations where the dog can encounter non-threatening experiences, friendly people and calm, relaxed dogs. He needs the opportunity to interact with everyone in a positive way. This will help him absorb new information, which will bring self-confidence to his daily life. You may find that clicker training (p. 116) will aid his development, and it will diminish his need for verbal and physical reassurance. As he progresses, remember to involve all of the family, including children. Repetition by each family member will enable him to enjoy interacting with everyone, and again this will lessen his dependency on you.

If he struggles whenever you leave him, you may find that the safest and kindest way to deal with this is to begin crate training him. With an older dog, this needs very careful handling as he needs to view the crate as a safe place, therefore his initial spells within a crate must be built up very slowly. But if you take the time to crate train him, he will begin to learn that his world does *not* fall apart when you are away from him, and this will make life better for you both.

Resist the temptation to emphasise when you are about to leave the house, as grand emotional gestures will only feed into his insecurities. Nor should you make a huge fuss of him on your return. Heightened emotions and energies will 'hallmark' you coming and going, and this will not help stabilise him. Pick and choose your times to fuss and engage with him, and encourage him to earn this affection, not to demand it or dictate its timing.

Make sure everyone gets a chance to feed, groom and play with the dog. This will reinforce the bonds he is making. And ensure the whole family agree on general rules or boundaries, as a consistent approach will help him be more certain about family expectations.

FEARFULNESS

Much as it is with clingy behaviours, fear is invariably a response from dogs that have had limited early socialisation, or bad experiences. The Shepherd processes information readily and fully, and negative experiences can have a profound effect on this bright, sensitive breed.

Clingy and fearful behaviours can overlap in many instances. However, one of the key differences between the two is that the clingy dog has developed a reliance on his owner to give him stability. Dogs that are *fearful* will often attempt to hide, and avoid the situation they are afraid of, and may have become so overwrought that they are not in a mental state to connect with the owner. The dog may flatten himself to the floor, urinate, whine and even bear teeth in a grimace.

If your dog is suffering from general nervousness, you will need to go back to the beginning with his socialisation. This is a process which is more readily accepted by puppies,

Training classes and regular practice will help boost your dog's confidence

and is discussed in chapter three. With an older dog it is imperative that the dog is gradually introduced to new experiences at a pace he can deal with.

Where a dog has developed a pronounced fear of an object, situation or sensory stimulus, reintroduction to the thing he is fearful of will need to be gradual. Fireworks are a prime example. Even a normally confident dog can become wild-eyed with fear on Fireworks Night. There are CDs available which can gradually introduce the dog to sounds which might trouble him. Such a process of desensitisation is to be recommended.

The same principle applies to other situations and stimuli. If you are aware that there is a certain situation which induces a state of fearfulness, desensitisation works for many dogs, through gradual reintroduction to the fearful stimuli. At every stage you will need to watch for signs that he is becoming uneasy. You will need to remain relaxed and unconcerned yourself, and resist the temptation to 'reassure' him. If you take things at a pace he can deal with, his adrenalin / cortisol production will decrease with time and repetition, and your calm presence will aid his recovery.

When his body stops producing a 'flight or fight response' (p. 87), his body language will calm noticeably, and at this point you can interact and offer praise. You will gradually increase his tolerance to the stimuli. This is best done with a professional who can help you read your dog's signals, and can help you interpret the messages you are also giving to your dog. Overcoming nervousness or deep-seated fears will take time and patience, and in addition to his reintroduction to individual fear stimuli, he will benefit from all manner of confidence-building exercises with all members of the family, much the same as the clingy dog will.

Remember that fear can lead to aggressive responses, and therefore nervous behaviours should always be taken seriously.

The use of calming herbal or homeopathic remedies and products such as D.A.P. infusers may also help in certain situations.

'DOMINANCE' / ILL MANNERS

The word 'dominance' has become a buzz-word over the past few decades, and is often used inappropriately. For the purposes of this chapter, we will look at some instances where 'dominance' issues have been used to describe ill manners (jumping up / mouthing / barking), through to general disinterest regarding obedience commands. In most cases these issues are not, in fact, caused by 'dominance', but by a lack of education during the formative stages, and by inappropriate responses to certain behaviours – usually by the owner and family. In all cases of ill manners, taking your dog back to classes is a good place to start, but be prepared to be honest with your trainer about general house rules (or lack of them) where your dog is concerned! In terms of 'disrespecting' formal obedience commands such as the recall, the same principle applies. Dogs that have had an inadequate or inconsistent early introduction to obedience, will have developed a sense of independence, and may have learned to ignore your commands. Re-training will not be about 'dominating' your dog in order to get him to do what you wish, but about finding positive ways in which you can re-educate him, so that you can all live in harmony.

Food theft is common in dogs that have not been given boundaries

It is important to note that dogs may become possessive over toys. This attitude can easily escalate to include becoming protective regarding your home, car and family. It is important to monitor your puppy's tendencies from very early on. Don't allow issues to grow unchecked. If you spot issues developing you are wise to discuss this with your trainer straightaway. It is common for little problems to escalate if left unaddressed. If you have an adult dog that guards his food bowls, you are wise to bring in a qualified behaviourist, as food guarding can become dangerous. When teaching puppies about food manners, we routinely drop a higher value feed into the bowl when puppies are feeding, as they learn to welcome our presence around the food bowl. This takes away any negative connotations of our presence at feed time, or of our hand near the food bowl. Feeding time should never be a battle of wills.

Good friends can 'play rough'! But supervision is important to ensure appropriate play at all times

JUMPING UP

Jumping up is often seen as a controlling behaviour, but can also be exhibited by clingy dogs. It is also a common 'conditioned' behaviour, in which the dog learns an unwanted behaviour due to negative reinforcement: (If the dog jumps up once for attention and is chastised by the person involved, that response is *still* a response – however negative.) Jumping up is also an appeasing gesture which can actually get worse if tackled as if it is a 'dominance' issue. It is a deeply annoying behaviour and is something which can be easily avoided if young puppies are taught to greet visitors and family in the 'sit' position. If puppies are never allowed to invade human space by body-climbing and jumping up, they will accept the rules readily.

In days of old there have been 'remedies' for this annoying situation, such as kneeing the dog in the chest, or hitting it with a rolled up newspaper on the head. Thankfully, dog training has moved well away from such methods. Learning to recognise the triggers is central to stopping any behaviour. Whilst the dog learns alternative and acceptable ways to greet people, the use of a negative punishment technique such as turning one's back on the dog as he jumps up can be initially effective.

The dog will need to be introduced to a controlled exercise of only receiving reward whilst he is actually in the 'sit' position. The more creative you can become once he has mastered the exercise at home, the better. (It will be helpful to engage the help of willing friends to greet you and the dog in a variety of settings.) It is best to introduce friends whilst the dog is on the lead so that you have more control over the situation. The dog can then be encouraged to sit calmly beside you, and only be allowed interaction with your visitor when he is fully calm. You must be consistent. Any jumping up must always be ignored, and sitting politely should always be praised.

Clicker training may aid the dog's understanding of your requirements in this situation, as rewards can be precisely delivered. Attempts to treat this bad habit with punitive methods will only produce tenuous results.

MOUTHING

The Shepherd is known for his persistence regarding mouthing or play-biting, which can escalate rapidly if clear boundaries are not established early on (see p. 94). Usually, this can be nipped in the bud, but during adolescence this can reappear. With the onset of adolescence come hormonal changes and second teething phase, both of which will add to the challenge! You will not want to end up with an adult dog who thinks it is okay to take hold of your arm or leg. This is a sign of utter disrespect at the very least, and can become dangerous if left unchecked.

Re-education will be important, and you are strongly advised to attend classes, or to seek advice from a qualified behaviourist. Practical things for you to examine will include your family's attitude towards your dog. Having a unified approach will enable him to become aware of what is expected of him by everyone.

One thing to look at is your approach to giving affection. Many dogs are subjected to indiscriminate fussing. If your dog never has to earn fuss and praise and he learns that he can demand this whenever he chooses, it is likely that mouthing will continue longer than with a puppy who learns that he has to earn the majority of his rewards, and who learns his place in the family.

Mouthing can also denote insecurity, as the dog 'takes hold' to take control of situations he is insecure within. If it is done as an expression of insecurity, he is less likely to use his teeth. Excitable, challenging dogs will be more inclined to use force and may puncture your skin.

BARKING

Barking is a natural form of communication, and is used in conjunction with body language to convey a broad range of meanings. For the domesticated dog, living side by side with humans, the vocal side of the dog's communication repertoire can lead to difficulties. The dog exhibits a range of vocalisations from growling, whinging, howling and barking, but it is the latter (especially when performed in a repetitive onslaught), which leads to problems for owner and neighbour alike.

Barking may have become a habit, unintentionally encouraged by the owner, and it is important to be aware of this issue when you respond to a puppy which is giving voice. If your puppy barks and you appear whilst he is barking, he is rewarded simply by your presence. If you chastise him, he is further 'rewarded', and it is likely that whenever he wants your attention he will therefore resort to becoming vocal. Some dogs bark as a result of boredom or stress. Others may feel the need to communicate to you that there is a perceived threat. Whatever the cause, excessive and unwanted barking can cause the relationship between dog and owner to deteriorate, and the sooner the situation is nipped in the bud, the better for all concerned.

Territorial barking

The German Shepherd is known to be a vocal breed. His guard instinct is strong, and (being naturally territorial) he is likely to bark at the door or gate when he thinks there is an unwelcome visitor. If the 'intruder' was merely walking past the premises or delivering something, they will subsequently move away from the premises of their own accord. However, the dog will feel as if he has achieved his aim in driving them away, and this will serve to reinforce his behaviour for the next visitor. In this instance, training your dog to cease barking on command can be useful, but you will need to be aware that this control will only be effective until the stimulus reappears again.

If you become stressed and shout at him, he will be left confused as your energies will be high and negative, and this will feed into his desire to remain on alert. It is surely more effective to create controlled visits to your house and reward him for greeting the visitor politely. It is a balance, as most owners welcome the German Shepherd into their lives partly because he is a deterrent for strangers, but barking at the door is subsequently seen as an undesirable trait.

'Nuisance' barking

The Shepherd thrives on company and stimulation, and therefore 'nuisance barking', whenever the dog is left unattended, presents as a real issue. Attention-seeking, stress or habit will cause the dog to bark in a repetitive manner, although the tone of his vocalisations will vary according to the root cause. Mental stimulation and physical exercise are the keys to tiring your dog before leaving him unattended. If you plan a training exercise in the park into his daily routine before leaving him, he is far less likely to be awake and pacing your garden in a state of boredom. If you leave him indoors, a radio may help desensitise him to any external stimuli.

Anti-bark collars are readily available through pet suppliers and online. These emit a spray of air or scent help to avert the dog's behaviour. This is an area of contention as some people leave this on the dog all day, thereby preventing any vocal expression for hours on end. Some dogs do learn to bark through this. They empty the canister quickly and carry on barking. Others channel their frustrations by becoming physically destructive. It is far better to ensure that your dog is mentally and physically tired before leaving him, and to leave him with things to channel his energies whilst you are gone. Stuffed kongs and buster cubes are a prime example. You can fill these with favourite treats and some of his daily ration of food, and it will take time and mental energy for your dog to play with these and empty them whilst you are out. He will begin to associate your absence with food reward. When you return home, remember to only enter the room where he has been left provided that he is quiet.

Many dogs get excited as soon as the owner gets their coat, car keys, or the collar and lead. This is perfectly understandable, and a little excitement is all part and parcel of dog ownership! However if he descends into boisterous and demanding barking, you will need to take some measures to desensitise him to some degree. During the day, it may prove helpful to pick up related items over and over again, to build in 'false starts'. He will gradually realise that this leads to nothing, and usually the message will be understood.

For dogs that are particularly persistent with nuisance barking, it may help to talk to your trainer about the correct usage of 'training discs'. Although generally considered outdated now, they may prove effective in some instances. These are a set of metal discs on a rope, which make a startling noise when thrown. If a dog is nuisance barking, throw the discs near to the dog to startle him into silence. Wait patiently and calmly and then quietly praise him for his silence.

Barking on lead

His sense of protectiveness over his own space and that of his owner may come to the fore when out on a lead, and so he may bark at people or other dogs whilst out walking. Again, this is common in the Shepherd, and invariably is caused by a lack of early socialisation. If your dog is fear-barking on lead, you are advised to talk to your trainer and friends to help you set up controlled situations to gradually desensitise him to the presence of people or dogs. It will be important to determine where his comfort zone is located. Initially, situations can be set up outside of this area so he can learn to relax and accept the presence of 'threatening' stimuli. Gradually the zone will decrease, and his tolerance will grow. If the dog is barking due to excitement, the training method may differ and will invariably involve working on the dog's ability to focus on you for treat, praise or toy, whilst people or other dogs walk towards you.

 Never allow yourself to become aggressive when these situations arise. Your heightened emotions serve only to make things worse.

AGGRESSION

This is an issue of considerable complexity. Aggression can be brought about by a wide variety of situations and stimuli, and much depends on the experiences that the dog has had, and the way it is handled. Aggression of all kinds should be treated seriously, and it is likely in most circumstances that professional help will be required. The reasoning behind the behaviour will need to be identified, and this can be complex in itself.

Aggression can stem from a wide range of factors. Controlling resources such as territory or food is a causal factor, as are intra-sexual behaviours – whereby two dogs of the same sex will become aggressive towards one another. (Bitch fights in particular are often determined and sustained, as the bitch is programmed to be prepared to fight with her life for her offspring.) Dogs in pain may exhibit aggressive behaviour. Fear may also escalate into aggressive responses.

Aggression can be directed towards people, which is of particular concern, and the breed is known for its suspiciousness towards strangers. Many German Shepherds are also reluctant to be overly familiar with other dogs and so aggression can be directed towards other dogs, both on and off leash. Both of these issues can be dealt with to a large extent during early puppy socialisation. This can be reinforced throughout adolescence, to firmly establish in the dog's mind that people and dogs are not a threat of any kind, and are to be greeted politely. Not all dogs get the best upbringing, and a combination of a lack of

The well socialised puppy is less likely
to be dog-aggressive later in life

143

education and weak handling can result in a Shepherd that becomes 'too big for his boots'. What seems insignificant in a puppy can become a major problem in the adult dog, so try to deal with all problems promptly. It will pay dividends later on!

🐾 If you are facing situations with a German Shepherd that is showing signs of aggression, you are wise to seek practical assistance from a qualified behaviourist.

The well-socialised dog is balanced, happy and non-aggressive

Part Five

Caring for your Shepherd

• Routine Health Care • First Aid • Diet and Nutrition •
• Complementary Therapies • Castration and Spaying •
• The Elderly Shepherd •

Routine Health Care

The healthy German Shepherd is a picture to behold. Bright-eyed, lithe and strong, he should appear energetic and alert and have a rich gleam to his coat.

You will clearly want to provide the very best of care for your dog throughout his life. By giving him a good quality diet and plentiful exercise, you will help to keep him in tip-top shape. Daily grooming will give you the opportunity to examine his body in detail and to be in a position to spot changes promptly. Other key areas of caring for your growing dog include making sure that he is vaccinated, wormed and given routine flea treatments. He will need fresh water to drink, and somewhere comfortable to rest.

In terms of his mental welfare, you will need to provide your dog with endless opportunities through which he can develop emotional stability – you will need to educate and train him, and to provide a broad and imaginative approach to his socialising process.

The conscientious owner will also take time out to become familiar with the rudiments of first aid, in case of emergency situations.

CHOOSING YOUR VET

From the moment your puppy arrives home with you, your veterinary surgeon will become one of the most important people in your life. Their assistance throughout your dog's life will no doubt be invaluable, and they are always the first port of call if illness or injury strikes. It is likely that two main issues will influence your choice of vet: Good recommendation from local dog owners will be important, and so too will accessibility. It is important that not only can you gain access to your vet easily and quickly in an emergency situation, but that you really feel you can trust the service provided and that you can communicate well with the staff.

It is always a good idea to make visits to local veterinary surgeries prior to bringing your puppy home. You will undoubtedly want to talk to staff on duty and obtain information about vaccinations and worming programmes.

Costs from practice to practice will vary according to the facilities, the numbers of surgeons and also any additional services offered, such as out of hours call-outs.

INSURANCE

Insuring your puppy is to be highly recommended. The German Shepherd is an active, enquiring, physical dog that is likely at some stage to experience illness or injury, or do damage to property. The cost of surgery on a broken leg for instance, can run into thousands of pounds.

Insurance costs vary greatly, as does the level of cover available. Conscientious breeders will arrange for your puppy to be covered by a good insurance plan, which the breeder will activate on the day the puppy leaves them. This ensures that puppy is covered during the first few weeks, whilst the owner has time to make enquiries about various policies and choose the one which suits their needs.

Be aware that policies do not provide cover for vaccinations and other routine treatments, but they will provide you with essential cover for illness or injury, as well as third party liability.

You can find details of pet insurance companies online and in canine monthly magazines. You could ask at your surgery for advice on reliable insurance companies, as they will have first-hand experience of successful claims made by their clients.

Be advised to read the small print, as exclusions to the policy may make the monthly figure very attractive but may leave you in great difficulty at some point in the future, should clauses in the contract leave you without the cover you need.

FIRST VISIT

Your first call to the vet with your puppy will probably be for a health check within 48 hours of purchase. It is important that this first check-up is a positive experience. Puppy is likely to visit the vet numerous times in his life and you would want these visits to be accompanied with as little fuss or trauma as possible. Making his first trip a pleasant one will go a long way to setting the stage for future veterinary encounters. If you have chosen your veterinary surgery well, you will find that staff members are only too keen to welcome your puppy and to put him at ease.

SG1 (GB) Draycore Uzi for Flyhart

Your vet will want to weigh the puppy. They will check puppy's heart and lungs, his eyes, ears and skin, and will look into his mouth for obvious structural issues such as an under or over-shot jaw. The vet will also want to check for umbilical hernias and hindleg dew claws. These are generally nothing for you to be alarmed by, but your vet will want to discuss any issue, however minor it may be. In male puppies the vet will want to note if both testicles have already descended, and if not, he will want to keep an eye on this situation. If the puppy does not have two fully descended testicles by 12–16 weeks of age, the vet will usually

Your vet will advise on worming products

discuss castrating the puppy at some point. The vet will also look at the general structure of your puppy, to see if he moves well and without discomfort.

This is a good opportunity for you to discuss the worming programme which your breeder will have started, and also for puppy to have his first vaccination. Your vet is likely to ask you about puppy's current diet, and will be only too happy to recommend a change if they feel that the diet is inadequate. Ensure that this visit is a good experience for puppy, and that he is rewarded with fuss and/or treats after he has been examined.

VACCINATIONS

Your puppy will initially have been protected from a variety of infections by antibodies passed to him from his mother, through her all-important colostrum (p. 234). Newborn puppies are protected by these maternal antibodies, *providing* that the bitch herself has been vaccinated. The level of antibodies present in the puppies' bloodstream begins to gradually decrease, leaving puppies at risk if they are not subsequently vaccinated. However, where maternal antibodies are still present at a significant level in the puppy's bloodstream at the point of vaccination, this can actually prevent the vaccine working effectively. This is one potential reason why a vaccinated dog may still become affected with the infectious diseases they are vaccinated against. Furthermore, immunity will wane for some diseases, and in some individuals, hence the need for repeat primary puppy vaccinations and for boosters at regular intervals – although the necessity for *yearly* vaccinations is currently under scrutiny, as this is cited as a causal factor in the breakdown of the immune system, and certain vaccines give protection for more than 12 months.

In the UK primary vaccinations will be given for core diseases, namely parvovirus, canine distemper, adenovirus and leptospirosis, and this usually takes place from around eight weeks of age. In the US, core diseases which are routinely vaccinated against are parvovirus, canine distemper, adenovirus, and rabies. Non-core diseases such as leptospirosis may also be recommended by veterinary surgeons depending on the determined risk levels. This can be influenced by the dog's lifestyle and by risk according to location.

It is important to be aware that puppies are *not* fully protected after a single vaccination. Most vets will suggest your puppy has a course of vaccinations which will require you to visit the vet several times. Your puppy will not be covered until the course is complete, and invariably not until at *least* a further seven days have passed after the final injection. Care is needed to ensure that your puppy is not exposed to the risk of infectious disease in the meanwhile, so he should not be placed down on the floor (away from the confines of your home) until that time.

Following each vaccination, you may find that your puppy is a little more tired than usual. Keep a close eye for any adverse signs following vaccination. These are thankfully rare, but it is wise to be vigilant. Always talk to your vet if you have any serious concerns.

 Vaccinating against these life-threatening canine diseases will not only protect your puppy from developing a potentially fatal disease, it will also help to prevent the spread of infection.

Bursting with good health

Parvovirus

This virus first emerged during the late 1970s, and thousands of puppies and adult dogs died before an effective vaccine became available. The disease is caused by canine parvovirus type 2 (CPV-2) and continues to be seen sporadically in the UK, mainly in unvaccinated dogs. Currently there are three known strains circulating: CPV-2a, CPV-2b and CPV-2c. Evidence shows that current vaccines provide adequate protection against all known strains, provided that an individual puppy has completed its vaccination course and has responded as expected.

Parvovirus attacks white blood cells, the intestinal tract, and vital organs. In very young puppies it has the potential to affect the heart muscles. Death can occur very quickly as a consequence of this disease, and veterinary treatment is to be sought immediately that symptoms present themselves to give affected animals the best chance of survival.

It is a disease which is mostly seen in young puppies, but any adult dog that is not vaccinated is still at risk. Feared by breeders, it is a tough virus which spreads rapidly through a kennels, and can be carried from home to home on footwear and clothing which have been in contact with infected faecal matter. The virus is transmitted via the mouth of a dog that has direct contact with either infected faecal matter or with inanimate contaminated objects (such as boots, cage floors, bedding etc). The disease is most commonly characterised by acute, persistent vomiting and diarrhoea. The diarrhoea often contains blood, and characteristically will have a foul, sour odour. Puppies become dehydrated rapidly, and this can prove fatal.

Intravenous fluids, or the introduction of electrolytes in drinking water, are the most important treatments, and may save multiple fatalities in a litter. Antibiotics are also invariably prescribed, as the damaged gut can allow bacteria to gain access to the bloodstream. A drug called Interferon is also sometimes given by vets, to improve the affected animal's chances of survival. Despite such measures, a significant proportion of infected puppies will die from this disease.

Distemper

The canine distemper virus (CDV) is a highly contagious, potentially fatal virus which is similar to the virus which causes measles in humans, and also distemper in seals. It not only occurs in domestic dogs, but affects foxes and other wildlife. It is multi-systemic, attacking gastrointestinal, respiratory and nervous systems.

Early symptoms therefore include:

- Cough
- Nasal and eye discharge
- Diarrhoea
- Vomiting
- Anorexia
- Lethargy

Advanced stage symptoms include neurological signs such as muscle twitching. High fever and seizures may also occur. Another symptom associated with this condition is a thickening of nose and pad leather, leading to the common name of 'hard pad'. CDV is transmitted by the inhalation of aerosol droplets during close dog to dog contact.

There is no available treatment for CDV. However, supportive therapy (intravenous fluids) will help with dehydration in less serious cases. Having your puppy vaccinated is to be strongly advised.

CDV has a worldwide distribution, but vaccination has been highly successful at making this a very rare disease.

Infectious canine hepatitis (ICH)

Infectious canine hepatitis is a highly contagious viral disease, which affects the liver and other organs. It is caused by the canine adenovirus type 1 (CAV-1). It is transmitted by dog to dog contact, and it is also spread in urine, blood, saliva and faeces of many animals. This virus can also cause disease in wolves, coyotes, foxes and bears.

Symptoms include:

- Nausea
- Vomiting
- Anorexia
- Jaundice
- Tenderness and swelling of the abdomen
- Pale faeces

In severe acute disease a high fever / runny eyes / yellowing of eyes / pale gums / enlarged abdomen / fits and coma may be seen. The virus can damage both the liver and kidneys. Dogs can still shed the virus through their urine for many months after recovering. There is no cure. However, treatment of symptoms includes fasting, antibiotics and intravenous fluid therapy.

CAV-1 is closely linked to the similar canine adenovirus-2 (CAV-2), which is one of the causes of kennel cough. Modern-day dog vaccines contain CAV-2 virus, which is close enough to CAV-1 to also give good protection against infectious canine hepatitis.

Leptospirosis

This is a highly infectious disease caused by bacteria, which can affect both dogs and man. The two main types of leptospirosis which cause serious illness in dogs are *Leptospira icterro haemorrhagiae* (Weil's disease) and *Leptospira canicola*.

Your dog will need to be vaccinated against waterborne diseases

Rats are the main carrier of the disease. Urine from infected animals often contaminates waterways, pools and other damp environments. Dogs that drink from, or swim in, contaminated water sources can easily become unwell. Symptoms range from vomiting and diarrhoea, to jaundice, fever and organ failure. Severe cases prove rapidly fatal if they are left untreated, and prompt attention is needed for such cases to stand any chance of survival. Treatment will typically include appropriate antibiotic and intravenous fluid therapies.

Vaccination against this condition will include two doses of vaccine as a puppy, and a repeat dose which is given every twelve months. Where leptospirosis is endemic, boosters may be given twice yearly.

Rabies

Rabies is caused by a virus which can affect humans and other mammals, such as dogs, foxes, wolves and bats. Although much progress has been made in reducing the incidence of this disease in Europe over the past few decades, it still occurs, particularly in Eastern Europe and the Balkans. It can be passed via bites and scratches from an infected animal, and its symptoms are highly disturbing, as it is a virus which attacks the central nervous system. Initial signs vary depending on the species affected, but neurological signs progress and involve changes in behaviour, agitation, spasm, convulsion, paralysis and death.

The incubation period is highly variable, but can take several months to manifest after the infected bite. Once symptoms are present, the virus will usually prove fatal. Rabies is a notifiable disease in the UK, in that the Department of Food and Rural Affairs (DEFRA) must be notified if the disease is suspected.

This much feared viral disease is thankfully almost unheard of in the UK due to the strict quarantine laws regarding imported animals. However, in recent years, a scheme has been developed which allows greater freedom of movement of pets in and out of the UK. PETS, (the Pet Travel Scheme) is the system which has been developed to allow dogs, and other animals, to enter the UK without having to go through quarantine. People who are holidaying within the EU (and certain specified non EU countries) can take their pets out of the UK and return, without needing to use quarantine. This is providing that any dog coming into the UK meets the strict criteria laid down by the Pet Travel Scheme. If they fail to meet the standards laid down, the dog has to be placed into quarantine. At the time of writing, all dogs have to be micro-chipped, vaccinated against rabies and blood tested to demonstrate evidence that the dog's immune system has responded an adequate level of protection against the rabies virus. See www.defra.gov.uk for the full and up-to-date information and guidance regarding travelling into the UK with your pet.

In the US, rabies vaccinations are one of the core vaccines given to puppies and to adult dogs at their yearly booster, and dogs entering the US must be vaccinated against the disease at least 30 days before entry into the country. Failing this, the owner is required to complete a 'confinement agreement' which states that they will keep the dog confined. 30 days have to elapse from the point of vaccination before the dog is released from confinement. Dogs entering from rabies-free countries are exempt from this provided that they have lived in that country for a minimum of six months. See www.cdc.gov/animalimportation/dogs.html

Kennel cough

This is the commonly used term for canine infectious tracheobronchitis. It is a disease of the dog's respiratory tract. The presence of one or more infectious agents results in irritation of the trachea (windpipe) and the upper bronchi, and it is readily transmitted by coughing or by direct dog to dog contact. As its name suggests, kennel cough is hallmarked by a deep-throated cough, which can sound as if there is an obstruction to clear. The cough is dry, harsh and usually very persistent. Infection spreads rapidly anywhere where multiple dogs mix. Ideal environments for the rapid spread of the disease include boarding kennels, dog shows and trials, veterinary clinics, and rescue centres, regardless of their attention to detail regarding hygiene practices. Mixing with other dogs in the park will also be a risk. Both the viruses and the bacteria associated with kennel cough take time to incubate, and apparently healthy dogs may therefore pass it on without necessarily showing symptoms themselves. Dogs who have fully recovered may shed the bacteria for many months following recovery.

Vaccines against one of the viral causes of kennel cough (CAV-2) are given in primary vaccines for puppies, and in booster vaccines. In addition, an intra-nasal vaccine may be given as drops up the nose, to protect against the most significant infectious causes. This includes protection against the bacteria *Bordetella Bronchiseptica*, and sometimes also protects against the main virus involved, canine parainfluenza.

The intra-nasal vaccine can be given prior to putting dogs into kennels, and forms part of the immunisations required by many boarding kennels. Be sure to discuss individual kennel's requirements regarding timescales of administering the intranasal vaccine, as this appears to vary from kennel to kennel. Administering the vaccine at the time of the annual booster is increasingly offered and may be a prudent step with the added advantage of convenience, since the immunity afforded by nasal vaccines now lasts a full 12 months.

Some cases of kennel cough require no treatment, as the symptoms are often mild and self limiting. More commonly, the signs of kennel cough will also include lack of energy, lack of appetite and a slight temperature. Persistent and serious cases may well develop into pneumonia, and of particular concern are the elderly dog, very young puppies and dogs with already weakened immune systems.

Liquid cough medicines are sometimes employed to help the irritation caused by the disease, but it is important to consult your vet before administering any medicine not intended for use in the dog. Antibiotic treatment, administered by the vet, may be an aid in combating bacterial causes, reducing the spread of infection and perhaps shortening the course of disease.

EXTERNAL PARASITES

Ctenocephalides felis
Image courtesy of
Bayer Animal Health

Fleas

The flea is the most commonly seen canine external parasite. In the UK, the most common species of flea found on dogs and cats is *Ctenocephalides felis*. *Ctenocephalides canis* is more commonly found on dogs in Ireland. Fleas can cause a wide range of problems for their host and his owner, as they readily infest not only dogs and cats, but their owners and the family home too! They also act as an intermediate host for the tapeworm, *Dipylidium caninum*. Adult fleas can be found in the dog's coat where they suck blood. They are also found in the carpet. Fleas lay their eggs in the soft furnishings of the home and also in dogs' bedding material. Larvae will hatch in a matter of days in the right environment, and a serious infestation can occur rapidly if left untreated. Adult fleas will bite human skin.

Fleas are frequently not visible in the dog's coat, but their presence will usually be heralded by the dog scratching frequently, or nibbling at areas of his body. By combing your dog with a flea comb, you may find adult fleas (or their droppings, which are black and very small). If you place the droppings on a piece of wet paper you will see red or reddish brown swirls developing. This is because the dried droppings contain blood.

Some dogs will barely react to the presence of fleas, but at the extreme end of the scale a severe infestation can cause serious blood loss and complex skin infections. Dogs will cause major trauma to the skin by constant scratching and biting which can result in a very itchy 'hot spot'. Mentally, this is extremely traumatic and exhausting for the dog. Some dogs will develop a flea allergy. This is caused by a reaction not to the flea itself, but to flea saliva. Steroids are often given to block the allergic reaction and to give relief from the itching. Antibiotics would be given in the case of secondary skin infections.

Your vet will be able to discuss the most effective treatments available. There are a wide range of preventative and treatment options on the market, including oral, 'spot-on's, sprays, shampoos, and flea collars. There are also treatment sprays and shampoos for your home.

Lice

Canine lice are different to the lice found on humans, as they are host-specific. Transmission is usually from one infected dog to another, or by louse eggs being passed via grooming brushes. There are two types of canine lice. *Trichodectes canis* is a biting louse that feeds on skin or from skin flakes. *Linognatus setosus* is a sucking louse which feeds on the host's blood. The latter are more irritating to the dog.

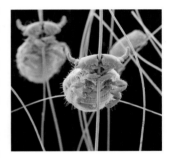

Trichodectes canis
Image courtesy of
Bayer Animal Health

The parasites lay their eggs (termed nits) on the dog's hair shaft. These are usually more noticeable than the louse itself. The life cycle of the louse takes place solely on the dog, and not in our environment like the flea. Lice can cause your dog to have a scurfy, dry coat, and some hair loss may be seen. In severe cases dogs will suffer from anaemia. Preventative treatments will help keep your pet free from lice.

Ticks

The tick is a small wingless ectoparasite that is a member of the arachnid family. Ticks are larger than other mites and there are around 800 known species across the world. They are divided into hard shell and soft shell ticks. Ticks suck blood from their host and can anchor themselves to the host, proving notoriously difficult to remove. Ticks are commonly found in woodland or areas of dense heather and fern. They are found in large populations where deer roam. In Europe, the main ticks seen are *Ixodes ricinus*, whilst in the US *Ixodes scapularis* is more widespread.

Prompt removal of ticks is crucial to the prevention of the various diseases which they spread worldwide, including babesiosis, ehrlichiosis and Lyme's disease.

Preventative control in tick infested areas includes acaricidal collars and topical acaricides e.g. Frontline® (acaricides are pesticides which kill both mite and ticks). Tick removal is best done with a tick removing tool. Alternatively use petroleum jelly or baby oil, and smother the tick before gently removing it with fine pointed tweezers. Do not pull quickly or you may leave the head embedded in your dog's skin.

MANGE

Demodex canis
Image courtesy of
Bayer Animal Health

The word mange comes from the French word *démanger* which means 'to itch'. There are several varieties of parasitic mite which embed themselves in skin or hair follicles, of which two forms, demodectic and sarcoptic, cause the most commonly seen skin complaints in dogs. Demodectic mange, or red mange, is caused by the mite *Demodex canis,* which lives in hair follicles. Sarcoptic mange, or scabies, is caused by the mite *Sarcoptes Scabiei,* which also causes human scabies. This usually presents as the most severe form of the condition.

Mites cause inflammation and itching, particularly in sarcoptic mange where the females burrow to lay their eggs beneath the skin's surface. This causes intense irritation. Demodectic mange is predominantly seen in dogs with a weakened immune system, causing generalised hair loss, lethargy, swollen lymph nodes, and diseased lymphatic system. Scratching as a result causes thickening of the skin and infections which need antibiotic and steroid treatments.

Traditionally, medicated lime-sulphur dips were used, but currently Ivermectin treatments are now routinely prescribed for scabies. Medicated baths to soothe irritated skin are also to be advised. Amitraz (Aludex®) washes are used to treat demodex and scabies. NB Amitraz is toxic if ingested, and its contra-indications should be discussed with your vet before using. Both Ivermectin treatments and Amitraz washes are only available on prescription from the veterinary surgeon.

Mange is very debilitating, and in its most advanced stages is a tremendously painful condition, often proving fatal if left untreated. It should be treated early to avoid acute suffering.

INTERNAL PARASITES

Roundworm

Also termed ascarids, these worms have a round body and can grow to several inches in length. They are 'spaghetti-like' in appearance. There are two types of roundworm which infect dogs: *Toxocara canis*, and *Toxascaris leoninae* (which also infects cats). Mature roundworms inhabit the dog's intestinal tract, where they feed on undigested food material in the small intestine. They can cause diarrhoea, vomiting and unthriftiness, leading to severe malnutrition in rare cases.

Worm burdens can cause the abdomen to appear distended, and can also cause an intussusception which can prove fatal. Of significant importance is the potential damage they can cause to children. Worm larvae, ingested by children playing in an infected area, can migrate through the body, disseminating to virtually every organ. They can cause detachment of the retina (a condition known as ocular larva migrans). This can cause blindness in extreme cases. It is advisable not to let children play in the area of your garden where pets defecate, and to thoroughly wash their hands after handling cats or dogs.

Worm eggs containing larvae are passed in faeces and can be ingested by dogs through the normal grooming process. In an adult dog, the worm larvae migrate into the body forming cysts which can lay dormant for years, before migrating back into the intestine.

Encysted larvae are also passed to nursing puppies from infected milk and across the placenta from infected mothers to their growing foetuses. Another mode of infection can come from a dog feeding on a carcass which is carrying larvae.

Medications may kill the worms outright and they are then digested and passed in the dog's stools. Other medications inhibit the worm's ability to latch onto the wall of the intestine, and they may be passed whole in the dog's faeces. The worms can sometimes be seen wriggling when passed, however they will die quickly. It is essential for dog owners to adhere to a regular worming regime as no worming product will protect a dog from being infected long term. Your vet can discuss with you the various worming products available.

Tapeworm

There are several types of tapeworm. The type most commonly found in dogs is *Dipylidium caninum*, and it requires the flea as an intermediate host in order to complete its life cycle. The tapeworm, as its name suggests, is flat-bodied and resembles a length of tape. The tapeworm can grow to approximately 8 inches. Its body is made up of small segments, the last sections of which are mobile and break off intermittently. These sections contain literally thousands of eggs. They are to be seen moving around the anus area or in the stools, where they dry out and burst, scattering the eggs. Tapeworm eggs are ingested by flea larvae, in which the new tapeworm (cysticeroid) develops. As the dog chews at irritated skin, he eats the flea, and the tapeworm larvae attach themselves to the lining of the dog's intestine.

Tapeworm infestation may cause unthriftiness and weight loss if present in large quantities. The most effective treatments include oral or injectable medication, available from veterinary practices, combined with a methodical approach to flea treatments for the dog and for his environment.

Hookworm

The most commonly found species of hookworm found in the UK is the northern hookworm (*Uncinaria stenocephala*). These worms are small and thin and, as the name suggests, they hook themselves on tightly to the wall of the host's intestine where they feed on blood. Larvae in contaminated soil are the prime site of infestation, and are also passed through the uterus and the milk into developing puppies.

Uncinaria stenocephala
Image courtesy of
Bayer Animal Health

Whipworm

The most commonly found species of whipworm in the UK is *Trichuris vulpis*. These worms are thin at the head end, with the posterior end being thickened like a whip handle. Infestations occur by ingesting food or water contaminated with eggs. The larvae develop into adults in the large intestine and burrow their mouthparts into the wall of the intestine where they suck blood. Eggs laid are passed in the faeces ready to infect the next dog.

Trichuris vulpis
Image courtesy of
Bayer Animal Health

157

Heartworm

Thankfully rare in the UK, these nevertheless present as a serious problem elsewhere across the world where mosquitoes spread disease. It is caused by the parasitic roundworm *Dirofilaria immitis*. This not only represents a huge threat to dogs, but to other animals and humans. It is an easily preventable disease, but is complex to treat effectively.

Lungworm

Angiostrongylus vasorum
Image courtesy of
Bayer Animal Health

Caused by the *Angiostrongylus vasorum* lungworm, this life threatening condition is on the increase in the UK. It is spread by slugs and snails, and less commonly by frogs. The dog has to eat infected hosts in order to become infected themselves, and the ingested larvae migrate and develop. Adult worms are found in the heart and lungs.

Symptoms include breathing difficulties, coughing, and lack of energy. Anaemia and poor blood clotting can manifest, as can seizures, lack of appetite, sickness and diarrhoea.

Monthly 'spot on' treatments, available from your vet, can be prescribed to kill the lungworm. Moreover, the same product which kills lungworm has recently received a new license indication, and now *prevents* Angiostrongylosis (the disease which arises from infection by the *Angiostrongylus vasorum* lungworm.

Giardia

The *giardia* parasite is a tenacious organism which can affect humans and other mammals. *Giardia lamblia* colonises and reproduces in the small intestine causing a condition called *giardiasis*. The presence of the *giardia* protozoans causes chronic and persistent diarrhoea and can also cause serious malabsorption of nutrients. Testing is to be done intermittently as the organism only sheds periodically, and initial tests can prove inconclusive. Broad spectrum wormers containing fenbendazole such as Panacur®, prescribed by your vet, will be used to treat the infestation. The antibiotic metronidazole (brand name Flagyl®), is also used by vets in the treatment of this condition.

ROUTINE CHECKS

Eyes

The eye of a healthy dog is bright, and clear of debris or discharge. The German Shepherd typically has a brown eye, although the pigment may range from dark brown through to a warm amber. Dogs with dilute coloured coats are likely to also have significantly paler eyes. The white of the eye (which is not fully visible without physical examination), should not be discoloured or inflamed. Foreign bodies such as dust or grass seeds will cause your dog to paw at the eye, or rub the eye area on the floor. The affected dog may 'squint' and the eye area is likely to become wet with watery discharge. Initial flushing of the eye with sterile saline solution may alleviate the problem, but any persistent signs of discomfort, redness, swelling or discharge should be discussed with your vet.

Ears

The German Shepherd puppy initially has folded ears. Over the first few weeks in his new home these should ideally become erect, although as the puppy goes through teething stages, the ear carriage may be periodically affected. If your puppy has 'soft ear' – an inherited condition – his ear carriage will be permanently affected and will therefore not become erect. Soft ear is not a medical condition and can therefore not be 'treated' as such. In terms of normal development, ear carriage will be intermittent for some time, but gradually the puppy will mature through his teething stages and will have good erect ear carriage typical of the breed. With ears that are having a little trouble staying fully upright, it is possible that supporting the ear, by taping it in its vertical position, may help to some degree. There are many sites on the Internet that specifically cover the various options for this process.

Ear carriage will be eratic during the teething process

General care of your dog's ears will help avoid the build up of wax or debris which can lead to painful ear infections. The regular use of ear cleaning fluid will break down ear wax which can be wiped away using a ball of cotton wool or gamgee. Alternatively you can use purpose-made ear wipes. Do not insert cotton buds into the ear canal as this can be counter-productive: you may push infected matter further into the ear canal, or damage the delicate structure of the inner ear. Waxy build-up, mite infestation and infections caused by grass seeds are the commonest cause of ear complaints. These can all be avoided through vigilant health care practices.

If the ear is infected, you will see reddening and possibly some swelling inside the ear canal, and your dog will usually paw at the ear in distress. He may also rub his head on the floor and furnishings, shake the head repeatedly, and hold the affected ear at an unusual angle. All of these are symptomatic of irritation or pain. Veterinary treatment will be required if the ear is infected.

Teeth and gums

Checking your dog's teeth and gums regularly will help you keep an eye on the development of plaque, and avoid 'gingivitis'. This is a painful inflammation of the gum area. Ask friends and family to perform checks on your dog's teeth too, as the more familiar he is with having his mouth touched, the less of an ordeal it will be when he has a dental check-up at the vets. When examining your dog's teeth watch closely for debris lodged in the roof of the mouth, and for signs of fractured teeth. Bad breath can be a sign of tooth decay, so it is wise to have him checked out if his breath becomes foul smelling.

The diet you choose for your dog will play its part in keeping his teeth healthy: if you are feeding a quality complete diet you are likely to find that the kibble contains calcium chelators (e.g. sodium polyphosphate). Calcium chelators bind and remove unwanted calcium, which is a foundation block for plaque. If you are feeding according to raw feeding principles, the addition of raw, meaty bones into your dog's diet is reputed to help in the management of plaque build-up, as will smoked bones which are readily available from a good pet food supplier. There are many products now available to help keep your dog's teeth in tip-top order, from toys to dental chews such as Nylabone® and Dentastix®. Toothpastes and brushes are also available for regular use, and if brushing is introduced early on into your puppy's daily routines, he is likely to accept this with little fuss. This will keep your dog's teeth in the best of condition.

While puppy is growing he will inevitably lose his milk teeth from around four months of age. It is important that you monitor this, as occasionally new teeth are blocked from emerging correctly if milk teeth are a little stubborn about leaving! Give puppy plenty to chew on, as this will help remove the milk teeth and help soothe sore gums. Puppy teething rings, knotted rope toys and hide chews will all aid healthy tooth development during this period. NB Always monitor your puppy when you give him bones or chews.

Feet

It is essential to check your dog's feet on a regular basis. You will need to ensure that his nails are kept short, and that there is no debris in between his toes which could cause infection and irritation. Check his pads regularly for splits and embedded foreign bodies. Nail trimming should be started during his puppyhood. It is good practice to get puppies used to the handling and inspection of the feet from day one. As nail clipping under duress can lead to cutting a nail painfully short, it is important that the dog is at ease with the process, so it can be performed with greater accuracy. Always keep your clippers sharp, and only take off a small amount of nail at a time so that you do not cut the 'quick'. This can be painful for the dog, and may lead to future problems when cutting his nails. Don't forget to trim front leg dew claws (and any on the rear legs if these are present), as these can quickly become long and may cut into the dog's flesh if they are left unattended. If you do unfortunately clip a little too short and cause bleeding, apply silver nitrate to the end of the nail. Dogs which are lead-walked on hard surfaces will need their nails trimmed less regularly than those who are exercised on fields and country tracks.

Anal glands

These glands are situated at either side of the dog's anal opening, at approximately '4 o'clock and 8 o'clock'. Their purpose is to deposit fluids which scent marks where a dog defecates. Anal glands may become blocked following a bout of diarrhoea or constipation, and this causes irritation and itching. The affected dog usually responds to this by rubbing his bottom along the ground, or gnawing at his anus, in an attempt to alleviate discomfort. Squeezing the glands, in order to empty them, is a procedure usually best carried out by your vet. It is wise to review your dog's diet if you find that he suffers regularly from this condition, as it is likely that there is insufficient fibre in the diet.

 It is important to check on your dog's perianal area as a part of your routine health checks. A distressing and painful condition called anal furunculosis is well known in the breed, and early diagnosis is crucial to successful treatment (p. 245).

Coat and skin

Brushing your dog on a daily basis will help keep the skin and coat in top condition. It will also help you spot the presence of parasites and prevent the unattended spread of skin complaints. It will also prevent 'mats' occurring, especially in the long coated Shepherd. A healthy dog will usually only moult heavily twice a year, but as the Shepherd is a double-coated breed, you can expect them to continue to shed hairs throughout the year. Bitches in season will go through a heavy moult prior to their expected heat, and dogs that have been spayed or neutered tend to develop a characteristic woolliness to their coat.

We use a metal toothed brush with which we back-comb throughout the dog's body, loosening all dead hairs and exposing any areas of dry or flaky skin. (As an alternative, you can massage the coat throughout, to achieve the same result.) If the dog is in a heavy moult – particularly if your dog is long coated – you might follow this with a metal toothed rake. These are designed to smoothly glide through the coat, picking up the shedding undercoat, without snagging. A slicker brush or fine toothed metal comb will pick up the majority of loose hairs. Finally, a soft bristled brush or grooming glove will lift the final hairs and give a bloom to the coat. When brushing the head area, it is best to use a soft nylon brush. When grooming the back of ears, tail and leg areas, you can use a metal-toothed comb or small slicker brush. Remember to reward your dog following a grooming session.

Everyone has their preferences regarding the 'tools of the trade' and how to best use them, but this method has continued to stand our dogs in good stead for decades. Regular shampooing of a healthy adult dog is not a necessity and can initially strip valuable oil from the coat. Once every six months or so, if needed, is usually more than enough. However on a practical level, shampooing is sometimes needed if the dog has rolled in something unsavoury! It can also give welcome relief to a dog undergoing a heavy moult. There is a wide range of pet shampoos available, including medicated products, herbal and hypo-aller-genic ranges, and conditioners to match.

 Always take care not to allow shampoos to enter the eye or ear canals as this can cause intense irritation. Be sure that the dog does not ingest shampoo, especially if using a medicated product designed to eliminate parasites.

ADMINISTERING ORAL MEDICATION

Most dogs do not like the administration of medications and will produce an array of measures to avoid swallowing tablets and liquids alike. When giving tablets or capsules, we always coat these in butter or cream cheese. But some dogs will attempt to consume 'the good stuff' and spit out the pill, so always be vigilant and ensure that this is not the case!

Hold the top of the dog's muzzle with your hand. Tilt the dog's head towards the ceiling. Use the pill hand to gently open the dog's mouth and place the pill as far back as possible on his tongue. Quickly close the dog's mouth and hold it shut. He will breathe through his nose. (Take care not to accidentally put your hand over his nostrils.) Calmly rub his muzzle, gently stroke his throat or gently blow on his nose. This should stimulate his swallow reflex. Once he swallows, praise him and give him a treat. If you practise this regularly with small pieces of favoured foods, when the time comes to giving pills he will be conditioned to accepting the process, and will be less stressed by the ordeal.

The same initial process is used when administering liquid medication. Once the dog's mouth is open, insert a liquid dropper just behind the large canines, and advance the dropper into the mouth. Squeeze the dropper gently, and steadily release the liquid. If you squirt it too quickly you could make him 'gag'. Always give the dog a treat following this process. If you want to practise this as part of his grooming routine you could use a small amount of milk in the dropper.

Regular checks will keep your dog in good health

First Aid

It is possible that at some stage in his life, you may need to perform first aid on your dog. Invariably with minor issues this would only require a common sense approach, but being aware of basic first aid may just make the difference in the event of an emergency. It is wise to keep a first aid kit handy at home for injuries which might be sustained by your dog. A few human drugs can be useful in emergency situations but you should always discuss these with your vet before giving them to your dog. These include aspirin, Piriton®, and Benylin® cough syrup. First aid measures serve to keep the patient as stable as possible whilst veterinary assistance is sought. When giving first aid the most serious threats to life are treated first.

 Be prepared! If you are familiar with basic first aid administration, and are rehearsed regarding initial treatments for serious situations, you will ease suffering, and you could save your dog's life. Stay as calm as possible. Your stress will inhibit clear responses by yourself, and may further stress your dog.

AIMS OF FIRST AID

* To preserve life
* To minimise suffering
* To prevent deterioration of the situation until professional help can be sought

ABC: AIRWAYS / BREATHING / CIRCULATION

Airways

Open the airways by gently extending the head and neck. Check for, and remove, any foreign bodies which might block the airway, whilst taking care not to get bitten. See 'Choking', below.

Breathing

Look for signs that the dog is breathing. Check that the chest is rising and falling, or place a mirror in front of his nose and check for condensation. If the dog is not breathing, place your hands around the muzzle to prevent air loss, and breathe forcibly into the nostrils. You should give 4 or 5 breaths at a rate of one breath every 4–5 seconds. Check to see if breathing has resumed. Check for a pulse. The easiest place to find this is on the inside of the back leg (femoral pulse). Alternatively, place your hand on the left side of the dog's chest to feel for the heart beat.

Circulation (CPR)

In the event that there is no pulse, the dog should be laid on his side on a firm surface. You should kneel behind him. Using the heel of your hand over the widest part of the chest compress the chest by about a third. You should aim for a rate of around 100 compressions per minute (sing the chorus to 'Stayin' Alive' by The Bee Gees in your head to provide you with a guide – Yes, really!). Give about 15 compressions then two breaths. Then repeat.

 Contact the vet. If possible, control any bleeding (see 'Wounds' and also 'Haemorrhage' below).

• CPR does not re-start the heart. It helps circulate oxygenated blood to the brain and heart muscle until help arrives.

FIRST AID KITS

Ideally you will carry a small kit with you at all times on your belt or in a rucksack. It should contain enough material to get your dog safely to the larger kit which should be at home or in your car. Prescribed medicines, ear cleaners etc should be stored in a different place to make access to your emergency kit easier.

Pocket first aid kit

• Cohesive bandage (e.g. Vet wrap)
• Padding layer (e.g. cotton wool)
• Sterile, low adherent dressing (e.g. Melolin®)
• Saline pods (from chemist)
• Tweezers,
• Strip of material (tights are good) to use as muzzle, tourniquet etc.
• Foil blanket
• Disposable gloves

Comprehensive first aid kit

• Larger amounts of the above
• Thermometer
• Round-ended scissors
• Muzzle
• Eye wash
• Sterile burn pads
• Sponges
• Antihistamine cream
• Liquid Benadryl®
• Silver nitrate

It is always good practice to have your own first aid kit

Medicine chest

- Elizabethan collar
- Electrolyte powders
- Syringe
- Prescribed medicines, flea and worm preparations etc.
- Tick remover

SITUATIONS REQUIRING FIRST AID / SOME COMMON AILMENTS

A large ball on a rope lessens the potential for accidents

Ball in throat

This is a common situation, given that the German Shepherd is invariably ball motivated. This is potentially a very dangerous situation with the airway being blocked by the ball, and by panic and stress causing shock. Be careful when trying to remove a ball from a dog's throat as you may be inadvertently bitten. If you have no assistance available, use a roll of bandage between the canine teeth to wedge the mouth open. It is usually impossible to grasp the ball via the mouth, so if this is the case, place your fingers either side of the dog's larynx (voice box) where you will probably feel the ball. Apply a firm sharp pressure to dislodge it. If unsuccessful you will clearly need to obtain immediate veterinary assistance.

Bites

Where fleas and ticks are present in very small numbers, bites made on your dog's skin may only require localised cleaning with a saline solution and the application of antihistamine cream. The crucial issue is to address the cause of the problem. With a serious infestation, treatment of the skin would also necessitate antibiotic and steroid treatments to reduce inflammation and swelling.

In the case of animal bites such as rodent, cat or dog bites, cleaning of the wound with saline solution is to be advised. The application of antibacterial or antiseptic cream would also form part of the treatment, providing that the wound does not require stitching. Bites frequently result in abscesses, which are sites of deep infection and are usually foul smelling and painful. These may need poulticing, lancing, flushing and antibiotic treatments from your vet. In the case of serious wounding see below for advice about tending open wounds.

Broken nails / dew claws

Nails can easily become broken, especially if they have been left to grow too long! Bleeding from a broken nail may initially appear far worse than it actually is, and will usually stop of its own accord. These can be effectively treated by gently removing the torn part of the nail

165

if possible, and applying silver nitrate. It is always a good idea to muzzle the dog before tackling a broken nail, especially as many dogs generally do not like any interference with their nails. If the nail requires veterinary attention, apply a light dressing to reduce the chance of further infection until you see your vet. Surgery may be required if the whole structure has been torn away from the leg.

Burns and scalds

Burns are caused by dry, extreme heat, corrosive substances or electric shock. Scalds are caused by moist heat, e.g. boiling water or steam. Burns and scalds will cause rapidly inflamed and moist areas of skin, which are tender to the touch at best and unbearably painful or life-threatening at worst (as dogs who suffer extreme burns and scalds may also suffer from shock).

Treat with cool water as quickly as possible for at least ten minutes. Do not over-cool the dog – simply cool the area only. If the dog requires immediate veterinary treatment, cover the affected area with wet sterile gauze or cold, wet towels to bring the heat down in the affected area, and to prevent contamination with dirt etc. Do not interfere with the burn. Do not apply creams, lotions or powders. If possible, following cooling, apply sterile pad or cling film to the area and seek veterinary assistance. Watch for shock at all times with serious burns and scalds.

Choking

Most 'choking' dogs in fact have kennel cough. Obstruction of the airway, other than by balls, is extremely rare. Obstructions such as bones or pieces of toy in the mouth can be removed by wedging the mouth open with a roll of bandage then using the handle of a spoon to flick the object out. But don't attempt to remove an object you cannot see and identify, as dogs have small bones at the base of their tongue and these can easily be mistaken for a foreign body.

Playing with sticks and branches can be hazardous

Occasionally, greedy eaters will choke on food. In these cases this obstruction of the oesophagus (food pipe) is not usually as severe as obstruction of the airway, although the dog may still panic. Offer warm water and massage the throat until the blockage clears. Lumps of bone or pieces of toy may necessitate prompt veterinary attention.

Constipation

Characterised by frequent, unsuccessful attempts to empty the bowels, constipation can be uncomfortable and even painful for your dog. It is evident from a number of symptoms, namely infrequent success with passing stools, straining whilst having a bowel movement, and the production of hard dry stools. The most frequent cause of constipation is a lack of fibre in the diet, or eating bones. It can also be caused by a variety of other issues, such as ingesting a foreign body (stones, rocks, toys).

Some medications will cause constipation, as will the presence of an enlarged prostrate. Dehydration will also cause constipation, so ensure that water is

Puppies readily ingest sand, stones and debris

accessible at all times. In general terms, the addition of more fibre into your dog's diet will assist the passage of stools. For a one off instance of constipation, the administration of a teaspoon of liquid paraffin should help the bowels to move again. For more persistent cases, high fibre complete diets are readily available.

Coughing

A wide range of issues can cause coughing in dogs. Some of these are potentially fatal, so it is wise to keep a close eye on persistent coughing fits and discuss with your vet. Causes include inhalation of dust, the presence of foreign bodies, ingestion of irritant plants or stinging insects, poisons, kennel cough and distemper. Parasites such as lung and heartworm will produce bouts of coughing, as will heart disease, allergies and hairballs. Treatment clearly depends on the nature of the condition causing the cough. Brief relief can usually be given with an initial dose of warm honey or Benylin® cough syrup in most cases, while vet advice is sought.

Diarrhoea

Most dogs will have a bout of diarrhoea during their lifetime, and usually it is of little consequence and lasts only a few days. Prolonged, acute or frequent bouts of diarrhoea can be attributed to a wide variety of causes such as poor diet, stress, internal parasites and viruses. Where a short bout of diarrhoea occurs, unaccompanied by other symptoms, it is usually treatable by simply withdrawing food for 12–24 hours, and by reintroducing bland food such as chicken and rice for a further 24–48 hours. Probiotic foods, such as live yoghurt, will replace good bacteria in the gut. It is important to ensure that drinking water is always available as the dog will lose precious fluids while he is suffering from diarrhoea. It is also advisable to introduce electrolytes into the water. These are available in soluble powder form which you can obtain from your vet, and they are an essential part of your medicine chest. Made up with water, these will quickly replace vital minerals to the blood stream.

You should seek advice from your vet under the following circumstances:

• If the diarrhoea is persistent
• If there are other signs of illness

- If there are signs of pain
- If there is blood in the faeces

NB If the patient is a puppy you should always consult your vet. Regardless of the cause, dehydration from diarrhoea can kill a puppy.

Eye injury

Eyes can become inflamed for a wide number of reasons:

The eye is sensitive to injury

- Foreign bodies
- Allergic reaction to stings or chemicals
- Disease such as conjunctivitis or glaucoma
- Inward growing lashes

As the eye is so fragile and easily damaged, veterinary advice is always to be sought if you have the slightest doubt whatsoever about the cause. Temporary soreness can be caused by dust or a sting in the eye area, and can be rectified by flushing with saline solution, and by the administration of antihistamine cream to the area around the eye if required. However, for any situation where trauma to the eyeball is suspected, or if there is an object embedded in the eye, this is best left to a professional. Prevent further trauma caused by the dog scratching at the eyeball, by bandaging the dew claw and leg on the side of the affected eye, and/or using an Elizabethan collar, whilst the dog is transported to the vet.

Fractures

A fracture is a crack or break in a bone. This can occur anywhere in the body and is particularly significant when it is a limb that is affected, or the head or the spine.

There are several types of fracture:

- Greenstick fractures (hairline). These are small fine cracks within the bone. The bone remains basically intact, but is cracked.
- Compound fractures. The broken bone protrudes through the skin.
- Closed fractures. The surrounding skin and tissue remain intact.
- Epiphyseal fractures. These are commonly found in developing dogs. Soft areas known as growth plates are the weakest part of the bone, and are easily fractured.

Causes of fracture are poor diet (e.g. rickets), and trauma (e.g. traffic accident, jumping or falling from a height).

Symptoms depend on which bone is fractured and how badly, and can include:

* Pain
* Lameness
* Loss of function of the limb
* Swelling
* A grating feeling / sound from the affected limb.
  The latter is termed 'crepitus'

Broken bones should be immobilised wherever possible before the injured dog is taken to a vet. Homemade splints can be made from any stiff material (e.g. rolled-up newspaper), bound firmly with tape or string then incorporated into a bandage. Open fractures should be gently covered in a sterile dressing and bandage to prevent contamination. Do not attempt to clean an open fracture.

Stretchers can be made from blankets, coats or boards to assist you in transporting badly injured dogs to the vet in most cases. You will undoubtedly require assistance to help you move the dog and to keep it calm in the car. Your vet will treat the injury accordingly, depending on the nature and position of the fracture. This can involve pain relief, casts, splints, screws and pins etc. Fractures in puppies heal more readily than in older dogs.

Haemorrhage

Bleeding can be internal or external. Dogs with suspected internal bleeding (e.g. spleen, brain, chest etc), should be referred to a vet immediately.

External bleeding from arteries will be bright red and pressurised. From veins, the bleeding will be a deeper red and will not be pumping. Some bleeds look more serious than they actually are. For example, a tear to an ear may initially cause huge concern as the dog shakes his head and splatters blood everywhere. Wounds from any extremity may appear worrying until further inspection proves otherwise.

Apply pressure to the site of a bleeding wound, by using sterile dressing or a clean handkerchief. Use the flat of the hand or fingers to apply pressure. Do not concern yourself about cleaning the wound at this time. Stemming the blood flow is of prime importance.

Pressure can be applied to 'pressure points', i.e. on the artery supplying the site, if you are able to identify its position. If the laceration is severe, a tourniquet may be applied as a last resort. This is placed just above the wound, and should be placed tightly enough to stem the flow, but not so tight as to damage tissue. The tourniquet should be released every ten minutes to allow circulation to resume. It may be that you find that the haemorrhage has ceased.

 Always be vigilant for signs of shock. Seek veterinary attention immediately in cases of severe blood loss. Minor wounds can be treated at home with bandaging, but never use creams or powders on a wound which may need stitching.

Hyperthermia (heatstroke)

The normal parameters for canine temperature are between 38 °C–39.2° C. A dog's temperature can easily rise and lead to heatstroke, as dogs do not have a very effective cooling system. Unlike humans, dogs cannot sweat. Cooling occurs through panting and through heat loss through the pads.

Also termed 'sunstroke', symptoms of heatstroke include:

- High body temperature
- Salivation
- High anxiety
- Disorientation
- Collapse

Shade and water are vital on hot summer days

Heat stroke can occur by the dog playing excessively on a hot day, by having no shade in which to cool down during the summer. It can occur by not having access to cold water to drink in warm weather. Dogs should never, ever be left in a car on a hot day as temperatures quickly rise, and a dog left inside a car will overheat and die in a matter of minutes.

Cooling the dog's body down is the top priority whilst vet assistance is sought. Use cool (but not cold) water applied directly to the body, but do *not* immerse the dog in cold water as this can add to stress and can also cause shock. If the dog is conscious offer tepid water as cold water can cause stomach cramps. All cases of heatstroke should be seen by a vet as organ damage can occur.

Hypothermia

Commonly seen in puppies, hypothermia is the opposite of hyperthermia. The patient has a very low body temperature. The patient should be wrapped to prevent further heat loss (bubble wrap is excellent), but not actively warmed as this can actually draw heat away from vital organs. Warm food or water will help mild cases. Dogs with severe hypothermia will need veterinary treatment. In these instances a warmed intravenous drip will be utilised to bring the body's temperature back to normal levels.

Poisoning

Accidental poisoning of dogs is fairly common as they are frequently exposed to a variety of toxic chemicals in our homes. Dogs will drink or eat toxic substances such as medicines, household chemicals (e.g. drain solvents and antifreeze), poisonous plants, and pesticides laid for slugs and rodents. Symptoms will include:

- Vomiting
- Diarrhoea
- Anorexia
- Swollen tongue
- Excessive salivation
- Disorientation
- Seizure

Successful treatment depends largely on correct identification of the poison, which can prove difficult. Making the dog vomit (by using either a solution of salt, washing soda or mustard) is a common reaction from most owners, but this is dangerous if the source of the poisoning is not known. If it is a corrosive substance, regurgitation of the substance may cause further injury to the throat, mouth or digestive tract. In all cases, veterinary assistance or advice should be sought before taking any action. If the dog vomits, it is wise to collect a sample and take with you to the surgery. If the source remains unknown, the vet will treat the symptoms accordingly. Activated charcoal can be given by the vet, and may prevent further absorption of the poison.

Poisons commonly found in the home:

Bleach / Cleaning fluids / Deodorisers / Disinfectants / Drain cleaners
Hair dyes / Nail polish removers / Shaving creams / Deodorants / Bubble bath
Antifreeze / Windscreen fluids / Petrol / Diesel / Kerosene
Paint / Paint stripper / Wallpaper paste
Matches / Lighter fluids
Rodent poisons / Slug bait / Weedkillers / Insecticides / Mothballs
Prescription / non-prescription medications
Acids / Ammonia / Antiseptics
Furniture polish / Shoe polish
Chocolate / Sugar-free gum
Avocado / Onions/ Some wild mushrooms
Tea / Coffee / Yeast
Walnuts / Almonds
Rhubarb plants / Potato plants/Bulb origin flowers, e.g. Daffodil
Jasmine / Yew / Wisteria

Chocolate is highly toxic to dogs

Shock

This is a collective term used to describe symptoms which arise when the flow of blood in the body becomes inadequate to meet the body's needs. Causes of shock can include haemorrhage, acute dehydration, heatstroke, and severe pain. It is a common consequence of trauma following car injury or electric shock.

Symptoms include:

- Cold, pale mucous membranes
- Weak, rapid breathing
- Shallow, laboured breathing

The pulse is likely to be weak and rapid, exceeding 140 beats per minute as the body attempts to compensate for inadequate circulation by speeding up the heart. The dog can quickly lapse into unconsciousness, and dogs in shock can die very quickly. Keep the dog quiet and calm. Ensure he is kept warm by covering the body with a light blanket. Seek veterinary assistance immediately. If possible, keep the dog's head lower than the body, keep airways open, and administer CPR if appropriate to do so. It is important to control external bleeding. Only muzzle the patient if absolutely necessary, as this can cause further distress and inhibit breathing. Above all, try to stay calm because your demeanour will impact on your patient.

Snake bite

In the UK the only venomous snake is the adder. But as pet passports are now available and as we venture into pastures new with our dogs, an awareness of other poisonous snakes is to be recommended prior to travel. In all instances of poisonous snake bite, it is crucial to keep the dog as still and calm as possible and to seek immediate veterinary help. If the bite is on a leg and you can't carry or stretcher the dog, apply a firm bandage before walking him. This will reduce circulation to the area and help limit the spread of poison. Do not try to suck out poison, as this can make the situation worse.

Stings

There are three key areas to dealing with bee and wasp stings: locate the stinger; identify the insect, and neutralise the venom. If the stinger is still present it is best to scrape this away from the site rather than using tweezers, as using tweezers might pump more venom into the area. A credit card is one of the best tools for this purpose! In terms of time-honoured remedies, wasp stings are said to respond best to a solution of vinegar or lemon juice to reduce the pain. For bee stings, make a paste from baking soda and water (or use toothpaste) and apply to the site. Using ice packs in both instances will cool the area and reduce swelling.

For a more modern approach, Piriton® is a safe, effective antihistamine for dogs, but you should always clear its usage with your vet. A dose of 4–8mg (1–2 tablets) is enough for a large dog, and this can be repeated in 8–12 hours if needed. If there are any issues such as weakness, disorientation, vomiting or problems with breathing, veterinary assistance should be sought immediately, as this is likely to be the onset of anaphylactic shock which is life threatening. In any situation where the dog is stung in the mouth, vet assistance should be sought regardless, as airways can become restricted due to localised swelling.

Stroke

When blood fails to reach parts of the brain due to blockage or bleed, dogs can suffer from a stroke just as humans can. This can be very frightening to observe, but although there is no way to reverse or repair any damage caused to the brain, many dogs will recover their motor function and movement quite quickly.

Symptoms may prove different than those seen in human sufferers. We tend to suffer facial paralysis and loss of speech, whereas dogs may exhibit head tilt, loss of balance, circling and falling over. Keep your dog warm and calm if you suspect a stroke, and prevent further injury should he be physically unstable. Seek immediate veterinary advice. Your vet will do diagnostic tests, and urine and blood samples will be taken to rule out other diseases which can exhibit similar symptoms. A full diagnosis may well follow with CT/MRI scans and a spinal tap.

A condition called canine vestibular syndrome will need to be ruled out, as this mimics stroke but is, in fact, caused by inflammation of the nerves between the inner ear and the cerebellum which controls balance. Blood tests will rule out issues such as diabetes or thyroid dysfunction which may present similar symptoms.

Prevention of stroke is always to be borne in mind especially with older dogs, and this can be best achieved through good diet, exercise and also by keeping the dog's weight down. Caring for a dog following stroke will require that he is generally given plenty of positive encouragement as he finds his feet again. Security and routine will also be important.

Wounds

The main objectives of treating wounds are to stop the bleeding and to prevent infection. Given that wounds may be extremely painful, you may need to muzzle or restrain your dog whilst giving treatment. It is important to say that if serious bleeding persists for more than 5–10 minutes (or if the dog is in shock), it is important to get the dog to the vet immediately. This is also the case where wounds are deep or if they contain large foreign bodies, which you should never attempt to remove yourself. See 'Haemorrhage' (above) for prevention of blood loss from the wound area.

In terms of the general treatment of wounds once the blood flow is under control, small abrasions would require flushing with saline or warm water plus the application of antiseptic lotion. Large abrasions would require flushing but may also need stitching, so powders and lotions should not be applied. It is unlikely that your vet will stitch wounds which are over 12 hours old and so these should be cleansed thoroughly and treated with antiseptic lotions. Do not flush wounds with hydrogen peroxide as this will prevent blood clots from forming. With all wounds, clipping or cutting of the hair around the site will help the healing process by helping keep contamination at bay. All wounds on the foot should be bandaged to prevent further contamination. Veterinary advice regarding deep wounds should be sought so that appropriate interventions can be taken, i.e. suturing, removal of foreign bodies, and the administration of pain relief and antibiotics.

Vomiting

Hallmarked by the forceful ejection of gastric contents, vomiting has a variety of root causes. If your dog vomits once, there is not likely to be a problem – as all dogs will vomit if they have eaten too much, too quickly – but frequent or persistent vomiting should be taken seriously. It is important in these instances to determine the dog's general well-being. Is he still bright and alert, or is the vomiting accompanied by listlessness, lethargy or diarrhoea? Is there blood in the vomit? If vomiting persists, the dog is likely to become dehydrated, and it should be taken seriously. Common causes include overeating, worms and parasites, a sensitive digestive system, foreign bodies, diseases of the central nervous system, infections of the stomach, and gastric torsion (p. 251).

Treatments in most circumstances will include starvation of the patient, and rehydration using soluble electrolytes combined with a slow, bland re-introduction to food over several days. If the root cause is a more serious illness, medical treatments will be as appropriate.

Being sure of first aid principles will help keep your dog safe and well

Diet and Nutrition

Feeding your dog a nutritionally appropriate diet is crucial to his physical and mental well being. Of that, there can be no debate. Yet, what it is that actually *constitutes* the best canine diet leaves many owners bewildered. It is clear that domesticated dogs are dependent on us to provide them with a nutritious diet, but despite the ever-growing array of options, many dogs are still offered inappropriate foodstuffs for their age, activity levels, and even for their breed. The subject of canine nutrition is widely and hotly debated by owners and breeders alike, and has inspired its own wealth of research material and literature.

HISTORICAL CHANGES

The canine diet has undergone significant scrutiny and development over the past century, reflecting the changing roles of the domesticated dog, our own food fashions, and progress made within research into canine nutrition. In recent times, the age of the Internet has had its part to play too: owners are now able to search through vast realms of information trying to determine what is fact and what is fad, whilst on heartfelt missions to feed their dogs the very best.

In terms of historical development, the canine diet has thankfully developed from the days when dogs were fed on scraps, bread and bones, with no thought given to their nutritional needs. In the late 1800s the concept of the canine biscuit evolved, with the introduction of Spratts 'Patent Meat Fibrine Dog Cakes®'. These were made of wheat, vegetables, beetroot and beef blood. In the early 1900s the FH Biscuit Company was established. They developed a recipe created by an American butcher, and patented the recipe under the name of 'Malatoid®' in 1911. It later became known as 'Milkbone®', and dominated the market in the 1920s and 30s. During the first part of the 20th century, a variety of pet foods gradually became available. Canned horsemeat was in plentiful supply after the First World War, and canned dog food in general represented the majority of the market during the 1940s.

After the Second World War, people began to place great emphasis on leisure time, and therefore foods for dog and man became quick and convenient. The dog's place as a 'luxury item' also reflected people's growing affluence, and the demand for commercial pet foods increased hand-in-hand with the rapid rise in the purchase of pedigree dogs. During the past fifty years or so, the commercially available canine diet has moved through various fashions from tinned dog meats to pre-packaged meat products, and on to dry, nutritionally appropriate, 'complete' diets.

So where are we now? Scientifically formulated diets have been introduced over the past two decades, to suit various breeds, ages and levels of activity. Therapeutic or clinical diets have been developed to help in the nutritional management of dogs with many illnesses and

conditions from obesity to gastro-intestinal disorders. Certain pet food manufacturers focus their attentions on producing holistic and hypo-allergenic products. This reflects ever-changing trends towards nutrition generally, and demonstrates a growing belief that quality products and fewer preservatives are better for our own bodies, and for those of our beloved pets.

In certain respects, some owners may have almost come full circle: complete diets are increasingly rejected by dog owners who feel that they want a more 'natural' solution to feeding their dog. But, unlike the 'natural diets' of times past, current raw feeding regimes are advised on, and promoted by, some nutritionists and veterinary surgeons.

THE ESSENTIAL COMPONENTS

The dog is classified as a carnivore because its natural diet (stemming from its wolf ancestry) would be made up of the carcasses of prey animals. Biochemically, physiologically and in terms of dentition this classification is well evidenced. However, although dogs have the teeth and digestive system designed to process meat and bone, they will consume plant and fruit material in the wild in the absence of prey.

The dog has a large and expandable stomach, with a more acidic level than in the human stomach. The actual value depends very much on the make-up of the meal, the size of the meal and the frequency of feeding. Evolution has designed the canine gut to be suited to bone digestion. In contrast to our own small intestine, that of the dog is short and less readily suited to carbohydrate digestion. The gut flora of the dog also differs from our own in that it is more limited, but may simply reflect the small range of the wild dog's primary diet. Dietary adjustments, however, will induce rapid changes in the gut flora, which will depend on the new dietary make-up.

Through a varied diet, the 'building blocks' for good health are provided. The basic components to any dog's diet (proteins, fats, carbohydrates, vitamins, minerals and water), are the same building blocks which make up our own dietary requirements. However, given that the canine capacity for processing certain foodstuffs differs from our own, our own diet is not entirely suitable for our canine companions. Being aware of the essential components which make up your dog's nutritional needs can only enhance your decisions, as you will want to provide him with the very best.

Proteins

Dogs require amino acids which are the components or building blocks of protein. Different forms of protein (e.g. eggs, vegetable proteins, fish, chicken etc.) are made up of different amounts and ratios of amino acid. These are needed in the adult dog to replace proteins that are used up each day by normal life processes, such as enzymes, hormones, skin and intestinal cells, whilst in the puppy there is an additional requirement to produce new tissue (i.e. growth). Twenty amino acids are considered as being needed for good health in the dog. Half of these can be synthesised by the dog's own body from primitive building blocks. The other half are termed 'essential' amino acids, as they must be provided in the diet and cannot be synthesised by the animal. The 'essential' amino acids consist of arginine, histidine, isoleucine, leucine, lysine, methionine, phenyl-alanine, threonine, tryptophan, and valine.

Proteins should come from a variety of sources, as different food sources provide different amounts of amino acids. There is no such thing as a perfect protein, and therefore there is a need for a mix of protein sources to provide a balance of amino acids in the diet. Animal sources of protein, such as chicken, beef and fish are better than plant sources for a canine diet, as animal proteins are generally more readily processed by the dog's digestive system than are plant sources. However, it is important to note that not all animal proteins are good protein sources. Tendons and connective tissues for example may be left undigested and passed out in the stools. Be aware also that claims of '25% meat' will not give you the full picture in terms of protein levels. This may actually be as low as 4 or 5% protein as fresh meat contains a high percentage of water. Animal proteins increase palatability, and therefore encourage the dog to eat more readily. Protein intake affects growth rate, therefore an excessively high protein, high calorie diet given to growing puppies can readily lead to skeletal abnormalities and diseases if fed inappropriately.

Fats

Fats are vital for good health, and are available through animal fats, vegetable oils, and fish oils. Omega 3 fatty acids, found predominantly in fish oils, are crucial to physical and mental well-being as they are important for the functioning of the nervous system, and also the immune system. Omega 6 fatty acids, found mainly in vegetable oils, are important in maintaining coat and skin quality, and fat metabolism. Fats increase the palatability of the diet, and they also store 'fat soluble vitamins'. Dietary fat is a concentrated energy (calorie) source: the energy yield of fat is approximately 9kcal/g (kilocalories per gram). By contrast the energy yield of protein is close to 4kcal/g. The use of fat *supplements* (used to increase calorific intake without increasing volume of food intake), should be viewed with caution, as high-fat diets could lead to obesity if the dog is not suitably exercised or the food is fed at an inappropriate amount. They can also lead to health issues such as pancreatitis.

However, the active dog is tolerant of large amounts of fat in the diet and indeed benefits from such. The dog relies on fat as an energy source, both at rest and at high levels of activity as well. It is a fat-adapted animal that best performs on high proportions of calories from fat. Conversely, continuous use of body fat stores is associated with rapid weight loss, and in these semi-starvation circumstances, immune function can be compromised if the nutrition provided does not meet the energy needs of the dog in question.

Carbohydrates

Carbohydrates in the diet serve to provide energy and bulk. They have been shown to be conditionally essential in the breeding animal and their role in gut health and the immune system is now well understood. (This latter role is the basis of pre-biotics.) Simple carbohydrates (also called sugars) are found in milk, fruit, honey etc, and provide rapid energy sources, whilst complex carbohydrates include starches and dietary fibres, found in grains, vegetables and some fruits.

They can be further divided into four groups:

- Absorbable: mono-saccharides, and sugar alcohols
- Digestible: sugars such as lactose, sucrose and maltose, and starch
- Fermentable: oligosaccharides, resistant starch
- Non fermentable: hemicelluloses, cellulose

The first two groups are energy sources, whilst the last two form components of dietary fibre. The fermentable group also has prebiotic properties and thus contributes to intestinal health.

Carbohydrates are used as readily available, excellent sources of energy. The dog has a metabolic need for glucose, which can be synthesised from protein in the diet, but the body converts simple carbohydrates to glucose more readily and this means that the amino acids (precursors for glucose) can be used for other functions within the body.

Dogs, like humans, cannot digest all the carbohydrates in cereals, but there are certain benefits to this as this is how whole grain works as a pre-biotic. These carbohydrates are not digested, but fermented in the hind gut, with the products of digestion being absorbed to provide a modest amount of energy. This benefits the hind gut and the immune system: oligosaccharides provide a food source for 'bifidobacteria'. These are a 'good bacteria' and they play a key role in the gut as they produce substances which kill harmful bacteria. They are also thought to reduce the risk of harmful substances being absorbed by the colon lining, and therefore help support against infection.

Indigestible carbohydrates form a substance known as dietary fibre. In the canine diet this can come from the cell skeleton of a wide variety of plant materials, the outer layer of grains, fruits, root crops and vegetables, and even some of the less digestible connective tissue of animals. Mostly, it is the cell wall materials of these foods. Dietary fibre is highly beneficial in the control of obesity as undigested fibre provides bulk and speeds up the transit of waste matter through the colon, and some calories are therefore expelled undigested. Poorly fermented, indigestible fibre also holds water like a sponge. This results in waste matter remaining soft and bulky, rather than hard and dry, and it is easily passed from the body.

Dogs can digest starch, but benefit from the cereal being cooked to gelatinise the starch into digestible, less complex carbohydrates. Milling and grinding do not achieve this; however they can speed up enzymic processes by increasing the available surface area of those carbohydrates which can be digested.

Puppies have the enzymes to utilise lactose (milk sugar), but adult dogs do not. However, the reverse is true for starch as the puppy lacks the enzymes, but the adult has them. Bitch's milk, which provides essential nutrition for newborn puppies, is significantly lower in lactose than cow's milk. Consequently cow's milk should not be used as a bitch milk substitute. Their ability to digest milk sugar wanes over time and it is well known that adult dogs can develop diarrhoea when given cow's milk. Yoghurt is the exception to this issue, as yoghurt is a form of milk where the lactose has been pre-fermented and is more readily digestible.

Poor quality cereals usually form the basis of lower grade dog foods, as these are cheap and provide bulk. Typically, in a lower grade feed, the carbohydrate source would be oats. Corn is used in hypo-allergenic diets and certain clinical diets, especially when the dog presents with intolerances to rice. It is also used in some premium diets. Brown rice has higher fibre content than white rice, and is therefore useful in weight management diets. Wheat is not used in some natural products as it has been linked to inducing adverse reactions or hypersensitivities. Barley is often used in diets to help manage diabetic patients as it has a very low glycaemic index.

Vitamins

Vitamins are the key to the functioning of most metabolic processes. They can be 'fat soluble', whereby they are stored in the fat cells in the body (e.g. vitamins A, D, E and K). These can cause serious problems if over-supplemented in the diet. For example an excess of vitamin A in the pregnant bitch can result in foetal abnormalities. Vitamins can also be 'water soluble' (e.g. the B-group vitamins and vitamin C) and these are readily eliminated from the body. NB Dogs can synthesise vitamin C and it is therefore not a dietary requirement.

A broad overview of their roles can be summarised as follows:

Energy supply
- Vitamin B1 is vital for releasing energy from starchy foods.
- Vitamin B2, B6 and niacin help release energy from proteins and fat.
- Vitamin B12 and folic acid are involved in the formation of red blood cells and are therefore key to high performance. In dogs, as in humans, folic acid has a role to play in reducing the risk of congenital problems such as cleft palate.

Build and repair:
- Vitamin C supports the metabolism in building and maintaining body structures like bones, tissues and blood cells
- Vitamins D, K and Biotin strengthen bone and skin structures. NB Dogs do not synthesise significant amounts of vitamin D, and thus it must form part of the diet.

Defence and support:
- Vitamins A, C and E are powerful antioxidants supporting organs and tissue by neutralising free radicals.
- Vitamin C is essential for a strong immune system and oral health.

Regulation of activity:
- B-group vitamins and choline are of major importance for high metabolic activity and the synthesis of neurotransmitters.
- Balanced vitamin nutrition contributes to weight control, high performance and physiological strength.

Minerals

Minerals, like vitamins, have many functions in the dog, from structural to catalysts for biochemical reactions. Two of the most important minerals are calcium and phosphorous, which must be available in the diet in the correct amount and in the correct ratio, or they will not be used properly. The desired calcium–phosphorous ratio is in the range of 1:1 to 2:1. This is finely balanced in quality complete feeds, but presents a genuine dilemma to those who choose to feed a raw diet without the addition of bones. Calcium is vital within the diet for promoting healthy bone growth and maintenance. Phosphorous in addition to bone has a vital role in energy transfers within the cell. When either of these minerals is deficient in the diet, the body draws on reserves from the skeleton, compromising bone modelling and remodelling. In puppies this can lead to skeletal abnormalities and in the older dog to orthopaedic problems. It is worth noting that with modern complete balanced feeds it is *overfeeding* that predisposes similar problems in the puppy, and this is a more common cause of abnormal bone development than errors in calcium or phosphorus supply. In raw diets, meat contains a

A balanced diet is vital for a growing puppy

high level of phosphorous and needs to be balanced out by calcium supplementation in order that the proper ratio is achieved. This can be provided in a commercial supplement powder, and via ground eggshells, seaweed or bonemeal. (NB The latter also contains phosphorous.) Vitamin D is essential for intestinal absorption of calcium and phosphorous, but if provided in excess there is a significant risk of further imbalance as calcium uptake will increase readily.

- Calcium and phosphorus are vital to the rigidity of teeth and bones, whilst magnesium is involved in their formation.
- Phosphorous is also involved in cell and sub-cell membrane structure, DNA and RNA and energy metabolism.
- Calcium, magnesium, potassium and sodium are involved in nerve impulse transmission, muscle contraction, and cell signalling as well as acid base balance, cell membrane transport and the balance of water in the cells and the blood.
- Sulphur is involved in protein formation and amino acid structure.
- Micro minerals in general are involved in enzymes and or protein / hormone structure and function, for example iron in haemoglobin, iodine in thyroid hormones, and zinc in keratin structure. Some of the effects of micro minerals can be seen in outward appearance such as coat quality.

Water

The dog's lean body mass is made up of approximately 70% water, and other tissues range from 70–90% water. Water is vital for survival, and as little as a 10% loss can be fatal. It keeps the body hydrated, regulates temperature, and provides the means for nutrition and oxygen to be transported throughout the body. Water also acts as a solvent that facilitates cellular reactions and acts as a transport medium for nutrients and end products of metabolism. A dog's need for water per day is said to be in the order of 40–70 mg per kilogram of body-weight. However, this can vary according to the dog's age, activity level and coat type. It is also affected by climate, and by the conditions within your home. More importantly it goes up to nearer 150mg/kg bodyweight during lactation, as milk is mainly water. Fresh water should always be available and a healthy dog will regulate his intake as is needed. Dogs which are dehydrated are medically at risk. A dog can survive for many weeks without food, but will die within only a few days of being deprived of water.

DIETARY ISSUES IN THE GERMAN SHEPHERD DOG

The Shepherd is known to suffer from food allergies and intolerances. This can be frustrating and time consuming to tackle, but once the actual cause has been identified, the sufferer will usually fare well on the correct diet. The concept of 'elimination' diets is explained overleaf.

The Shepherd is also known to be prone to certain disorders which affect the digestion and/or absorption of food. Conditions such as exocrine pancreatic insufficiency, pancreatitis and small intestinal bacterial overgrowth can have a profound effect on the digestive process and are looked at in more detail in chapter six. Regardless of condition, the affected dog's diet will need to be medically appropriate, and your vet will advise the best way forward once diagnosis has been reached.

Gastric torsion (otherwise known as 'bloat') is a major concern when looking at your Shepherd's diet (p. 251). This medical emergency is common in the breed, and there are several causal factors, of which breed conformation and management of feed regimes play a significant part. There have been many studies which incriminate diet but no clear association has been proven. The *way* in which diet is fed is probably much more significant, e.g. single large meals / overeating / kibble size / elevated bowls / exercise following a meal. Previous gastric injury is also pertinent to the likely incidence of this condition.

Prevention is widely believed to be best achieved by feeding the dog a large kibble, which he has to break down before swallowing. 'Aerophagia' is believed to present a significant risk factor in gastric torsion. The dog is less likely to inhale air if he is not gulping food down quickly. With all adult Shepherds, it is wise to feed two meals a day, and restrict vigorous exercise for two hours either side of feeding.

'Complete' foods

There are a wide variety of reasons why people choose complete diets. Some will simply feel that complete diets offer them the best chance to feed their dog appropriately, and that this will eliminate worries and mistakes on the owner's part. Complete diets have been developed with the aim that the dog is provided with a balanced diet every day. This is endorsed by many vets, nutritionists, pet food manufacturers, and by owners from all walks of life.

If you are leaning towards feeding your dog on a

With the right diet, your dog will gleam with health

complete diet, you need to be aware that there are a wide range of these products on the market, from the highly researched product through to feedstuffs that are of poor nutritional value. Super premium grade and tailored nutrition diets will invariably have been well researched, and produced from good quality ingredients which are palatable and digestible. Expect to pay a high price for these products, but you will usually find that you feed less of the product each day, and your dog's faeces are likely to be firm and less voluminous than you would find on a poor grade diet. This is usually a sign that the dog is processing the food correctly and efficiently.

Do remember that simply choosing a super premium complete diet may not be the whole answer. Your dog may dislike it, get bored of it, or may be allergic or intolerant to it. Re-examine your choices throughout your dog's life, as although you may be buying the most expensive food, this still might not result in a happy, healthy dog. It is true to say that there is a huge range of superb products on the market, but it pays to be aware that not all 'complete' diets are quality products. Cheaper complete foods may be bulked out with poor quality ingredients.

Some owners find that their dog's lifestyle is best suited to a complete diet. With pregnant bitches, working dogs and puppies in particular, appropriate, accessible nutrition is of vital importance. Opting for high quality, complete foods in these instances keeps things simple and gives many owners peace of mind. Dogs that are competing may stay away from home regularly, and complete foods provide a practical solution. If your dog has a delicate stomach, there is much to be said for a complete diet which is a 'constant' within the changes elsewhere in your dog's life.

Many breeders opt for complete diets. The breeder will promote the food with their buyers, in the hope that the puppies will be reared on a quality product, which will provide them with correct nutrition while they are at their formative stages.

Clinical diets will afford you the opportunity to know that your dog's health condition is supported through his diet, and this will alleviate a great deal of worry whilst your dog is unwell. It is always important to consult with your veterinary surgeon before and whilst feeding a therapeutic diet: some diets (if fed long term), may result in problems if the dog does not require the particular food any longer.

Hypo-allergenic foods

There is a ready demand for canine products which are free of ingredients likely to cause adverse reactions. The German Shepherd suffers frequently from food allergies, and exhibits a wide range of symptoms such as:

- Itchy, flaky skin
- Dull coat
- Licking of paws
- Diarrhoea or flatulence
- Lethargy and depression

Like humans, dogs may at some stage in their life develop an allergy or intolerance to certain foodstuffs. In order for this occur, the animal must have been previously exposed to that food allergen at some point in time. Dogs may therefore become allergic to a foodstuff which it has eaten for many years without any problem. Allergies can arise whether the diet is a super premium or economy based diet. Because allergies will differ from dog to dog, it is not possible to create a hypo-allergenic diet which suits every dog.

The dog can only develop an allergy or intolerance to a particular food where there is a glycoprotein (carbohydrate/protein) or intact protein present. The speed of the onset of the adverse reaction, and its subsequent reduction in response once the protein is removed, indicates the nature of the immune response and that an immunoglobulin (IgE) is involved.

Hydrolysed Protein Diets

For a protein to be an allergenic agent it must be large enough (10–70kDa) to trigger the immune response. If the molecule can be reduced in size ($\cong$ 6kDa), as in the case of certain hydrolysed proteins, then the risk of an immune reaction to it is substantially reduced or even eliminated. As a consequence, it is possible to produce protein hydrolysates (such as soy hydrolysates) that will not trigger an adverse reaction and thus can be used as a general hypoallergenic diet, which may suit some dogs.

Selected Protein Diets

Selected protein diets invariably contain only one protein source such as duck, fish, chicken or lamb, and they may also contain brown rice or tapioca as a carbohydrate source. They do not contain dairy products nor wheat or gluten, because these are widely recognised to cause allergic reactions. The diet may also be formulated using a 'novel' ingredient such as venison. (A novel ingredient is one which the dog is unlikely to have previously eaten, and has therefore not built up a resistance to it.)

This could also be utilised as an 'elimination diet' protein source, to determine the cause of the allergy. (An elimination diet is one where all likely allergenic agents are removed from the recipe.) If your dog is suspected of having dietary sensitivity of some kind, it may be suggested that such a diet might get to the root cause. Elimination diets (whether hydrolysed or select protein), use the principle of removing ingredients from the diet which are suspected of causing an adverse reaction. This reaction can be caused by food allergies, but also by food intolerance. Key ingredients known to cause allergies include:

- Wheat
- Nut oils
- Dairy products
- Eggs
- Beef

In cases of suspected intolerances (or allergy), it is recommended that a select or hydrolysed protein diet be fed for a minimum of 12 weeks. During this period it is important that the dog is fed nothing else, and has no access to scraps, bins etc. If symptoms resolve over the next 12 week period, food should then be introduced gradually one ingredient at a time over a number of days. If symptoms reappear after the feeding of one particular ingredient then that is assumed to be the source of the problem. In reality most owners opt for the feeding of select protein or hydrolysed protein diets for the lifetime of the animal.

Holistic foods

There are a wide variety of interpretations of the term 'holistic'. However, when referring to holistic animal feeds, the term is used to illustrate that the whole body is supported by the product. Whereas some complete feeds make claims to support specific areas such as the immune system, digestive tract, urinary tract, or the skin, the holistic product aims to support the body as a whole without bias.

Raw feeding

Dietary deficiencies are unlikely to just happen in a matter of days. They occur over time, and many owners feel that their dog may not want, or need, a uniform diet every day of their life. This thinking has led many owners to move away from complete feeding, and to look at more 'natural' methods of feeding their dog. As with all canine diets, raw feeding methods have staunch supporters and critics.

'Prey-model feeding' describes the practice of feeding a diet which is generally made up of raw meat, bones and organs. Owners who have opted for this model believe that feeding their dogs in this manner not only provides a nutritionally superior food source, but that it is biologically appropriate for the species. The whole prey may be used, for example rabbit or poultry. The general recommendation is that the diet consists of a predominance of meat, bone and organs, with some vegetable component to the diet, derived from the digestive system of the prey animal.

The 'BARF' diet was devised by Australian vet Dr Ian Billinghurst, and is an acronym for 'Biologically Appropriate Raw Food', or 'Bones And Raw Food'. In the BARF method of feeding, around three-quarters of the diet consists of raw meaty bones (a good example being chicken necks or wings, but remember that *cooked* bones splinter readily and should not be fed). The remaining diet consists of offal, meat, eggs, dairy produce, fruit and vegetables.

Neither diet has grain as a component. Cooked or processed foods are ideally omitted.

Dog owners who opt for raw feeding methods are of the thinking that dogs (like humans) do not require every single meal to be a balanced offering in its own right. The thinking is that a variety of ingredients will provide adequate and appropriate nutrition, which will balance itself over time. Benefits are said to include increased energy levels, alongside improvements in skin, coat, and dental hygiene. Stools are argued to be less voluminous and have less odour than those fed on complete diets. Puppies are said to grow at a steady rate and not given to damaging growth spirts. Risks are said to include dental fractures, oesophageal or intestinal obstruction and perforation. Bacteria and parasites are also argued to be an increased risk to dog and human alike.

The 'pros and cons' of feeding raw diets gives rise to some of the most heated debates on any canine subject. For anyone contemplating raw feeding, be aware that this involves careful preparation so that important nutrients are not overlooked. For example, if the ethos is misinterpreted and the dog is merely feed raw meat, the dog is seriously at risk, as vital nutrients in the diet are omitted. But if the diet is well-researched, dogs fare extremely well on raw diets the world over.

There is already a range of literature available which covers the subject in depth.

AN OUTLINE OF CHANGING NEEDS

0–8 weeks

Newborn puppies need colostrum from the first flush of their mother's milk (p. 234). This provides much needed antibodies. Bitches' milk is rich in essential proteins, fats and vitamins. Newborn puppies are able to process lactose during the first few weeks, but as they approach weaning this mechanism changes. The puppies' capacity to digest lactose decreases, and cow's milk in particular will almost certainly cause diarrhoea, as the lactose content is higher than in bitches' milk. In cases of orphaned puppies, substitute puppy milk, which is based on the composition of bitches' milk, and is always a safer option then cow or goat milk.

Puppies usually can be fully weaned on to solids by six weeks and will need four feeds per day from this point. They are more easily weaned on to the starter or puppy product which has been fed to the bitch during late gestation and lactation.

The puppies' need for water will increase as they begin to wean from the bitch. Puppies need a quality, high protein diet, and the correct calcium–phosphorous ratio for good joint development. As a rule of thumb, puppies at this stage should be well covered but should never appear fat for their frame.

8–12 weeks

Four feeds a day

Your puppy's growth will increase rapidly at this stage. It is important that his feed regime keeps up with his growth demands or he will become overly 'rangy' and his development could be compromised. Keep watch on his rate of growth, which you will want to be steady, not given to erratic 'spurts'. Be aware that puppy needs steadily increasing quantities to help him achieve correct growth rates. Quality complete feeds have a guide of quantity to age/weight of dog, which are helpful. But this really only works if the puppy is weighed weekly and the food adjusted in accordance. It is also imperative at this stage that growth is not forced by excessive protein, nor that the puppy is allowed to become too heavy for his frame, as this is not good for joint development. If you are giving him a quality complete food, do not add vitamin or mineral supplements to the feed. You could cause major disturbances to puppy's development.

If you plan to feed your puppy in a different way from his breeder, be sure that you do not change your puppy's diet over immediately after he has moved home. This is highly likely to upset his stomach. Once he has fully settled in, you can make gradual changes over a period of 5–7 days.

12 weeks–6 months

Keep a careful eye on your puppy's development

Three feeds a day

This is a period of high demand nutritionally. Your puppy will pass through major changes anatomically in this period, and will go from a rounded bundle to a gangly adolescent in no time. Continue to be vigilant regarding growth spurts as these can leave the growing frame with a rakish appearance almost overnight. Vital nutrition is required for bone and muscle growth. You may find that his weight and muscle development are left behind if food intake is not appropriate. He should still be kept lean, but never allowed to become thin. Continue to ensure that your weekly quantities are increased without fail. Somewhere around 5–6 months will be the point at which the dog will eat the most food per day in his life.

6 months–15 months

Two feeds per day

At around six months the required number of feeds per day will fall from three to two. Some brands advise a changeover from puppy food to their junior brand at this stage, but you will find that most now adopt a 'puppy/junior' approach and the dog may remain on this from 8 weeks until he is around 15 months of age.

A condition called panosteitis is common during adolescence, which is commonly referred to as 'growing pains' and manifests as lameness (p. 258). If this is the case, you may find that your vet advises transferring to a diet where protein levels are lower, although all other nutritional needs must still be met for the growing dog.

At around 15–18 months, the recommendation would be to move the dog to an adult feed as the growth rate has slowed remarkably. The dog will continue to 'fill out' and mature, but this is a period of slow change.

It is always to be advised that adult Shepherds should be fed twice a day. This practice substantially reduces the likelihood of your dog developing gastric torsion.

Pregnancy and lactation

The nutritional demands of the bitch alter very little until the sixth week of pregnancy. Standard maintenance diets are adequate although diets are available for use from the bitch's heat through to day 43 of the pregnancy which include increased levels of folic acid and DHA to help in the development of the foetuses.

However, from around 6 weeks forward the bitch requires increasing quantities of food, in the region of approximately one and a half times her normal maintenance requirements. Many breeders change at this stage to a high grade puppy food. Her requirements *could* also be met by increasing the quantity of her normal food. However, as the puppies grow in her uterus her intestinal capacity decreases. It is therefore not always possible for the bitch to consume the volume of food required to make up the calories she requires, particularly if fed a wet diet. If she is transferred on to a puppy food, this will enable the bitch to consume high levels of nutrients in a densely rich product.

It is always a mistake to add calcium to the diet prior to whelping as ironically this can cause a condition caused eclampsia. This serious condition is caused by a lack of available calcium to the bitch, usually at the height of lactation (see p. 220).

The brood bitch has changing nutritional needs

During lactation, her energy requirements will increase with the growth of the puppies, until they reach the point of weaning. Her nutritional requirements will rise to three to four times that of her usual needs. You may find that feeding her 'ad lib' presents her with the opportunity to self regulate her needs during this time. Requirements are roughly maintenance plus a quarter of maintenance per puppy. It is important to note that her water requirements rise dramatically.

Your bitch will lose condition (including most of her coat) once the puppies are fully weaned, and can take many months to return to full health. A high quality diet is crucial for her prompt recovery.

The working / sports dog

This is very much governed by the individual situation. Every dog will have differing needs depending on the frequency and intensity of the training, competing and working which he is doing. It will also depend on the dog's individual make-up as some high drive dogs will literally drop weight overnight. Certainly, the active dog needs an increase of calories from fat, so that he is able to remain physically strong and mentally able to carry out required tasks, but in terms of quantity it will be down to the individual handler to assess the dog's needs on a regular basis, according to the demands being made on the dog at the time.

What remains crucial is that the food provided is of excellent quality, and able to support the demands made of the dog's muscles, joints, heart and other organs, and that it is able to keep him at an appropriate weight for his frame.

The overly lean dog will deplete his energy reserves rapidly, and the overweight dog is clearly at risk of injury and illness.

Feeding the older dog

Commonly, older dogs have a variety of issues, which can be supported or exacerbated by their diet.

Certain senior complete diets seek to help the dog who is ageing but clinically normal, by selecting specific nutrient profiles, ingredients or nutraceutical products.

As his demands for exercise decrease, be careful not to over-indulge him with food and treats as it is easy for him to become overweight. By the same token, if he is suffering with digestive disorders you may find he is more prone to upset stomachs and may actually find it hard to keep weight on his frame.

If the dog has a particular illness associated with their age, then clinical diets are readily available through your vet and can address some of the ailments of old age, such as decreased or impaired kidney function. There are also clinical diets to help in the nutritional management of dogs with diabetes or heart complaints which are common in older dogs. You may opt for holistic or hypo-allergenic diets, but whatever road you choose to go down, your dog will almost certainly benefit from a diet which supports his skin and coat, as both tend to deteriorate with the advancing years.

If your elderly dog has dental issues, his diet will need to be soft and manageable. Natural diets may need pulverising or liquidising. You will need to feed him at least twice a day, although you may find he needs his meals broken down even further. Some elderly dogs prefer to 'graze' throughout the day. Paying attention to oral hygiene is important at every stage of the dog's life, however it can become an even greater need in the elderly dog.

For those with mobility issues (and in addition to veterinary care) some owners report good outcomes from a dietary addition of glucosamine and chondroitin (p. 256), green lipped mussel extracts, gelatine, collagen hydrolysates and also Omega 3 fatty acids. These can all act as joint supporting agents in the diet.

SUMMARY

The history and development of the canine diet are fascinating subjects, and owners' responses to the diets on offer are on a very individual basis. The crucial issues are that your dog's diet must meet his individual requirements, and its components must be nutritionally accessible.

Whatever your final choice, be aware that you might not reap the results you had hoped for if you have not researched the diet carefully. Your complete food might actually be low grade, and your dog could therefore be without vital nutrients on a daily basis. If you are feeding a natural diet, you might easily omit crucial elements and therefore time, patience and care will be needed to devise home prepared regimes. A holistic or hypo-allergenic food will only give you and your dog peace of mind if it is the right product for his needs.

If essential nutrients are not present the animal can gradually become lethargic and out of condition. Skin, coat and demeanour may all be adversely affected, and the dog can be more inclined towards general ill-health. Puppies in particular will suffer from orthopaedic conditions if certain elements are missing from the diet, however overfeeding is probably a more common cause of abnormalities than true dietary deficiencies.

Research your dog's diet well, and you will surely be rewarded with a happy, healthy companion. If you talk to your vet, to nutritional advisors and to experienced dog owners for a broad outlook on canine diets, you will hopefully gain a wide overview of the issues. But above all, listen to what your dog is telling you. His physical condition and his attitude to life will speak volumes about how well he is faring on the diet you have chosen for him.

Complementary Therapies

Complementary therapies are also known as 'alternative' or 'holistic' therapies, treatments and medicines. They form part of a wide group of health care systems, products and also practices which are not presently considered to be a recognised part of conventional medicine.

Viewed by some with total conviction, they are also viewed by others with suspicion and even ridicule, because claims regarding the benefits of using some complementary therapies are not comprehensively supported by proven scientific evidence. However, the term encompasses therapies which are steeped in history and culture, and which are also based on folklore and spiritual beliefs. Complementary therapies are based on the assertion that the body has an innate capacity for self healing, and that the whole body forms the key to treatment. Mind, body, spirit and emotion will be looked at to find the treatment which best 'complements' conventional treatments.

Commonly used complementary therapies include herbal medicines, Chinese medicines, crystal therapies, acupuncture and many more besides. The aim is to stimulate the body's natural ability to self heal, by drawing on its own natural resources.

 If you wish to introduce complementary therapies to current treatment programmes for your dog, the therapist or practitioner will usually seek approval from your vet first, as the vet is still considered to be the primary carer. This is not the same as a veterinary referral, but it will afford the therapist the opportunity to ensure that the therapy will not be in conflict with existing treatments.

HERBAL REMEDIES

For many thousands of years, people have known of the benefits of using herbal remedies to improve their general health, treat wounds and ailments, and to ward off illness. Knowledge was passed by word of mouth from generation to generation, and herbal remedies became the precursor to developments in modern-day medicine. Over the past century, research and developments in modern treatments (for human and animal alike) have had an impact on ancient practices, and valuable knowledge was suppressed for a long time. Life often goes full circle however, and in the past few decades there has been an ever-increasing desire for alternatives and complements to modern-day medicines. This has led to the emergence of specialised markets to meet the need. There is a widespread demand for ethically and organically produced, high quality herbal remedies. Available as straight herbs (i.e. dried, or in a liquid form otherwise referred to as a 'tincture'), herbal remedies are also offered in encapsulated form, and when immensely diluted they are offered within homeopathic product ranges. Herbal treatments in the form of creams and lotions are also popular.

The German Shepherd is known to suffer from a wide range of conditions, and there are thousands of herbs which are reputed to be beneficial for many of these issues. Below are just some of the many herbs thought to provide benefits for certain conditions that the Shepherd may experience:

Immune system – Echinacea

Thought to be an immune stimulant, this is also said to be useful in treating skin problems, respiratory disorders and for post-viral infections. It is also thought to aid in the healing process of wounds.

Echinacea

General coat condition – Seaweed

There is a wide variety of seaweed from the oceans across the world. Said to improve coat condition and skin pigmentation. It is also thought to inhibit coprophagia (eating of faeces).

Digestion – Milk Thistle, Fenugreek, Fennel, Catnip, Chamomile

These are just some of the herbs thought to decrease sensitivity, support the system, and protect the liver against toxins.

Itchy skin condition – Nettle

Thought to cool and purify the blood. Used in the treatment of coat and skin in poor condition, as it is said to encourage regrowth in cases of coat loss.

Joint conditions – Devil's Claw Root

Devil's Claw Root

Thought to possess anti-inflammatory and analgesic properties, this is reputed to provide nutritional support for joints and muscles. It is a popular choice with owners of dogs with hip dysplasia (p. 252).

Hyperactivity / Anxiety – Chamomile, Valerian, Skullcap, Lemon Balm

Used to promote a sense of calm and well-being.

Urinary system – Juniper, Parsley

Thought to aid in the relaxation of muscle spasm, stimulate urine flow, and reduce uric acid build-up. Said to promote the healing of tissues damaged by infection or inflammation.
Cranberry is also used as this makes the urinary tract inhospitable to bacteria.

HOMEOPATHY

This ancient practice is based on the belief that 'like treats like'. In other words that something which makes someone unwell can be used, in extremely dilute measures, to stimulate the body's responses to fight the condition itself. Substances are diluted with water or alcohol, and are subject to ever increasing dilution to increase the remedies' 'potency'. Homeopathic vets take a three-year course, following qualifying as a conventional vet. Homeopathic medicine is a regulated practice, governed in the UK by the British Association of Homeopathic Veterinary Surgeons (www. bahvs.com).

Homeopathy is used in the treatment of the majority of chronic diseases, although certain conditions seen in the GSD, such as CDRM (p. 247), are unresponsive to treatment. The treatments of mental stress and auto-immune related conditions are at the forefront of homeopathic treatments. (These are causal factors in the body becoming vulnerable to disease.) Unlike conventional medicine which controls disease through continuous administration of drugs, homeopathy gives the body a source for healing itself and stimulates the body to recover. Of particular relevance to the German Shepherd are the treatments of skin, arthritic, gastric and bowel disorders.

HYDROTHERAPY

This highly popular therapy is known for its wide-reaching benefits, both to healthy individuals and for those with existing ailments. By offering the opportunity for non-weight-bearing exercise, hydrotherapy provides the body with the opportunity to build or maintain general fitness. It can be utilised by those who compete in canine sports as an additional means for the dog to benefit from a cardiovascular workout, *and* to improve muscle tone and joint mobility. For owners with dogs undergoing treatment for arthritic conditions, obesity and general weakness in the aftermath of surgical procedures, it is a gentle option. Hydrotherapy has less risk associated with its implementation than with other forms of exercise.

Hydrotherapy will assist in the treatment of dogs with certain respiratory disorders as it will strengthen the lungs. For dogs with neurological problems such as CDRM, it will assist in the maintenance of muscle tone as dogs that have limited usage of their hind limbs on land are frequently able to move through the water using both their fore and hind limbs.

Hydrotherapy is used to help in the treatment of many ailments

MASSAGE AND MANIPULATION

Various forms of massage and the manipulation of bones and joints are based on ancient practices. These practices are especially notable for their use in re-aligning the musculo-skeletal system and management of pain, and as part of a rehabilitation programme.

Massage may be offered in various forms, from ancient practices to more modern approaches:

- 'Shiatsu' massage for example, is based on the belief that lines of energy (meridians) run throughout the body, and that these lines can be manipulated by external forces to enhance energies and promote a sense of well-being and relaxation. It is growing in popularity in the UK.
- 'Reiki' healing is based on similar principles, and stems from a Japanese word which means 'Universal life energy'. It is an ancient method of passive healing, drawn from the belief that the earth's energies, stemming from 'shakras' or vortexes, can be channelled into the body to promote self-healing.
- 'McTimoney' animal manipulation is a technique aimed at re-aligning the musculo-skeletal system through manipulation of the bones and joints of the spine and pelvis. This enables the central nervous system (branches of which extend from the spine to all organs and systems of the body), to work properly. The techniques stem from McTimoney human chiropractic techniques, but McTimoney animal manipulation is a more recent profession, with a postgraduate course now offering an MSc in the subject. The McTimoney practitioner will use their hands to palpate for misalignments of the bones and will make light and fast adjustments. The lightness of the techniques ensures minimal discomfort and because of this, animals usually respond well.
- 'Deep Oscillation'® is a modern-day, proven technology which utilises the creation of electrostatic oscillations in the tissue of the patient. The technique can be used to aid manual massage, as the oscillations will penetrate deep into the tissue. Pioneered in Germany by physiotherapists Hans Seidl and Wolfgang Walder in collaboration with Physiomed Elektromedizin AG, Deep Oscillation® therapy was patented in 1988. PhysioPod UK Ltd holds sole UK rights. The practitioner is connected to the applicator by a small electrode and applies the electrostatic vibrations to the animal through a hand-held applicator. It is a non-traumatic and very gentle form of therapy, assisting in the management of many conditions such as arthritis, joint and muscle pain and the reduction of inflammation from bruising and swellings.

ACUPUNCTURE

Predominantly used to effect the relief of pain, acupuncture is an ancient remedy which can bring considerable results. The use of fine, long needles brings concern to newcomers, but there is little sensation when the needles are applied correctly, and it can be used to great effect. Acupuncture is also said to help with digestive and nervous disorders. The treatment of pain and inflammation caused by conditions such as arthritis may be of particular interest to the German Shepherd owner.

Castration and Spaying

You may be contemplating the prospect of having your bitch spayed or your dog castrated for any number of reasons. Both operations have genuine health benefits, but there are also certain issues which raise concerns, and you may want to consider these when making your decision.

Spaying and castration are surgical procedures offered by vets and promoted by many animal welfare organisations, as this is clearly the most effective method of canine birth control. Given that many thousands of strays are regularly destroyed due to escalating numbers of unwanted dogs, the situation causes huge concern amongst dog lovers worldwide.

Castration has long been associated with having a positive impact on unwanted canine behaviours, and spaying undeniably prevents potentially fatal conditions in the bitch. However, certain research indicates that there are various long-term conditions, and certain negative bevaviours, which can potentially follow either procedure.

This chapter aims to address some of the key issues amidst a complex subject which courts conflicting viewpoints.

CASTRATION (ORCHIDECTOMY)

Otherwise known as 'neutering', castration is an irreversible procedure in which the testicles are removed. This is a routine procedure which usually involves a day visit to the surgery, although the actual operation usually takes under an hour to perform. The dog will be put under anaesthetic, and a small incision will be made in front of his scrotal sac. The veterinary surgeon ties off associated blood vessels and the dog's testicles (testes) are removed. The sac which surrounds the testes is not removed, and this will gradually wither and disappear.

The testes are responsible for testosterone production. This is the hormone which is produced as the dog moves into adolescence and its presence in the body results in secondary sex-related behaviours, which can include:

Urinating with hind leg lifted / Increased levels of assertive responses / Mounting other dogs, people, or inanimate objects / Increased levels of aggressive responses

Stitches will be removed after around ten days, unless the wound has been closed using dissolvable sutures. Usually the patient will be given an antibiotic injection and painkillers, and will need little in the way of intervention from you during the following week, other than to check that his wound is healing well and that he does not attempt to remove his stitches by himself. It is usual practice for the dog to wear an 'Elizabethan collar' to help prevent him worrying at the area. His scrotum may swell during the recovery process as it is readily bruised, but this will subside, provided that there is no underlying infection.

It is important to state that castration is not the same operation as vasectomy. During vasectomy, the vessels leading from the testicles to the penis are cut, or tied off, in order that semen does not reach the penis. Castration, not vasectomy, involves the removal of the testes and therefore the elimination of male hormones from the bloodstream.

Some arguments for, and against, castration

As stated, there are certain medical benefits which arise from castration.

- It is the appropriate course of action when the dog has one or both testicles undescended, as the affected dog is at risk of developing testicular cancer.
- Neutered dogs have a reduced risk of the development of perianal fistulas (see p. 245).
- There is also a reduced risk of developing an enlarged prostate.

Conversely, neutered dogs are said to have an increased risk of developing the following conditions:

- Prostate cancer and urinary tract cancers.
- Hypothyroidism. This is caused by low levels of the hormone thyroid, which is produced by the thyroid gland. As the thyroid controls the metabolic rate, dogs that experience low thyroid levels have a reduced metabolic rate. This can lead to skin and coat changes including alopecia, lethargy, weight gain, and also neurological changes.
- Cardiac hemangiosarcoma. This is an aggressive, blood-fed sarcoma, which can lead to heart failure, arrhythmia and other heart conditions.

NB Dogs that are neutered *early* are said to be at an increased risk of developing other conditions. This is discussed overleaf.

Sterilised dogs and bitches are said to be at increased risk of suffering from obesity. Certainly obesity in dogs is a cause for major concern, and sterilising does increase the risk of dogs being overweight. The reasons for this are not yet fully understood. However, it is important to note that conscientious owners can limit this to a great extent by monitoring the dog's exercise and feed regimes, as any dog will gain weight if they are over-fed and given insufficient exercise. Sterilisation may also make your dog a little greedier, but if you monitor his diet and exercise appropriately, the risk of weight gain will be reduced. You may find that maintaining an optimum weight might prove more challenging than when the dog was intact, but it is important to remember that obesity can lead to serious health concerns, and so weight control is an essential part of caring for your dog.

Castration is thought by some to lower the hyperactivity of some dogs. This is arguably the least sound (and least ethical) reason for putting your dog through surgery. Giving your dog the regular opportunity for mental and physical stimulation is a far more acceptable and reliable way of calming the exuberant dog. If you want a laid-back dog, it is far better to choose a laid-back breed! The German Shepherd is first and foremost a working dog, with a brain and energy levels to match. Regardless, any lessening of activity levels causes a slowing of the metabolism, and contributes to the potential for weight gain mentioned above, along with its associated health risks.

Once the testes are removed, testosterone production ceases, and those behaviours driven by this hormone may steadily decrease. As certain secondary sexualised behaviours gradually diminish, the dog's changes in behaviour will benefit by being reinforced through training. For example, if your dog urine marks indoors castration may help decrease his desire to be territorial, but correcting his behaviour through training will make this far more effective.

From the birth-control point of view it will clearly prevent accidental matings and therefore unplanned litters, but so, too, will appropriate management of the dog. If your sole motivation for castrating your dog is to prevent unwanted litters, bear in mind that this can also be achieved by appropriate housing and fencing.

Neutering may assist in the management of certain behavioural issues, especially when used in conjunction with the re-training, but it is not the 'easy answer' to behavioural problems and should never be treated as such.

Castrating the 'aggressive' dog

It is a commonly held belief that castrating an aggressive dog will simply answer the issue. But aggression has a variety of root causes, and castration will not help alleviate the problem unless the underlying cause is linked to the production of testosterone – and in some cases this will still not answer the problem at all. Many situations where dogs exhibit aggressive displays can be attributed to a lack of socialisation. If you are unsure about why your dog is aggressive, you will need to discuss the situation with your vet. They may well recommend that you seek the advice of a qualified canine behaviourist to look at the issues your dog has, rather than merely embark on surgery.

It may be helpful to look briefly at some of the different situations where aggression might arise, to determine if surgery may actually be appropriate: (see p. 143).

Aggression towards other dogs is historically thought to be more common in intact males than in those who have been castrated. However, certain studies suggest that castration has no beneficial impact on lessening aggression, and indicate that the opposite may be the case. A steady programme of re-training may be more beneficial in changing the dog's attitude towards other dogs

It is useful to note that in the wild, males of most species show aggression to other males who invade their territory. They exhibit aggression in order to protect what they perceive to be their property. In the domesticated dog this can transfer into unacceptable behaviours such as guarding cars, children or his food. So it is important to 'think dog' at every opportunity.

These behaviours are normal to your dog but they have no place in your home, and in order to suppress these instincts, clear boundaries must be set at an early age. This is particularly true of this breed, and it is important to note that a castrated Shepherd is likely to retain his instinctive desire to protect home and family as this is part of his genetic make-up. It is the owner's responsibility to manage this instinct during puppy training so it does not become problematic, as castration is not a quick fix.

Nervous aggression is unlikely to respond to surgical intervention, and may actually be heightened following the procedure. Some studies indicate that fearful and anxious responses to a variety of social situations can be increased in the castrated dog. The anxious–aggressive dog displays aggression when afraid of a situation, and this is very likely to be caused by a lack of socialisation during his formative months, or due to trauma. If your dog exhibits fearful behaviours, and his only perceived form of defence is to exhibit aggressive displays, the best method of overcoming this is through a slow, steady and consistent re-education programme. This would involve desensitising the dog to those situations he finds threatening. It may be that he never fully attains full stability, but behavioural training can at least help him feel more balanced, and achieve a better quality of life for you both.

Castrated dogs are thought to have an altered scent, and may smell less masculine to other dogs. Intact males might therefore find him less worthy of a challenge. This may mean your dog is less frequently on the receiving end of other male posturing, and less inclined to initiate a fight himself. However, it can also mean that if your male smells more attractive to other males, they might attempt to mount him which can invite problems of its own!

It is now possible to castrate puppies at around 2–3 months and it is said that they have a faster surgical recovery rate than those castrated in maturity. However there are indicators that early neutering may have serious long-term consequences medically. Early neutering is said to be associated with the increased risk of:

• Osteosarcoma (bone cancer).
• Delay in the closure of growth plates, due to the lack of testosterone in the body, possibly leading to orthopaedic conditions later in life.

In terms of behaviours, it is fair to say that where a dog has already developed sexualised behaviours (or has been actually sexually active prior to castration), he is more likely to retain these 'drives', the older he is and the more experience he has had. But any perceived benefits regarding neutering a young dog *purely* because of his secondary sexualised behaviours, should be weighed against the potential long-term risks to the dog. Other options such as re-education should be explored in the first instance.

In summary: Castration can clearly be justified where there are medical conditions, such as undescended testicles or testicular tumours, and may be helpful in certain cases where there are behavioural concerns which could benefit from a 'joint approach' between surgery and retraining. However, if the dog is healthy and emotionally balanced, you may

This is a vital stage in your dog's development

want to think carefully about *why* you want him castrated. Discuss this with your vet so that you can make the right choice for your dog.

SPAYING (OVARIOHYSTERECTOMY)

Your bitch is likely to have her first season sometime between 8 and 12 months, although there can be deviations from this. She should then settle into twice-yearly seasons, which invariably last for approximately three weeks at a time. Bitches are generally in oestrus (i.e. the fertile period) midway through this time, and they remain so for three to five days. If your bitch does not quite fit the pattern exactly but is in good health throughout her seasons, then by all means check any concerns with your vet, but it is likely that this alone is not a reason for spaying her, should you have already planned to breed.

Spaying involves major surgery, to remove the entire reproductive tract. This will also remove the production of oestrogen and progesterone. Spaying is performed through a cut along the abdomen. If the bitch is very overweight, there may be an increased tendency toward bleeding or bruising. You are advised to ensure her weight is normal before surgery wherever possible.

Some arguments for, and against, spaying

The arguments for having a bitch spayed are extremely compelling:

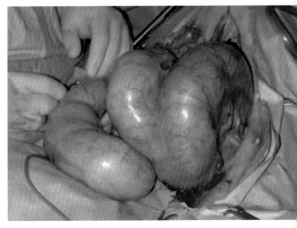

Spaying your bitch will eliminate the risk of pyometra

- The prime health risk with leaving any bitch unspayed is uterine infection. 'Pyometra' is a chronic infection of the uterus and occurs usually a month or so after a bitch has had her season. During her season, progesterone triggers changes within her body so that it prepares for potential pregnancy. This hormone primes the uterine wall to become engorged with blood, and the uterine immune function is also suppressed. The uterus is usually a sterile environment, whereas the vagina is a prime site of bacterial growth. During this period of change, bacteria can readily move from the vagina into the uterus causing catastrophic infection. Pyometra is life threatening, and rapid surgery is needed if the bitch is to survive. With an 'open pyometra', the cervix remains open and some of the pus is discharged from her vagina. With a 'closed pyometra' the cervix is closed and diagnosis can be more complicated. A bitch that develops pyometra will typically become overheated. Her temperature soars, as the body fights the infection in the womb. The womb gradually fills with pus, and may burst, sending poison through the blood stream. It is a horrendous situation which requires immediate veterinary intervention. It can be completely avoided by spaying pet bitches, and by spaying brood bitches at the end of their breeding life.
- Phantom pregnancies can occur in the unspayed bitch. She may or may not have been mated but, regardless, the body and mind can prepare for puppies being born and many bitches will change their behaviours, becoming focused on nesting and maybe gathering toys as surrogate pups. Some will produce milk. This can be a very distressing time for a bitch.
- Spaying reduces the chance of the bitch developing mammary tumours (see overleaf). It removes the small risk of uterine, cervical and ovarian tumours. It will also eliminate behaviours associated with oestrus. However, research suggests that certain negative behaviours (such as dominance aggression) are of increased incidence in the spayed bitch.

In terms of practicalities, problems arise with intact bitches for a variety of reasons. If you also own an intact male, and you wish to avoid puppies being conceived by error, then spaying the bitch is a sensible way forward. This enables you to avoid all of the difficulties which arise from this situation completely. The dogs can co-exist without any pressure, and without the risks of unplanned pregnancies. Even neutered males can become stressed if they live with a bitch that is in season every six months, as she will smell awfully exciting to him. A neutered male can, and will, still mate and 'tie' with a bitch, unless separated from her during the height of her season. Both intact and neutered males will experience tensions if housed near a bitch in season. They may call for her and possibly lose weight. Spaying your bitch eliminates all such management issues.

Spaying will also take away all hygiene issues caused by the bitch's season. Some bitches can be very clean when in season, but many are not, and they lose a bloody, often smelly, discharge. The scent of a bitch in the height of her season is also attractive to neighbourhood males, and it is advised that you do not walk her in public places at this time (partly to avoid unwanted attentions, but also because her public presence will cause problems for other walkers).

There is evidence to suggest that spaying increases the risk of developing the following conditions:

- Cardiac hemangiosarcoma and hypothyroidism (see above).
- Splenic hemangiosarcoma (an aggressive, blood-fed sarcoma).
- Orthopaedic conditions.
- Obesity – although appropriate diet and exercise will largely eradicate this risk. It is however a serious concern as obesity can lead to issues such as diabetes and pancreatitis.
- Urinary incontinence and urinary tract tumours. There is also an increased risk of developing cystitis, vaginitis and vaginal dermatitis.

Talk to your vet about the best time to spay your bitch

Spaying can actually be performed between 3–4 months of age. As her new owner, be aware that such early sterilisation is an additional stress to your puppy. Will she not have enough to contend with in terms of socialising, puppy classes and bonding with her family, without going through surgery at this important time?

The risk of developing mammary tumours rises with each successive season up to around two and a half years of age, and this is why some owners opt to spay the bitch at around 6 months. (NB If you are waiting until *after* your bitch has had a season, it is best to arrange spaying her *mid*-season. The blood supply to her uterus will therefore be given a chance to diminish. This will lessen any chance of her suffering a haemorrhage, during or after surgery.)

In terms of long-term health risks associated with early spaying, there is evidence to suggest that there is an increased risk of:

- Osteosarcoma (bone cancer)
- Orthopaedic disorders, and spay incontinence.

In summary: When considering sterilisation as an option, there are two significant risks to the intact female which intact males do not have to contend with. Pyometra and mammary tumours present a significant enough risk to the intact bitch that spaying is in the long-term interest of any bitch's health, if they are not going to be bred from. This makes the decision to spay far more clear-cut than when considering neutering the male dog. But it is still important to discuss any risks presented by early spaying with your vet, in conjunction with the benefits, so that you can make an informed decision about timescales for your bitch's surgery.

The Elderly Shepherd

For those of you who have already spent a part of your life with an elderly canine, you will already be aware that this can be a 'bittersweet' time with your best friend. Time creeps up on all of us eventually. For our canine friends, old age arrives far more quickly than our own twilight years do, and so we are likely to love and lose multiple dogs during our own lifetime. The life expectancy of a German Shepherd is generally around 12 years, although many will enjoy a considerably longer life.

This is a special time in your relationship, and looking after an elderly dog is an honour. His knowledge, gained at your side throughout his life, produces a great connection between dog and owner. The sense of telepathy which can be present is legendary, with dogs sensing when their owner will return, even after many weeks of separation. Dogs are said to respond to their owner's death with expressions of grief which mirror our own patterns of bereavement, including loss of appetite, lack of energy, and disinterest in surroundings. An elderly dog's connection to his owners may be transferred to new canine additions to the household, as mature dogs can be a huge source of stability and wisdom, imparting a lifetime's skills and manners to puppies.

Many dogs reach a greater age than in days gone by, and advances in canine nutrition and veterinary care clearly play their part. But the daily attention to detail which an owner provides *throughout* their dog's life is crucial to the animal's general well-being in old age, and to his longevity.

The care of the elderly dog is as vital as the care they needed in puppyhood. They will enjoy daily pleasures such as being brushed to perfection, but do take extra care: muscles and skin become increasingly frail and you will need to be increasingly gentle. By paying close attention to your dog's needs you are more likely to notice any dry areas or small sores which might arise. These will need prompt attention as open sores and wounds will be slower to heal than in the younger dog. His elbows and haunches in particular will need careful monitoring as calluses (areas of hardened skin) can form readily in these areas.

Your old friend is likely to be slower to react to your wishes, less fleet of foot and brain, but still as willing in his heart. You will begin to notice a variety of changes, such as in his sleep pattern or in his need to quench his thirst. He may gain or lose weight, and his eyesight or hearing might begin to fail.

You will inevitably need to make a range of practical changes as his needs begin to alter. Commonplace changes include providing extra bedding for comfort, providing extra toileting opportunities and making alterations to your own daily routines. The elderly dog will need a lower calorie, higher fibre diet than he had in his younger days. A specialised diet might be required if his digestive system becomes more sensitive, or if he develops a medical condition such as diabetes or poor function of the kidneys or liver. Soft, home-prepared meals will become the norm as his teeth deteriorate. Dental treatment (or endless tolerance!) may be required if his breath is less than sweet, although herbal products can help greatly if this odour is related to digestive disorders, rather than tooth decay. Keeping his teeth clean on a daily basis will enable you to spot the onset of abscesses or tooth decay. Older dogs often become sensitive to changes in the weather, and you may also find that incontinence becomes a daily occurrence.

Helpful 'gadgets' (such as ramps for the car and rubber mats on tiled floorings) are just some of the ways we try to make our old friend's latter days more comfortable, should their mobility begin to deteriorate.

Massage, physiotherapy and hydrotherapy are all elements which can bring relief to older dogs with muscular-skeletal conditions. So too can the inclusion of glucosamine, chondroitin and also devil's claw root to his daily dietary regime.

Older dogs often become increasingly sensitive and reactive to noises. If your dog becomes aware that he is less mobile and less able to defend himself and his family, he might become troubled by this shift in dynamics. As a result he could be distressed by your absence, and become more vocal.

Adversely, increasing deafness or loss of vision are commonplace. If this is the case, he will find it harder to adapt to changes of routine, and will need extra emotional support should you decide to move home during this period. If your old fellow *is* losing his hearing or sight, it is especially important that children in the family know not to surprise him, as this will surely trouble him and he may react negatively to this.

Keep a watchful eye regarding changes in his relationship with other family dogs. Be sensitive to his needs if you are planning to introduce a new puppy into the family. You are wise to do this whilst your older dog is mobile enough to enjoy the puppy's company. If you leave it until the older dog is far less mobile (and possibly in pain or losing his sight), you are likely to find that an exuberant puppy causes your older dog distress.

His demands for exercise and play will undoubtedly diminish as time progresses. His needs for mental stimulation will be simpler than when he was a boisterous adolescent, demanding to know all you could teach him about life. But he *will* surprise you once in a while, with bursts of puppy-like behaviour as if in defiance of his creeping decline. There are very few sights as rewarding as seeing your faithful old fellow having a mad five minutes on a beach as if he is eight weeks old and has never seen the sea before! You may find he suddenly starts to be 'naughty' occasionally, doing things which are more in keeping with his days of puppyhood, rather than his twilight years. Be prepared! And just as it is with our ageing relatives, if you let your dog sleep all day by the fire, he will age more quickly. By offering him the chance to enjoy sensible exercise, social interaction and play, he may stay young for longer than you ever dared hope for.

Common conditions found in the older dog

ARTHRITIS – Stiff, painful movement especially when rising or attempting to climb or jump / irritability / muscle wastage.

CANCERS – Abnormal swellings / Weight loss / Odour changes / Depression / Breathing or toileting difficulties.

CUSHING'S DISEASE – Increased thirst / Increased appetite / Hair loss or thinning / Fragile skin / Pot-belly / Possible incontinence.

DENTAL DISEASE – Bad breath / difficulty or reluctance with eating / loss of weight / irritability.

DIABETES – Increased thirst and urination / Increased appetite / Weakness or depression / Weight loss.

INCONTINENCE – This can be caused by loss of physical control of bladder, but can also be due to senility. It can evidence a wide range of conditions.

KIDNEY DISEASE – Increased thirst and urination / Vomiting and diarrhoea / Dark, tarry stools / Weight loss / Weakness.

LIVER DISEASE – Vomiting and diarrhoea / Appetite loss / Yellow gums or pale gums / Yellow skin and white of eyes / Pot-belly / Orange urine.

Also seen in older dogs is the onset of canine cognitive dysfunction (CCD). This is similar to Alzheimer's disease in humans, and affects the dog's general capacity to cope with his surroundings. He may become easily disorientated, begin to forget familiar people and places, and exhibit nervousness and aggression as a result of his anxieties. He will need a great deal of understanding as his emotional needs become more complex.

Commonly confused with the onset of hip dysplasia / arthritis, are the symptoms of a condition known as CDRM. This condition in hallmarked by increasing paralysis of the hindquarters / dragging of back feet / scuffing of the upper area of the hind toes / swaying and falling over, especially when changing direction. See p. 247 for fuller details on this condition.

Part Six
The Next Generation

• An Introduction to Breeding • Pregnancy and Whelping •
• Rearing Puppies • Breed Associated Conditions •

An Introduction to Breeding

If you are thinking about breeding from your dog or bitch, then the task of obtaining advice and guidance can seem daunting. There are many issues to consider, from ethics, housing and finances, through to veterinary care and hand rearing of puppies. There is not the space here to discuss genetics, but there is a wide range of literature already available which can introduce you to breeding principles. This chapter aims to address some of the health care and welfare issues which need consideraton.

WHY BREED?

The reasons are as varied as they are many, and ideally will lead to the perpetuation of quality and the betterment of the breed. Conversely it can lead to sickly or unwanted puppies being abandoned if it is a badly planned venture. In terms of contributing to the development of the breed, there will always be individuals that have achieved such success in the show ring, or demonstrated such outstanding working capacity, that it would be a loss to the breed if they did not contribute to the gene pool. In some instances, top quality siblings or other close relatives of successful dogs may also carry the bloodline forward.

Some owners are motivated by the idea of having a pup from a faithful companion. They may also be encouraged to do so by friends or family who want to book a puppy from the litter. There are others who are motivated purely by the prospect of monetary gain, but in reality it is highly unlikely to be lucrative. Mounting costs of vet assistance, stud fees and rearing the puppies leaves little to show for such hard work.

Imparting quality to the next generation:
Ch Nikonis Elektra and her two Champion sons, VA1 (GB) Nikonis Colin and V1 (GB) Nikonis Yago

You might be thinking that this will be educational for your children? It certainly can be wonderful if all goes well, but it pays to be aware that each stage may produce complications, and may not be the positive experience you had hoped for. Bitches in labour or nursing newborn pups can become stressed and possessive, even around those people they love the most. Whelping and rearing litters are not for the fainthearted!

Most dog owners have heard the phrase that 'all bitches should have one litter'. There is no evidence to support this. Bitches who do not have a litter of puppies still lead happy and fulfilled lives the world over. On the contrary, there are inevitably health risks to your bitch if you do put her in pup. Combined with your own inexperience this could lead to large vet bills and tragedy.

Finally, it might have been suggested to you that having a litter will improve your bitch's temperament. This is a fallacy, and it is more likely to enhance her protective and possessive traits. If she is a nervy dog, this is likely to be a recipe for disaster. Mating a dog or a bitch with an unsound temperament is never to be advised, as there is a genetic component to temperament which could be passed to the puppies.

 If you choose to take this path, it is prudent to remember that although most pregnancies and whelpings go relatively smoothly, it is vital to have experienced help at hand should problems arise.

CONSIDERATIONS

Rearing a litter

Do you have the right facilities to cope with a large litter of puppies? Initially very little space is required, but by six to eight weeks you will need considerable space to house the growing litter, as by this stage they are messy, vocal and highly energetic! In a cramped environment, hygiene can easily be compromised, causing health issues for the litter and for your family. In cramped surroundings the pups can also become bored, and the whole venture becomes a nightmare.

A play pen is ideal when raising puppies indoors

FINDING HOMES

Finding the right home for each of your puppies can be a painstaking job. Initial enquiries made months before may come to nothing for all sorts of reasons, and you might well find that you are left with multiple mouths to feed. The litter will need vaccinating and will be increasingly expensive to maintain, as growing puppies require large quantities of quality food. They can become fractious, and bored with their litter mates' company, at a time when they should be getting one-to-one attention in their new home.

Many people decide they want a puppy from their bitch, but end up giving litters away.

Rescue organisations are flooded on a daily basis with unwanted, neglected dogs and puppies. Sadly, the German Shepherd in particular is highly represented. Before you embark on this journey, be certain that you are able to find permanent homes for your puppies, so that your litter does not add to the awful statistics. If you want a pup that is related to your bitch, it may well be better to get one from an established breeder who can choose stud dog and bitch wisely, and who is fully equipped to cope with the demands of a large litter.

HEALTH

Having bred Shepherds for several years I experienced the joys of seeing my bitches raise healthy litters, from bloodlines that I had loved for decades. I also learned a very painful lesson, which is that *nothing* can ever be taken for granted, regardless of how well you feel you know a bloodline.

Health conditions can be carried by generation after generation of dogs from a trusted bloodline before re-emerging, only to cause immense heartache and sadness when they do. With the age of the Internet has come the availability of information which was far less readily accessible even a decade ago. This now ensures that breeders are given a wider opportunity to learn about such conditions, and to develop better breeding practices as a result. Regardless of individual passions in terms of type, coat colour or working attributes, health is very much at the forefront of the issue, and certain major conditions are being researched with the hope that diagnostic tests will someday become available.

For further advice, you will find that Kennel Clubs, Breed Councils and any number of breed advisors listed within popular monthly dog magazines can all provide valuable advice regarding health issues and ethics. Dog shows and breed clubs are a valuable source of information and inspiration. Talking to other breeders may inspire you – or may dampen your enthusiasm! But if you take advice from a variety of perspectives you will gain a wide picture of the issues at stake. Although the information gleaned will never actually *guarantee* a top quality litter, it may minimise certain risks considerably.

If you do decide to breed, you should arrange for your bitch to have her hips radiographed (X-rayed) and scored. There are a variety of schemes offered across the world, and these are discussed in depth later in the book*. Elbow scoring is also now recommended.

   *All health tests are discussed in more depth in 'Breed Associated Conditions'.

TEMPERAMENT

It is likely that most of your puppies will go into pet homes, probably where there are children. This means that you will need to be honest with yourself about your bitch's temperament, as any quirks could be passed on to her offspring. Whilst it is true to say that temperament can be very much down to early socialising, it is not the whole picture, as genetic make-up plays its part too. Therefore it is not ethical to sell puppies as pets if the parents' temperament is less than sound. Nor is it right to sell puppies from highly motivated, high drive dogs to inexperienced buyers. Attempting to match puppies to each buyer requires skill, and also attentiveness to the litter in question. Many of your buyers will not be able to discern issues such as 'drive' and 'attitude' in the cute bundle in front of them. You will need to assess your litter objectively, before explaining your thoughts to the buyer. This can prevent problems arising for you both at a later stage.

A gentle bitch and her puppy

'TYPE' AND 'DRIVE'

In the United Kingdom, as is the case in the United States, any German Shepherd puppy can be registered (providing of course that both parents are themselves registered with the respective Kennel Club and that they do not carry breed endorsements). As has been stated, this is a practice which is frowned upon by conscientious breeders, particularly in Germany, where attention to both the conformation and working potential of the Shepherd is undertaken with enormous dedication. With the increasing influx of bloodlines from Germany, dogs of 'International' type influence the development of the breed across the world.

However, in the UK, there are some owners and breeders who feel unwilling to abandon the dog of the 1970s and 1980s. These dogs have become known as 'English' type. Such dogs differ from International type, in particular with regard to topline and the ratio of height to length, although there are other factors too, such as strength of character. There is a similar divide in the US. The divergence of type from that which is recognised elsewhere has led to a larger, longer bodied and more upright dog. Some American breeders have a different vision for the breed, and pay little heed to the developments across the world. As in the UK, there is a wide difference of opinion within opposing camps and passions run high. Shepherds of International type have a distinctly glamorous movement, and are invariably higher in drive than some of their English or American counterparts, because German breeding places great importance on the working attributes of their national breed, and this influence is passed down from generation to generation.

Across the globe there are also enthusiasts who breed first and foremost for working/

sport attributes, and who concentrate far less on conformation as laid down by the Breed Standards. Such bloodlines are highly prized by trials enthusiasts. These dogs are invariably not for the novice owner and require a high commitment to training and socialisation as their drive to be active and productive is very strong.

Conscientious breeders aim to produce healthy puppies with beautiful construction. They will also hope that these pups will grow up with courage to burn, but with enough stability of character to make a gentle family companion. It is no easy task. The German Shepherd in 2011 is a breed of controversial diversity, and is the subject of considerable debate, but breeding puppies requires huge commitment *regardless of* whether you intend to breed for show, work, sport or pet homes. If you approach this venture with good intent, and seek out the best possible futures for your puppies, you will pave the way for them to become ambassadors for their breed.

PLANNING AHEAD

If you hope that your puppies will go on to show or work, then it is clear that you will be planning to breed from lines where successes have been forthcoming. This does not guarantee you or your puppy-buyers success, but it increases the likelihood of contributing to the gene pool in a positive and considered way. Successful dogs are occasionally born as a result of less well-considered matings, but they will be the exception rather than the rule.

Looking at bloodlines / choosing a stud dog

You will want to gain information on your bitch's bloodline to see if there are any issues which might arise in your own litter. If you study her pedigree and discuss it with her breeder you will hopefully gain insight into the attributes and failings of your bitch's ancestors. Her breeder can discuss with you those conformation issues which need careful attention, but you will be advised not to breed if the bitch clearly has major faults. Having the pedigree checked by an expert will help you identify health issues within the bloodline. It is wise to speak to your Breed Council about experts who offer this service, and about Breed Surveys (p. 31).

In terms of weaknesses and strengths, there will be areas of both which you will hope to address by choosing a suitable mate. It is not an exact science, as no dog is perfect, but by being honest about your bitch, and by carefully researching her mate, you will increase your chances of producing a quality litter. Selecting the stud dog may be largely influenced by your conversations with your breeder. They may already have had successful litters from a specific stud, and the calibre of the progeny may help you reach a decision. Breed clubs and Breed Councils produce yearbooks and you will find stud dogs advertised within these.

FARDOGART

Champion Ice vom Steinhauerberg
Owned by Videx GSD kennels

Attending shows or trials will also give you the opportunity to see multiple dogs and talk with breeders and enthusiasts, where you will be introduced to relevant terminology:

- If a dog is decribed as being 'inbred on', it means that this dog is seen on the pedigree more than once, and figures (such as 2–3) will denote that the dog appears in these generations, on opposite sides of the pedigree. If in-breeding is taken to the extreme, an outstanding bitch might be mated to her equally outstanding son, brother or father. She might possibly produce exceptional traits in her puppies, but the risk is high, in that faults are increasingly likely to be introduced. It is a practice which has been permitted in the past, but certain registries no longer allow this.
- 'Out-crossing' refers to the practice of selecting a mate from different ancestry, thereby introducing new genetic material into the breeding line. Choosing a mate for 'type' (i.e. similar physical traits to your bitch) may greatly influence the puppies' conformation, but it is wise to see some of the dog's progeny to see if he produces his own 'stamp' on his offspring, as this is not always the case. (If a dog has a significant ability to pass on certain traits, this is known as 'prepotency'. This is very important in a stud dog as the male can have a far greater impact on the breed than the bitch, as in his lifetime the male can produce many more offspring than the female.)

If you are interested in a particular stud dog, talk to his owner, or your Breed Council/registry about data regarding his hip production. This should always be looked at, as a dog with good hips may unfortunately not have a good track record when it comes to progeny results. Most stud dog owners now have their dogs elbow scored. He should have had a blood test for Haemophilia A, and he should have a strong but sound temperament. Nervousness and aggression are to be avoided at all costs. If he holds a SchH title and has been breed-surveyed, the picture will be an altogether fuller one.

 If your bitch is a maiden, it is wise to choose an experienced stud dog. You will not want your bitch's first mating to be a shambles, which could stress her or put her off for life.

Make arrangements in advance

Once you have narrowed the search, you will want to visit the stud dog at his home and discuss all arrangements with his owner for a future mating.

In terms of etiquette, you will usually be required to pay the stud fee after the first mating. You may be asked for a choice of puppy instead of payment. There are no hard and fast rules on this, but generally you will pay less than the price of a puppy if financial settlement is made at the time of mating. If you are asked for a puppy in payment, then it is a good idea to agree in writing beforehand if this is to be 'pick of the bitch puppies' for example. It is also wise to get in writing whether you will receive a free return mating if your bitch fails to conceive. What happens about payment if only a slip mating occurs? Perhaps payment will be delayed until you have your bitch scanned?

Make enquiries as to the protocol in passing on the 'free return' to another of your bitches, should the need arise. But be aware that some stud owners will be unhappy about this prospect if in their eyes the second bitch is inferior to the first. And if your second bitch is too closely related to the stud dog, is the owner happy to offer the services of another male instead? Clarity now, saves disputes later!

Talk to the stud owner about titre testing for a condition called brucellosis. This is a serious issue, as the bacteria *Brucella canis* is known to cause canine abortion. Some stud owners have their dog tested by their vet, and will want you to do the same.

The stud owner will usually sign the litter registration document after the first mating, and will also provide you with copies of the dog's pedigree and health test certificates.

CHOOSING A KENNEL NAME

Choosing individual registered names for puppies can prove extremely difficult, as if you choose a name for a dog which is already on the registry's database the name will be rejected. Choosing a kennel name (affix) will make registration of your puppies unique to you. It can take several months to process, so you will need to plan this well in advance.

THE BROOD BITCH

Seasons

Bitches usually have their first season at around ten months of age. This can vary greatly, as some bitches have this season as young as six months or well after their first birthday. These are the exceptions to the norm. It is common for this season to be short, and it invariably causes little concern (although you may notice mood swings around this time). Subsequent seasons usually last for approximately three weeks. Her seasons are likely to fall into a six-monthly cycle, although some bitches adopt a significantly shorter or longer cycle. Be aware that less than four months in between seasons can coincide with infertility. If her seasons are erratic or give rise to complications you are wise to discuss her viability for breeding with your vet.

Bitches are termed scientifically as being 'non-seasonal', referring to the fact that the breeding cycle occurs with no regard for the seasons of the year. They are also termed as 'dioestrous', meaning that they have two breeding cycles per year. This means they have limited chances for mating and conceiving. Polyoestrus animals, such as mice, horses and humans, cycle regularly throughout the year.

The canine season is divided into four, distinctly separate stages:

Pro-oestrus. During this stage, the bitch's oestrogen levels increase, and the follicles of the ovary begin to develop. The bitch becomes increasingly attractive to males but is sexually unreceptive. Her vulva swells, and she produces a bloody discharge. Pro-oestrus usually lasts around nine days. Towards the end of this stage, her progesterone levels begin to rise. Her oestrogen levels will peak two to three days before oestrus, and then decline. At the end of this stage the bitch will produce a surge of luteinising hormone (LH), which is produced by the pituitary gland in the brain.

Oestrus. During this stage, the bitch will become sexually receptive. Her vulva becomes soft, her oestrogen level drops. Ovulation begins approximately 48 hours after the LH surge.

Dioestrus. This stage starts around six to ten days after the LH surge and continues until progesterone level return to baseline levels – this occurs steadily in the non-pregnant bitch, or abruptly before the pregnant bitch whelps.

Anoestrus. This final stage in the cycle usually lasts around four months. It begins when the bitch's progesterone level falls to its baseline level, and continues until she begins her subsequent season. During anoestrus she is not attractive to other dogs, nor is she sexually receptive. Her vulva is small.

The brood bitch should be in excellent health

PREPARATIONS

Some breeders feel that is best to mate a bitch for the first time during her third season. But there is no hard and fast rule on this as bitches obviously mature at different rates. She may only have five months between seasons and so could be very young to cope with a litter. If you feel that her third season occurs when she is physically and mentally still developing, you are right to wait. Pregnancy itself, and the task of rearing a litter, are both very draining so if your bitch is still maturing it is wise to delay for six months. Most breeders feel that a first litter at around 24–30 months is ideal. Prior to mating, your bitch should be in great health. She will need to be fully up to date with her worming programme, and she should also be up to date with vaccinations.

 NB It is inadvisable to give yearly boosters during pregnancy.

As mentioned above, having your bitch tested for *Brucella canis* and other harmful bacteria is something you may wish to discuss with your vet. If a bitch is harbouring infection, this can interfere with conception and pregnancy. You may also talk to your vet about having your bitch examined for signs of vaginal stricture, which could present problems when the stud dog attempts penetration.

As your bitch approaches her expected season, she is likely to lose coat condition. This is completely normal. Once in season, her vulva becomes engorged, and will be warm to the touch, which has given rise to the term 'on heat'. Early discharge is bright red in colour. If you do a regular tissue test, by placing fresh white tissues over her vulva, you should notice that towards the point of ovulation (when she would be ready to mate) this discharge should change to a pinkish or straw colour. This is by no means an accurate test, however, as some bitches will show no change at all, so you should to talk to your vet about more reliable alternatives.

'PRE-MATE' TESTS

There are a variety of tests available which can help you determine your bitch's optimum date for mating. A blood test, performed during pro-oestrus, is advisable to be sure that everything is on track. The test will determine the amount of progesterone present in the blood. It has been found that a progesterone concentration of approximately 5.0 ng/ml indicates ovulation. Progesterone levels are at baseline (0–1.0 ng/ml) prior to the LH surge, and continue to rise throughout dioestrus. The sample of blood which has been taken from your bitch is compared to high and low progesterone 'standards' on a chart provided by the manufacturers of the testing kit used. This can then be performed every few days until a positive indication is reached. If you are taking your bitch to a stud dog, rather than using your own dog, it is important that such a test is performed. It saves the stud dog from having a bitch presented to him who is not quite ready to be mated, and saves you a wasted journey.

A more accurate test indicates the timing of the luteinising hormone surge. This peaks and falls away over a very short period of time, and, following the peak the bitch will ovulate approximately 48 hours later. It can therefore pinpoint the optimum time for fertilisation to take place. The immature ova (oocyte) which she releases cannot be fertilised for a further two days as these have to undergo further cell division and maturation before they become receptive to sperm penetration. The mature ova remain viable for 48–72 hours, and the bitch therefore is actually fertile for approximately four to seven days after the LH surge. Testing is performed daily because the surge takes place over 24 hours. It is undeniably more time consuming, invasive and expensive than other tests, but where timing is of the essence (for example when using frozen semen during AI), it can be a useful tool. Its availability in the UK is limited.

There are also a variety of home testing kits on the market:

Vaginal cytology

Swabs may be taken from the vagina during pro-oestrus, and the smear test obtained is examined under a microscope to determine changes in vaginal epithelium (the cells which line the uterus). As oestrogen levels rise during pro-oestrus, the vaginal epithelium become 'cornified'. This refers to the change in shape the cells undergo, as they enlarge, thicken and flatten. Nuclei are either small or absent. Around the optimum time for mating, cells show a typical shape and distribution.

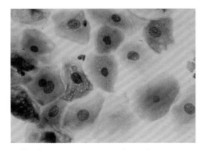

Early pro-oestrus showing non cornified cells

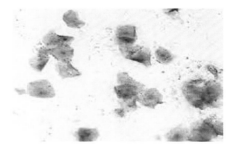

Cestrus. Cells are cornified

Saliva tests

As the bitch moves towards oestrus, her saliva holds important information about the presence of oestrogen in her body. A swab of saliva, dried under a microscope, will evidence a distinctive crystal 'ferning' pattern. This pattern precedes the LH surge by around two days, and continues until the end of oestrus.

Saliva test showing ferning pattern

PH tests

The ph of the canine vagina drops during ovulation. An indicator strip can be inserted into the bitch's vagina, and the indicator end will change hue to indicate vaginal ph status.

The usual recommendation is that the bitch is mated twice, invariably on her 11th and 13th day, but this is never an 'exact prescription'. Your ovulation tests will no doubt show that pinpointing the day of mating can lead to real surprises.

NB All tests have varying degrees of fallibility, which also includes human error. The best method is a combination of clinical examination, vaginal cytology and progesterone measurement.

THE MATING

If you have an experienced stud dog at home, he will undoubtedly indicate to you when the time is drawing near, but inexperienced dogs may mislead you by appearing keen too early. A bitch will indicate her readiness through body posture, and by lifting her tail to the side (known as 'flagging') and presenting her vulva. Invariably, she will stand for other bitches several days before she would stand for a male. Once she is nearing the point of ovulation she will stand for her accepted mate, with tail aside. You will also notice her lifting her hindquarters and 'winking' with her vulva. If given the opportunity she may attempt to excite the male with play. Most breeders do not to allow this to go on for very long, as if left unchecked this can exhaust or over-excite the dog. He might then be too tired to mate her or he might slip mate, especially if he is inexperienced. You will find that some stud owners prefer both dogs to be on lead during the whole process.

Some stud dogs prefer no physical contact from the handler while mating takes place, but it is always good practice to have two people present. Some breeders prefer 'assisted' matings – a practice designed to help the dog and bitch during the mating. One person will be there to reassure the bitch during 'the tie' (see below), and the other will be there to assist the male should he need some guidance. The bitch may also need steadying under the weight of the dog while mating takes place.

The stud owner will use a lubricating jelly on your bitch's vulva to assist penetration, and will invariably perform an internal examination on the bitch prior to offering her to the stud dog.

Once the dogs have been introduced, and she is indicating that she is keen to stand for him, you will usually be asked to hold your bitch's collar and stand facing her. You will be required to ensure that the bitch cannot turn on the dog as he mates her, and offer quiet words of reassurance. If the stud dog is accustomed to being handled throughout the mating, his owner will usually sit with your bitch's belly across their knee and will use one arm to offer further support should the bitch start to squirm during the tie. The other hand can be used to 'guide' the dog by encircling the vulva, if the stud dog is a little inexperienced. (Overly enthusiastic males may rub against the bitch's hindquarters and ejaculate prematurely.)

The stud dog will mount the bitch and grip her sides. He will draw his penis and attempt to locate her swollen vulva. At this stage the penis is not engorged. It is slender and is held rigid by a small bone called the 'baculum'. Once he has penetrated her, he will thrust more vigorously, and the penis will become engorged. The bulbous gland at the base of the penis also swells, the penis is held tightly within the bitch's body by her constrictor muscle while he ejaculates. This is known as 'the tie'. Normally the stud dog will bring his hind leg over the bitch's back until they are stood side to side, or back to back, whichever they feel most comfortable with. It is important to keep the period during the tie as relaxed as possible, and to reassure both dogs throughout. This saves either dog from having the discomfort of being dragged around backwards by the other. It is true that in the wild they would just 'get on with it', but you will want to ensure the safest practice for your dogs at this vulnerable time.

N.B. The male ejaculates in three fractions: Presperm fraction (clear prostatic fluid) / Sperm-rich fraction / Clear prostatic fluid.

The tie can last for more than an hour, but 15 to 30 minutes is more common, during which time the dog continues to ejaculate prostatic fluid. During the tie most males are quiet and calm, but towards the end he may become restless. Ensure that he does not pull away too soon or either dog could be injured. After they have separated, some breeders hold the bitch's hindquarters up a little for a few minutes to maximise the amount of fluid retained in her body. There is some debate as to the efficacy of this practice. She should then be offered a small drink of water and taken to your car so that she can rest while you attend to paperwork. She should not be allowed to urinate for at least half an hour. Obviously you will need to keep her separate from all other entire males until her season ends.

Problems / slip matings

If your bitch is very resistant to initial advances by the male, it is highly possible that you have brought her too early, or too late. Both situations can be avoided with accurate pre-mate testing.

If the timing is correct, but your bitch appears rather 'clingy', you may find that the stud owner asks you to vacate the room. This can be all it takes to settle the bitch down, and in most cases, she is more likely to accept the advances of the dog.

It is worth noting that if your bitch already lives with a male, she may be more reluctant to accept an 'arranged suitor'. Bitches can be resistant to the presence of the stud dog for a variety of other reasons. If she is a maiden bitch, it may be overwhelming for her. Allow her plenty of time to relax and feel at ease with the dog and you are likely to be successful.

Some bitches appear initially at ease with the male, and are keen to mate. However, once the tie actually begins some bitches panic. This can involve her attempting to get away from the dog (which of course she is unable to do), or to use her teeth in a moment of panic. You would never want a stud dog to be bitten in the face whilst tied, and so it is a sensible precaution to have a muzzle to hand before the mating begins. This can be slipped over the bitch's muzzle if she is showing signs of unease. It is a period of vulnerability for the male, and there is a real duty to keep him safe at this point. Breeders will have different viewpoints on this subject: many stud dog owners will insist on bitches being muzzled throughout, whilst others will be content for you to only muzzle your bitch if she becomes distressed.

Sometimes, an inexperienced or over enthusiastic male might 'slip mate'. This happens in two different ways:

- Firstly, he might appear to go through the initial stages of mating but fall away prior to ejaculation. He will withdraw his penis straight back into its sheath, and be keen to try again very quickly. Usually this occurs in young males who get over excited and thrust erratically.
- The second scenario is where the dog might be too eager to 'turn' and he falls away whilst ejaculating. His penis is fully engorged, the bulbous gland is swollen just as if he had tied within the bitch's body, and he will continue to lose seminal fluid. He will find it uncomfortable to move, and he is rather vulnerable at this point. It is a good idea to remove the bitch from the room and let the dog relax at his own pace. It may take some time for his penis to return to its sheath. Please do not be tempted to try to hasten this with cold water sprays. It may help him if KY jelly is administered to the base of the penis. When his penis has returned to its sheath, it is sensible to give him a period of rest before trying again.

 Pregnancy can still result from some slip matings, but most owners will hope for dog and bitch to tie successfully.

Return mating

It is common practice to return with your bitch 48 hours later for a second mating. This is to ensure cover over a period of several days during which ovulation is occurring. The dog's semen is active for around five days depending on various factors. Mating on successive days is unnecessary. Avoid entering into arrangements where your bitch is left in a kennelled situation for three days with a stud dog. This is a lazy way of doing stud work, and is traumatic for the bitch who is mated over and over again unnecessarily. If the stud dog is not interested in her on the second visit, it is likely that her period of ovulation is over. Hopefully she will have conceived from her first mating. Many breeders choose to take their bitch for a single mating only.

The bitch will now enter dioestrus and, regardless of whether she is pregnant or not, her body will continue to produce progesterone for many weeks. She is at risk at this time due to increased potential for uterine infections, as the cervix has been open and is vulnerable to bacteria. Non-pregnant bitches may experience a phantom pregnancy during this period.

You will want to choose a quality male to sire your litter.
V4 (GB) Astroflash Cato

ARTIFICIAL INSEMINATION

Artificial insemination using fresh, fresh-chilled or frozen semen has gained in popularity and accessibility over the past two decades, with advances made in all aspects of semen collection, storage, and in the techniques used for insemination.

It is clear that freezing the semen of a top quality stud dog has huge benefits. Frozen semen can be used long after a valuable dog has died, or become injured. From a logistics point of view, transporting semen across the globe provides breeding opportunities which otherwise would never be possible. Frozen semen is potentially viable for generations, and the possibilities for this to influence the gene pool years down the line are as endless as they are astounding, as lost traits can be brought back into lines. A clear advantage is that with advances in diagnostic testing for conditions, choices can be made many years down the line, once inherited health issues are known. A.I. has other clear practical advantages, in that valuable stud dogs are less at risk from injury or infection during this process.

In terms of time scales, fresh semen can live within the bitch's reproductive tract for approximately five days. Fresh-chilled semen, mixed with a semen extender and cooled to 40 degrees farenheight, has the advantage that it can be transported to a bitch a good distance away. But it can only live for 24–72 hours once it is back to body temperature. Frozen semen is also mixed with a semen extender, which protects the cells while frozen. It is then preserved in units known as pellets or straws, which are stored in liquid nitrogen containers. Once thawed to body temperature, the sperm have a short lifespan of approximately 12–24 hours. It is easy to see why it is useful to pinpoint a bitch's LH surge accurately if using frozen semen as the window of opportunity is incredibly short.

Pregnancy and Whelping

The nine weeks of the canine pregnancy can seem to last for ever. But this time provides you with a good opportunity to read up on the subject and talk to those who have had experience of whelping and rearing puppies. Never be afraid to ask questions of breeders and vets, as most people will be only too glad to help you with advice and guidance.

There are specialist whelping books available which cover the subject in infinitely more depth than there is space for here. Below is a general guide to the main issues which you will face during your bitch's pregnancy and during the whelping process.

GESTATION

The average gestation period for dogs is 63 days but this varies according to breed. For a German Shepherd, 61 days is the figure generally accepted, carrying a +2 or -2 day variation without giving rise to concern. Reports of variations of a week or so are common, but these figures are often measured from the day of the first mating, and this may well be the reason for the wide variation in results. Gestation is the length of time from fertilisation to birth, not from mating to birth, and therefore if the bitch is mated several days prior to fertilisation (having only just produced immature ova), the end figure can seem artificially long. In developmental terms, a *slightly* prolonged pregnancy will be of less concern to a breeder than a premature birth. (The lungs of the unborn foetus develop fully in the last days of the pregnancy, and premature puppies are therefore likely to experience significant respiratory distress.) However, it is always wise to discuss the situation with your vet if the bitch goes beyond her due date.

EARLY / MID PREGNANCY

You should continue to feed your bitch with a healthy diet, but do not give her greater quantities at this moment in time. Resist the temptation to add vitamin and mineral supplements. You are likely to do far more harm than good. One of the commonest mistakes is to add fish oils or liver oils to the diet. These are a high source of vitamin A, which is known to produce mid-line developmental defects in the foetus such as cleft palate and harelip when used as a supplement in early pregnancy. Vitamin D supplements can also seriously compromise foetal development, thus causing a variety of abnormalities.

It is also a commonly made error to think that the bitch needs calcium supplements to assist with milk development. Her need for calcium will increase once she is feeding her pups, but this should *not* be tampered with before she gives birth. The addition of calcium during the pregnancy can actually increase the likelihood of causing a potentially fatal condition:'eclampsia' (also known as milk fever) is a genuine medical emergency caused by hypocalcemia, which usually occurs at the height of lactation. Affected bitches become restless, anxious and wild eyed. Excessive salivation and loss of co-ordination are followed by convulsion and collapse. Her temperature will soar. Your vet will administer injections of calcium and glucose, and even in cases where it looks as if all hope is lost, the response to this is frequently spectacular. Failure to seek veterinary assistance will undoubtedly result in a fatal conclusion.

Your bitch can be exercised sensibly during the pregnancy. This is to be encouraged as it helps her through any early sickness periods, and it keeps her mentally and physically well for the event that lies ahead. You might choose to avoid walking her in busy public areas, as although she will be protected by her vaccinations she should not be exposed to viruses needlessly. (Even if they do not affect the dam, they might affect the foetuses.) At this stage, most breeders retire their bitches from the public gaze, with shows and working trials being avoided. Many also avoid showing or working other dogs from the kennels, to further limit the risks of viruses being carried home.

Early indicators that she is pregnant can include morning sickness and resulting food refusal. Her vulva is likely to remain soft and large for longer than it would do ordinarily. She may be quieter, and sleep more than she would usually. Other indicators as to her condition include a visible change in her teat size and colouration, and some bitches develop a white (or clear), odourless discharge from their vulva. Around mid-term, the hair on her flanks will tend to stand out away from the body, and you should begin to notice a visible change in her shape. But some bitches have no outward signs and you will be left wondering!

If you are keen for more definitive answers, your veterinary surgeon can examine your bitch by palpating her abdomen. This can take place at around three weeks, as at this stage it is possible to feel the spherical swellings which contain the developing embryos, membranes and fluid. This is unadvisable by all but the most experienced of hands though, as the embryos are at a fragile and vital stage in their development. This can be undertaken between three and five weeks, but beyond this stage the thickening of the uterus makes palpation impossible.

It is common to have an ultrasound scan performed, and this normally done at around four weeks. This is a non-invasive and painless procedure, during which foetal masses and heartbeats can be clearly seen. After day 45 foetal skulls and spines are visible on a

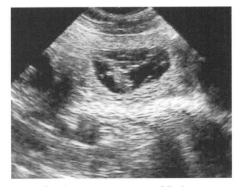

Canine pregnancy at 25 days

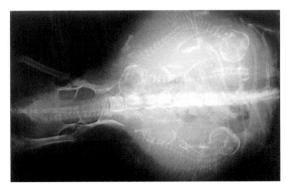

Radiograph of canine pregnancy

radiograph. Calcification of the skeleton continues to progress, and leg bones can be observed from around day 50.

There is much to be said for the above examinations, in that the approximate number of pups can be determined, as can important information about their development. But if you have any doubts about your bitch's stress levels you are wise not to put her through any of these procedures, as stress can be dangerous for the foetuses.

Canine Herpes Virus

It is prudent to arrange for your bitch to have a canine herpes vaccination. This is usually given at around ten days after the first mating, and is then given again approximately ten days before the expected due date. CHV causes infertility, reabsorption, abortion, stillbirth, and 'fading puppy' syndrome. It also causes kennel cough. It lives in the respiratory and reproductive tracts of adult dogs, and can be transmitted to the foetus in utero, or as they travel through the birth canal. It can also be passed to a newborn pup via the dam's nasal secretions. Affected newborn puppies will almost certainly not survive. The CHV virus thrives in lower body temperatures, and as newborn puppies cannot mount a fever response until they are around three weeks of age, they are particularly vulnerable. If they contract the virus before this time it is likely that they will 'fade'. They will fail to suckle, appear increasingly listless, and they produce yellow-green diarrhoea. They will almost certainly die. Puppies that develop the condition after three weeks of age are more likely to exhibit respiratory distress, and are more likely to survive. There is no cure available, but supportive treatments can be offered for affected puppies. They will need to be kept warm, and fluid/anti-diarrhoeal therapies may be useful if the pups are of an age where they can mount their own response to the virus.

The virus can become dormant and will then resurface at times of stress. Adult dogs may cough and sneeze, and they may also have genital blisters or discharge, but some show no symptoms at all. The CHV vaccine, given at intervals to the pregnant bitch, protects her unborn puppies, but the CHV virus is only one of many reasons why a bitch might lose her litter.

Some infectious causes of canine abortion:
Brucella canis / Canine distemper / *E. coli* / *Streptococcus* species / *Mycoplasma* and *Ureaplasma* species.

Some non-infectious causes of canine abortion:
Hormonal imbalance / Inadequate nutrition / Hereditary or congenital abnormalities / Chemical agents / Traumas / Stress.

You may never know that your bitch has actually lost her litter as there are often no outward signs. If you had not had a scan performed on your bitch you may think that she was simply never pregnant in the first place. It is possible, however, that you might notice that she produces unusual colour or loose stools, has a suspect vaginal discharge, or that she is depressed mentally or physically, including a loss of appetite. In these instances, seek advice from your vet in case treatment is needed, as abortion/reabsorption can lead to the development of serious conditions such as pyometra (p. 199).

Between weeks five and six you should begin to change your bitch's diet to that of a good quality complete puppy food, which will give more accessible nutrition for herself and the puppies in her womb (p. 186). Her dietary requirements by six weeks mean that she would have to consume vast quantities of her usual food, at a time when her belly is already burdened with puppies. Transferring her on to puppy food means she will gain a higher calorific diet for less bulk.

PREPARATIONS

 Be sure to contact your vet as your bitch nears full term, so that arrangements can be discussed regarding on-call services should you need them.

- Phone and important phone numbers
- Spare vet bed / towels / newspapers for the whelping box
- Small, soft towels for drying off the puppies
- A small box with heat pad or hot water bottle / soft blanket or vet bed
- Container with lid for discarded placentas
- Container with lid for any puppies who are born dead (NB If you plan to ask your vet for post mortems do not freeze the bodies)
- Laundry basket for soiled towels
- A bowl of warm water / Hibiscrub® hand wash / towel
- KY Jelly, in case of difficult presentations
- Surgical gloves / blunt ended scissors
- Umbilical clamps / sterile dental floss
- Digital thermometer
- Glucose drink or puppy milk drink for the bitch
- A set of scales, notebook and pen, to record puppy weights
- Nail polish or ribbon for identification of puppies
- Clock
- Nutri drops
- Puppy milk formula / feeding bottles / syringe / teats
- Baby suction bulb (for aspirating mucus from the mouth)
- Book / magazines for those long quiet spells!
- Camera
- It is useful to set up tea-making facilities / snacks, as you will not want to leave her side once she starts whelping.

 You might like to pad your car out with newspaper covered in layers of vet bed. Have a small crate ready to put the puppy box into, should you need to transport your bitch and pups to the vet.

Prior to labour, it is useful to shave the hair around the dam's hindquarters, especially if she is long coated, as puppies can easily become tangled in long hair. A cohesive tail bandage, such as is used on horses, is invaluable for keeping the tail area clean during and immediately after birth. Your bitch will have already shed most of her belly hair, but some breeders choose to shave any remaining hairs.

Whelping area and box

Prepare the whelping area in a quiet corner of the house at least a week before the puppies are due, in order that the dam gets fully used to this in good time. It is important to note that if your bitch feels vulnerable in her surroundings this can have devastating consequences. If she feels under threat from another family dog, or if she feels that her whelping area is in anyway unsafe, this can lead to the loss of the litter. For many bitches, especially one having her first litter, it can be vital to keep her separate from her 'pack' in the weeks beforehand.

We have always put our whelping box into a side room with a baby gate across the doorway. The expectant bitch can then be shut away from other pets for short periods, to sleep, feed, and grow accustomed to her whelping area. A good site for this would be a quiet utility or study room which is close enough to the main flow of the household to give reassurance, yet is private enough to give the dam peace of mind in the early days with her newborns. It is a good idea to put up a camp bed for yourself, in order that the bitch and puppies' every need can be monitored at this fragile time. We always camp out with the bitch and pups for up to two weeks. Leaving a litter unattended for long periods (especially with a mother who is inexperienced or on a particularly large litter) is likely to result in crush injuries or death to puppies.

Whelping boxes should be constructed of materials which are easy to keep clean, and will need to be approximately 4ft x 4ft, by 18 inches high. You will want to make the front panel adjustable, so that in the first weeks the dam can climb in and out of the box without damaging her undercarriage. This will need to be heightened as the puppies grow, and as the dam spends less and less time with her offspring. The box should have 'pig rails' at approximately 5 inch height, around the inner edge. These help puppies avoid being crushed in the early days. Newborn puppies have a tendency to crawl under their mother's tail and around behind her if they fail to find a teat, or if they are in search of somewhere warm. With a Shepherd bitch weighing 25 kilos or more, and a newborn pup weighing around half a kilo, it is easy to see how a tired bitch can inadvertently suffocate her offspring as she stretches out to sleep, or after she turns around in the box. If you feel unable to construct a box, there is a wide range available commerically, to suit all pockets.

You will have chosen either a heat lamp or heat pad, and will need to follow the individual manufacturer's instructions carefully, as providing the right temperature for the puppies is crucial to their survival (p. 234). It is also worth mentioning that you will need a fine mesh cover for heat lamps in case the bulb shatters at any stage.

LATE PREGNANCY

Exercise continues to be important to help maintain general fitness and muscle tone. However your bitch's desire for this will inevitably decrease and no doubt she will let you know when she no longer feels up to going out for a walk. Some bitches, however, remain incredibly active tight until the end of the pregnancy. You will notice that her spine becomes noticeably more prominent. This is due to the developing foetuses dropping lower into her belly. The weight pulls the flesh taut over her spine, making it clearly visible. This is noting to be alarmed by, and unless accompanied by other symptoms is not indicative of weight loss.

In the last week you may find that your bitch becomes increasingly picky with her food. Try adding small tasters of her favourite meat or stock. Soaked food often seems more palatable. In the last 24–48 hours she may stop eating completely and might even vomit if offered food. This is perfectly normal and should not give rise to concern unless accompanied with other symptoms such as a worrying discharge, or rise in temperature. She will need fresh water available at all times, and will need to urinate more frequently as the pressure on her bladder from her heavy uterus increases.

Pre-whelping behaviours

The bitch's greatest need at this time is to gather herself mentally and physically for what she knows lies ahead. As she is probably not wishing to take food, and is weary from weeks of carrying her young, it is rest and deep sleep that she needs. If you find that she wants to be away from you a lot of the time and avoids fuss and contact, do not be unduly alarmed. She is genetically programmed to seek a quiet place away from everyone at this time, and your plans to be involved in the birth are entirely unnatural to her. It will be your job to blend into the whelping process with as little fuss as is possible, thereby enabling her to cope with and welcome your involvement. She is arguably your best friend ordinarily, but whelping brings forth a deep seated, primitive set of responses, and she may well lose her emotional connection to you for a while.

Your bitch will feel the need to 'nest'. She may begin digging, thereby giving the impression that the birth is close by when in fact it may still be days away. Do not chastise her for this desire, even if she uproots your favourite plants! It is a natural response to her body's changes. In the wild she would be digging her chosen site in which to give birth. Provide her with lots of shredded newspaper in her box as this helps her to satisfy the need, and is easily removed and replaced with vet bed once you know that whelping is imminent. Do not despair if she seems to have chosen an entirely inappropriate spot for her digging spells. Once you confine her to her room during actual labour, she will undoubtedly settle and will concentrate on the job in hand. She will completely forget that she had made plans of her own to give birth behind your best sofa!

She may make attempts to tear her bedding with her teeth, in response to increasing discomfort. It can be helpful to reassure her, but you will probably find she simply wants to do it her own way. Watching her dismantle your tenderly arranged bedding can be frustrating, but it is perfectly natural. As with digging, 'shredding' can take place for short periods but can also last for hours, so don't be in too much of a hurry to attempt to sort her bed out afterwards – you may have to do it all over again!

In the last few days her teats will become fully enlarged, and some bitches will leak milk. Prior to whelping you may notice a clear fluid being expelled from her vulva. You might have seen some discharge during the pregnancy, but now it will increase significantly. This indicates that the mucoid plug which seals the cervix is dissolving. It is a sure sign that birth is close. If there is a dark green or bloody discharge which precedes the first puppy, it is imperative that you phone your vet. In this instance it is likely that she is suffering from a placental abruption. This is where the placenta breaks away from the uterus before its due time, and can result in blood loss for the bitch, and oxygen starvation for the puppy.

It is useful to take your bitch's temperature in the days leading up to the birth, to help give you a better idea of how things are progressing. Her temperature normally would be around 38.3°C (101.5°F), but during the last days of pregnancy this begins to drop. When it reaches around 37.5°C, (99.5°F) labour will usually begin within 24 hours. During the final 12 hours, the reading will drop further. You will notice her panting as she lowers her temperature.

It perhaps goes without saying that a glass thermometer should never be used as these are unsafe. Always use a thermometer designed for veterinary purposes. Plastic digital ones are by far the best as they emit a soft audible bleep when the temperature is read. You have accuracy and ease of reading – not a desperate attempt to see the thin line of mercury against a ceiling light, as in days of old!

The puppies also undergo final changes and begin to stress as their space becomes crowded. You may notice a lot of movement from them during this time. It is the puppies who trigger the birth process, not their mother. (The presence of the stress hormone cortisol begins the initial process of labour.) There will then follow a period of calm 'meditation', whereby the panting slows, the puppies become still, and the expectant mother seems to focus on somewhere far away in her mind.

WHELPING

 Whelping is best done with an experienced breeder present or close to hand, in case there are concerns. It is a specialised subject, with its own wealth of superb literature. Below is a simple outline of the process, with a guide through a 'normal' birth, and a glimpse into more difficult scenarios. It is not an exhaustive guide, because there are no substitutes for having experienced practical assistance to hand, and a vet on standby for emergencies.

It is important to note that the majority of German Shepherds are good whelpers, but it is vital to stay with the dam throughout the process. First litters in particular can bring huge surprises. For example, your normally gentle bitch may become frantic and rough whilst breaking cords, or may become clumsy in response to pain and adrenalin. Some have seemingly no idea of what to do with the first puppy, and will need you to take positive action, whilst reassuring her gently.

First stage labour will see your bitch becoming increasingly restless. She will pace, dig, shiver and pant and may appear panicky as her temperature drops and her cervix dilates.

She is likely to refuse food, and may vomit during this time. This usually occurs over a 6–12 hour period although maiden bitches may experience this for longer.

As her cervix reaches full dilation, second stage labour begins, during which her puppies will be expelled from her uterus. The puppies are each contained in individual sacs of amniotic fluid. The sacs usually break prior to the puppy being pushed through the birth canal (although occasionally puppies are born whilst still contained fully in the amniotic sac). As the membrane around the puppy ruptures, amniotic fluid released assists the lubrication of the birth canal.

Once this membrane has actually broken it is important that the first puppy is born quickly. Taking into account the length of time it takes to travel to your vet, you are advised to call him promptly if you have any doubts, so that arrangements can be quickly made. The timing between subsequent puppies should also be closely monitored. If your bitch is resting calmly between puppies you can usually expect safe intervals of up to three hours between pups although half-hourly intervals between puppies is more normal for a strong, healthy bitch. If she is pushing continuously, and straining with no signs of success, it is wise to ring your vet within 10 minutes of such pushing as it is likely there is a problem.

This is why having an experienced breeder with you during your first whelping is so important. Timing and signs can be misleading if you are simply 'going by the book'. A three and a half hour wait with a bitch who is resting between contractions might represent little problem, but a relatively short wait with a bitch who is straining hard could present a grave risk to bitch and her unborn pups.

Preceding the birth of each puppy, abdominal contractions begin in earnest and the dam will concentrate, probably dig at her bedding and lick herself frequently. She will 'shiver' with each contraction, and you will see the spasm running down her flanks. As contractions intensify, she may crouch with back and tail arched as she begins to push. She will turn round repeatedly in the box, lie down, and then get up again. She may utter a guttural groan

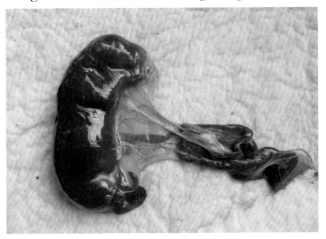

A puppy encased in its membrane and wth placenta attached

with the strongest contractions. Most bitches finally lie down to pass the puppy, but others actually give birth from the crouched position mentioned above, which can be alarming to novice breeders, but is unlikely to result in injury.

Puppies can be born in a variety of presentations. Ideally the puppy will be born head first, although many are born feet first (breech birth) without this leading to complication. Presented like this, the birth should be smooth and without concern, unless of course the puppy is too large for the bitch to pass it, or if she is at a stage in the proceedings where she is too tired to push any longer. The puppy is enclosed within its protective membrane and the placenta is attached by a cord to puppy's abdomen.

Some bitches prefer no interference from their owner as each pup enters the world. Some are adept at tearing the cord and sac, and they instantly attend to the newborn with rough licking. This stimulates blood supply to the organs, and stimulates the lungs into operation. If your bitch is either too rough or not attentive enough, you will need to tear the sac around the puppy's mouth and ensure that his airways are completely clear of mucus.

If you need to break the cord yourself, this is best done by tying off the cord with sterile dental floss. Make a knot about an inch from the puppy's abdomen, and tear or cut the cord with blunt scissors beyond this knot. Dip the end of the cord in iodine. You will need to rub the puppy with a dry towel to stimulate him into breathing. Hold him with his head pointing downward to help any mucus drain from his airway, and rub *firmly!* Once he utters his first cry, most bitches will stir into action and will want to lick him clean and dry. Occasionally a bitch will look on with disinterest, or panic. You will need to tend to the puppy's needs while the bitch becomes accustomed to the puppy's presence. Usually once the second puppy arrives, the dam will have settled and will want to be fully involved with subsequent births.

 You will need to make sure you do all of the above with the minimum of fuss. Blending in calmly with the whelping experience, keeps your bitch's stress levels at a minimum.

Dystocia / Inertia

Dystocia means 'difficult birth'. Complications occasionally arise with breech birth, and in presentations where the head is twisted sideways or down into the chest. If the puppy's body is bent, or if his hip or shoulder becomes wedged during his passage into the birth canal, these can all present serious problems. With help at hand, you may lubricate the dam's vagina in between contractions with lubricating jelly or baby oil. During breech presentation, using a clean, gloved, index finger, you can gently try to help the puppy forward as the next contraction occurs. You may find that in poorly presented births, you are able to hook a finger around the puppy and reposition him for a safer passage into the world. However, if you find that a puppy is poorly presented, and you are unable to realign or reposition him, you should seek help immediately. The whelp, bitch and other unborn puppies are at risk if you fail to seek help when a puppy cannot be passed.

Dystocia can also be caused by inertia, which refers to the failure of the uterine muscles to expel the foetuses. Inertia can be termed as primary or secondary. If your bitch fails to begin labour at full term, she has primary complete inertia. If some of the puppies have been born, but others remain due to uterine exhaustion, this is termed secondary inertia.

Many factors can lead to inertia. In primary inertia for example, the uterus might fail to respond to signals from the foetuses, or there might be insufficient stimulation for her labour to progress – especially if there is a dead puppy or very small litter. Secondary inertia is frequently caused where the dam is overweight, or has been fed on a poor diet. Nervous bitches can suffer from inertia, as can older bitches. If your bitch is out of condition, and lacking in muscle tone, she may simply be unable to sustain contractions, and it is highly possible that puppies will be stillborn as prolonged labour can lead to oxygen starvation in the foetus. This suffering of bitch and puppies is needless.

Oxytocin / 'feathering'

If your bitch experiences inertia, your vet is likely to give her an injectable hormone called oxytocin. This hormone is normally released in the body during labour and it stimulates uterine contractions. Oxytocin injections are used by the vet in certain situations where the bitch has an absence of, or weak, contractions. It is also used after labour to expel any remaining placental matter from the uterus. It will only be used where the bitch's cervix is fully dilated, and if the puppies and dam are stable.

If your bitch has strong contractions and it is evident that there is an obstruction causing failure to pass a puppy, oxytocin will not be used. It will not be used if there is a puppy in the birth canal. In most instances, a vet may choose to use oxytocin if a bitch has shown weak (or an absence of) contractions for over three hours. If there is a continued lack of viable contractions despite the administration of oxytocin, the vet will advise that your bitch undergoes a Caesarean section.

'Feathering' may also assist your bitch if her contractions are weak. Be sure that your hands are clean, and if you carefully insert your gloved index finger into her vulva, you will find that gently rubbing along the top wall of the vagina will usually stimulate contractions to begin again.

Milk production

Some bitches do not produce milk until whelping finishes. However, it is more likely, as you place each newborn pup on the 'milk bar' in between births, that they will find milk present in abundance. As each one suckles, the dam will produce further oxytocin which helps to strengthen her contractions. You may find that some puppies are unable to latch on at first. If you support their wobbling head and frame, and use your other hand to express milk from the teat, most puppies rapidly get the idea. They will then use their front feet to stimulate a constant flow of milk to the teat.

It can be helpful to remove the feeding puppies into a safe, warm box each time that their mother pushes a new pup into the world. As she stands up, crouches or lies down, her prime focus is on the next birth, and those puppies already born can be crushed in the process. If the box is warm and welcoming they will settle quickly, and if it is kept in the immediate vicinity the bitch is unlikely to fret. Once she has settled with the new pup, the others can be returned to her. It sounds intrusive and involved, but it takes seconds to transfer them back and forth, and may save a life. However, if your bitch is distressed by this action, stop immediately and simply keep a close vigil on those in the whelping box while she moves about in preparation for subsequent births.

 Be aware that bitches are often slow to produce milk following a Caesarean section.

Most bitches attempt to break the cord and eat the placenta

The placenta

Most bitches will attempt to eat the placenta following the birth of each pup. You may not even notice this with some bitches, as placentas can be passed with the pup, in between births, or even with the next puppy. As she will constantly be cleaning herself and removing the sac from the newborns, the afterbirth often gets eaten at the same time. In the wild she would have eaten these for vital nutrients and proteins. However, if your bitch is allowed to consume all of the placentas throughout the birth, she will probably develop an upset stomach. If possible, allow her to consume a few of the placentas to provide her with protein, but after the first four or five, discard those that you can remove from her discreetly. It is important to attempt to monitor the number of placentas passed, as retained placentas can cause uterine infections.

Has labour finished?

You will need to keep an eye on your bitch once she has passed the 'last' puppy. If you are unable to feel any further puppies within her abdomen but she still appears restless you are wise to take her to your vet. Some bitches will not have enough energy left to pass remaining puppies, so remain vigilant and take action if she is showing any signs of distress. Usually, once a bitch has finished labour, she will be relaxed and keen to take some food to replenish her reserves.

If you are unsure, your vet can check for foetal heartbeats, and scan your bitch. If necessary he will administer oxytocin providing the situation permits it. If this action would be detrimental to your bitch, a Caesarean section would be performed to remove remaining puppies. Your vet might also give you the option of spaying your bitch at this time, if there are good reasons to do so.

The bitch's appetite

She will need high protein meals from day one, and yet some bitches are tremendously reluctant to eat in the 24 hours following the birth. Many breeders opt for chicken-based, home-prepared meals (or high protein 'recovery' meals which are available from most vets) to encourage the bitch's appetite in the first few days. The benefit of the latter is that she can eat small quantities and still get high protein and trace elements. This can be mixed gradually with complete puppy food to wean her back on to this once she is ready. It is difficult to replicate the carefully researched nutrition found in quality puppy foods, and it is therefore advisable to get her back on to this as soon as possible. She will need to stay on puppy food whilst nursing the litter. After the puppies have left, she will usually drop condition markedly, and will need a quality diet to help her body repair.

IMPORTANT POST–PARTUM ISSUES

You will need to bathe your bitch's rear end at some point in the first day or so. This is advisable for a multitude of reasons, including the removal of bacteria, helping to reduce odour, and also to make your bitch more comfortable. You will also be better able to monitor her vaginal discharge more readily over the ensuing days if she is bathed fairly frequently. It is vital to monitor her discharge over the next week to ten days. She will lose brown and dark red matter for several days, which has a distinctive metallic odour to it. This is perfectly normal. However, if this appears to not be decreasing, or if the discharge becomes bright red or foul smelling, you should speak to your vet immediately.

Metritis

This is a bacterial infection which causes inflammation of the uterine lining. Metritis can be caused by retained placental matter or a retained foetus and is a genuine medical emergency. Delayed treatment can lead to septicaemia, shock and even death. Metritis can also occur following abortion of puppies. Bacteria enters the uterus through the cervix whilst it is still open and the resulting infection leads to a range of symptoms varying from loss of appetite and lethargy, to raging temperature, depression vomiting and diarrhoea. Other key symptoms include a blood and pus filled discharge. Veterinary attention should be sought immediately.

Cleft palate

Cleft palate is an abnormality of the nasal and oral cavities (cleft of the secondary palate). The bones of the roof of the puppy's mouth fail to form correctly during gestation for a variety of reasons, and the resulting fissure between the cavities allows fluid and food to pass from the mouth into the sinuses. Cleft palate puppies are usually noted in the first few days following birth as they 'bubble' milk back through their nose as they feed.

Some cleft puppies will die within a few days if the breeder does not bottle or tube feed as they will quite literally starve to death, or die of aspiration pneumonia. Others survive perfectly well, although they too may suffer from respiratory infections. Some breeders will intervene and tube feed the affected puppy until around five weeks of age, at which point attempts can be made to wean them on to softened food. Close attention will need to be paid to hygiene of the hole as debris can get caught causing infection or discomfort. Surgical reconstruction can be performed by a specialist surgeon, in some cases with excellent results, although this can be very expensive.

It has been scientifically proven that excess vitamin A in the bitch's diet during pregnancy is a cause of cleft palate in her puppies. So too are a variety of other causes such as deficiency of vitamin B$_{12}$, usage of antihistamines or steroids, exposure to insecticides and viral infections, all during the early weeks of pregnancy. If embryonic development is disturbed at a critical stage, any part of the foetus's body may fail to then develop correctly. Cleft palate is also associated with harelip (known as a cleft of the primary palate), and other midline closure defects such as missing toes and skull deformities.

Umbilical hernias

The umbilical hernia is the most common type of hernia found in the dog. These result as a consequence of part of the muscular abdominal wall remaining open after birth, usually around the umbilicus ('belly button'). An area of fatty tissue (or, in rare cases, an abdominal organ) protrudes through this opening covered by layers of skin and subcutaneous fat. If only fatty tissue protrudes, this usually causes no problem for the puppy. However, herniated organs can become entrapped, twisted or otherwise blocked and this can be very serious. As a guide, if the hernia can be pushed back under gentle pressure without resentment it is called 'reducible'. If it cannot, it is termed 'irreducible'. If herniated tissue is squeezed by the hole in the muscle through which it pokes it can lose its blood supply and become 'strangulated', often causing pain and depression – a situation which requires urgent surgery.

Umbilical hernias might be partially genetic in origin, but might also be the result of rough tearing and cleaning by the bitch. If the hernia itself does not pose a health issue, it can be simply resolved under anaesthetic when the dog is sterilised. Many small hernias become insignificant within a few months.

General care of the bitch

Keep an eye on the dam's temperature in the first week in particular, and be sure to familiarise yourself with the sigs of eclampsia (p. 220) as this requires prompt attention by a vet.

Check her teats regularly for signs of heat or hardness. 'Mastitis' is a very painful condition and if this occurs your bitch may need antibiotic treatment. If spotted early, mastitis can also be successfully treated using warm and cold compresses. If the blocked teat is then milked by hand, the milk should begin to flow. Allow a hungry puppy to suckle until the affected treat softens.

Your bitch may revert to digging a few days following the birth. Do not become alarmed – she is not about to give birth to late puppies! Her womb is contracting steadily back to its normal size (known as 'involution'), and the resulting discomfort prompts the urge to dig again. This will settle in a matter of days. If possible, give her a separate area with shredded paper or old blankets in the whelping room to allow her to carry out this task. Failure to do so will inevitably result in her digging all around her puppies, making them fractious and putting them at risk. Involution takes place over several weeks, but it is the initial stages which appear to cause the most discomfort. Some research suggests that it may take around six weeks to complete, but it is likely that your vet would not consider spaying your bitch (unless complications arise) until 12 weeks post-partum, to be absolutely certain that her uterus is back to its normal size.

She will hardly sleep at all in the first few days, and you will find she stirs to check on the puppies even when they are sleeping and quiet. Just when you think all is calm, she will begin washing them, and will scatter them all over the box. Be calm and steady with her, as your presence will enable her to realise that *she* can rest while her puppies sleep.

You may find you need to bring food and water to her where she lies for the first few days, and that you will have to put her on a lead in order to persuade her to go outside to the toilet. She will be reluctant to leave the puppies, even for a moment, but gradually she will develop trust in the process. Just be patient with her, and you are likely to find that in three or four days you all have a nice routine, and that she will eat, drink and toilet normally.

You are likely to have plenty of people who wish to visit during and immediately after the birth. But visitors will stress the vast majority of bitches and you would do well to wait until she is really up to it. This may be a week or more in some instances. Remember that every visitor brings the risk of infection with them.

Following a Caesarean section, some bitches are reluctant to accept their offspring, especially if the whole litter was born this way. If your bitch has not gone through a natural birth it may take time before her maternal instincts take over. Do not force the issue. Be calm and supportive of her, and make introductions with extreme care. If reintroducing the puppies proves impossible, see the following chapter for advice on hand rearing your litter. As an alternative, you might choose to seek a foster mother through your vet, or through local breed clubs.

Rearing Puppies

The German Shepherd bitch is invariably a diligent and loving mother. If she has been kept fit and well, both before and during her pregnancy, she will no doubt nurse her puppies to perfection. But there are times when bitches experience difficulties producing milk, and sometimes a litter can simply be too large for the dam to feed without assistance. Regardless, there is always plenty for the conscientious breeder to do, and you will soon find that you are consumed by the joys of rearing your litter. Being prepared is always the key to being able to take each day in your stride.

Enjoy! It is a magical time.

COLOSTRUM / MECONIUM

Whenever possible, it is important that newborn puppies get their fill of their mother's creamy yellow, pre-milk fluid. This is called colostrum and it is present during the first 24–48 hours after whelping. It is high in proteins, vitamins, and antibodies which help the puppies to fight infection during these vulnerable first weeks. The strength of these antibodies lessens as the weeks pass and ultimately they are of no efficacy whatsoever, hence the need for puppy vaccines. Colostrum also acts as a laxative, which helps the puppies pass meconium (waste matter from their time in utero). Meconium is dark brown and rather 'tarry', but the faeces that will follow are bright yellow in colour and are granular in texture. Gradually, faeces become yellowish-brown, and will change in colour once again when the puppy is introduced to solid food.

BODY TEMPERATURE – A GENERAL GUIDE

Beautiful puppies under a heat lamp

Newborn puppies have no control over their body temperature during the first few weeks of life. This should be between 35.5–36 °C. You will need to maintain this artificially, by keeping the area in the whelping box at around 26.5–28 °C during the first week. Make sure that the heat source is placed such that the bitch and puppies can move away from it if they need to. The temperature can be reduced gradually to 22–24 °C by the fourth week. You should continue to ensure that the environmental temperature is kept at around 21.5° C from this point forwards.

The importance of providing a reliable

heat source should not be underestimated. This will enable the puppies to maintain a rectal temp of around 36 °C which climbs steadily until the puppies' temperature reaches around 37.8 °C at around three weeks of age. At this stage two important changes occur. The puppies will begin to have control over their temperature, and they are finally able to produce a 'fever response'. Their body can thus produce heat of its own which enables the puppy to fight infection. Prior to this, they are highly vulnerable, and a chill can quickly lead to death. You should never feed a puppy who is chilled, as their rectal temperature needs to be above 35 °C for digestion to occur.

If your puppies are being hand reared, then you will need to be especially vigilant as they unable to gain extra body heat from the bitch. Keep a constant temperature of around 28.5–30 °C in the box during the first two weeks, and lower this steadily as time progresses, monitoring the puppies' responses carefully.

PREMATURE BIRTH / RESPIRATORY PROBLEMS

Puppies born prematurely are invariably underweight. They have reduced hair development on belly, legs and muzzle. They usually have bright red feet and belly, and flaccid skin caused by dehydration. Premature puppies will need considerable nursing care by the breeder. If they are left with their mother they are unlikely to survive. There is usually a reduced suck reflex, and puppies may simply not have the drive or strength to search for their mother's milk. As the lungs develop in the final days in the womb, respiratory difficulties are common in premature puppies. Affected pups would require steroid or antibiotic therapy, and intensive care support at the veterinary surgery. Many healthy, strong dogs are the end product of intensive veterinary care following premature birth, but others do not survive. Some breeders feel that they should let nature decide, and that such stock would be weakened by the experience in any case. It is a very personal judgement.

MOTHERLY LOVE

During their first few weeks of life, your German Shepherd puppies will ideally be tended to by their mother, with support as required from you. If she has an average litter of around six to eight puppies, she is unlikely to need you to substitute her efforts by hand rearing. However, if she has a large litter, or if she is not producing quite enough milk, you will need to become involved. The best way to support the bitch is by rotating the litter (feeding some by hand while she nurses the others). The puppies can be swapped over at the next feed time so that they all get the benefit of their mother's milk in equal measure. Your life will not be your own any longer, as feed time takes place every two hours come night or day, but your support is necessary if the litter is to become healthy and well covered.

A healthy puppy's frame should be filled out, with no sign of dehydration or unthriftiness. Coats should be shiny and the puppies themselves should be active. Even in the early days, before they are able to stand up fully and walk, they should be actively seeking the teat, and shuffling around the box trying to find the best spot to sleep in! Their movement in the first two weeks is very distinctive. Their limbs cannot carry their own body weight yet, so they wobble from side to side in order to move around the box.

Puppies soon learn not to use their bedding as a toilet area, providing that a small area of newspaper is available in the corner of the box. But for the first week at least, they will use their bedding as a toilet area. If you use 'vet bed' (p. 75), this will help keep the puppies dry during this period, as the urine will soak through the bedding and onto newspaper underneath. If you do not use vet bed you will soon realise that other bedding materials get soaked rapidly. Bedding will need to be changed several times a day regardless of material. Puppies produce a high volume of urine, and the area can quickly start to harbour odour and germs.

The puppies' eyes will open at around 10–14 days, but it takes several more days before they begin to focus. They do not like bright lights at this stage so be aware of this when you make choices about your heat source. Between weeks one and two, the ear canal begins to open and gradually the pups will become more aware of their environment. At around three weeks they will begin to bark! Teeth begin to erupt at three to four weeks. By four weeks they will begin to play, although their responses and reflexes take at least another two weeks to develop, and for playtime to really gather momentum.

It is important to clip the points from puppies' front claws at two weeks of age as this helps the bitch to stay free of painful tears and scratches while she is feeding them. You should monitor this weekly as some will need doing again.

WORMING

As puppies will carry a worm burden from their time in the womb, it is crucial that they are wormed at regular intervals. Use a quality wormer such as Panacur®, Milbemax® or Drontal® puppy. Most worming programmes advise worming puppies at two, four, six and eight weeks whilst with the breeder. You will then hand this task over to your buyer, so that they can plan further worming programmes with their own vet. The chapter on 'Routine Health Care' discusses this more fully.

WEANING

Weaning should be a gradual process, with the bitch spending less and less time with her offspring. It is natural process but should be handed with sensitivity. The whole process usually takes around 3 weeks, but some bitches will take a little longer.

Do not simply take your bitch away from her puppies to wean them. It is important that she continues to suckle her pups, in decreasing measure, whilst you undertake the process of weaning them on to solid food. By weaning them gradually and by increasing the dam's exercise, you will encourage her mind and body to deal with the situation. The nutrition she provides is crucial whilst the puppies learn to adapt to solid food, and the continued bond between bitch and pups is very important. Puppies can be weaned fully by around six weeks, and if the bitch only has short access to the puppies from this point forwards, she will lose her milk naturally.

Most puppies possess the ability to lap from around two and a half weeks, but weaning does not usually start in earnest for a further week. If your pups are to be reared on a complete puppy food, you will need to soak the pellets with warm water. For the first week this will need mashing into a porridge-like meal, and should be served warm while puppies begin to make the transition from their mother's warm milk. All breeders have their own preferences for weaning their puppies, but we feed four times per day, paying particular attention to weights of puppies and corresponding quantities of food given through the day. By six weeks most bitches will not be supplementing the food you are giving, so you will need to be vigilant in ensuring that each puppy is getting enough to eat. It is very easy to underfeed, and you may think about dividing puppies into smaller groups, or even feeding them individually if you are at all concerned about the litter developing evenly. Watch closely during weaning for any puppies

First meals need to be porridge-like

who regurgitate their meal. This could be due to a serious condition called megaoesophagus (p. 257). Soak the puppy kibble with less fluid as the weeks progress, and you can also leave dry kibble down in between mealtimes.

New owners should be encourated to replicate the diet you have chosen, at the very least until the puppy has settled into their new home. It is a good idea to explain that puppy's appetite may wane briefly in the first few days. Many puppy buyers do not realise that the excitement and stress of moving home can lead to disinterest in food. A classic error is to start introducing alternative food. This is to be avoided at all costs. Puppies usually settle after a few days of being in their new home and get back to eating normally if the new owner does not start experimenting with food. The last thing anyone wants is a puppy developing diarrhoea. Owners should be encouraged to keep to the routine with food and resist the temptation to change the diet in the early days.

Puppies are usually weaned by six weeks of age

As already discussed, bitches can develop mastitis at any stage of feeding puppies, but the weaning stage leaves them vulnerable to this uncomfortable condition. Keep a close eye on her as the puppies change over to solid food.

HAND REARING

In the event that your bitch is unable (or unwilling) to tend to the litter you have a large job ahead of you. This will involve total commitment as this is a 24 hour-a-day undertaking! If the dam is unable to feed her babies but can still assist with all *other* aspects of rearing them, it is wise to let her do so. She will be invaluable in keeping them clean, and will also teach them important lessons in terms of behaviour, bonding and play.

You will need to use a quality puppy milk substitute powder, such as 'Whelpi®' or Royal Canin 'Babydog milk'®. Puppy milk powders are very specific in their directions regarding mixing and quantities. It is imperative that these are adhered to. It is sensible to weigh the puppies daily, and to mark the puppies so that you can keep track of individual weight fluctuations.

Newborn pups will need feeding every two hours or so, and they will need to sleep on a thermostatically controlled heat pad in between each feed. These pads are available through good pet suppliers, dog magazines and also via the internet. They are a more reliable source of heat than water bottles or heat bags, as they will not overheat, nor underheat your puppies at this vulnerable time. Ensure that puppies can move away from the pad a little to regulate their own temperature, as all have differing needs just as babies do. Some people prefer to use infra-red lamps, which is perfectly fine but be especially careful to monitor the temperature in the box. (p. 234)

Mix your puppy milk as directed by the manufacturer, ensuring that it is smooth in texture and at the correct temperature. If puppy has not yet suckled from its mother you may find that it takes to a fake teat more readily. Dip the teat in milk after filling up the bottle, to encourage the pup to latch on tightly. This can be extremely frustrating in the first few attempts! Newborn puppies wobble uncontrollably, and some will fail to take the teat over and over again, wailing in frustration. Be patient and they will get there in the end. Some puppies prefer to be held fully while feeding, some prefer less intervention. However, you will need to gently support the puppy's head. Hand feeding is a delicate process. Above all, you will need to ensure that milk is not taken too quickly or this can lead to choking. Newborn puppies are also susceptible to aspiration pneumonia if they inhale fluids.

It is not only the method you use which is important, but the fact that the puppies are at ease with your attempts. If a puppy only takes a few mouthfuls and then resists, check the milk temperature repeatedly. Some puppies resist feeding as soon as the milk starts to cool. Certain puppies may only want tiny amounts in the beginning. If this is the case let them take what they can, and return to this reluctant feeder in between the others. Be calm and patient, and this will reap great rewards. You may feel helpless if you have never done this before, but the sight of all your puppies sleeping after a successful hand feeding session is one of the most rewarding moments you will experience as a breeder.

During and after feeding, and also after periods of sleep, the bitch would lick her puppies' bottoms, as this stimulates the puppy to defecate and urinate. It is essential to their survival that you are aware of this if you are hand rearing: use a cotton wool pad soaked in warm water, and wipe the area to stimulate elimination. Failure to do this will result in the puppy's death, as toxins build quickly. Puppies can excrete without the need for stimulation from around two weeks of age.

Hand reared puppies will not have the benefit of being washed regularly by their mother. Replicate this by using a damp flannel on their coats on a regular basis. Use warm water with a weak solution of mild baby shampoo to keep their coats fresh, and to prevent dry skin occurring. It is particularly useful to do this as they begin weaning, as they will undoubtedly get covered in food in the early days.

Confidence in abundance!

The singular hand reared puppy is likely to have issues of its own which should be noted. When a puppy is reared without sibling or maternal contact, it becomes imprinted on humans: it learns to see the human who rears it as its parent. As we do not possess the skills inherent to the pup's natural parent, it is easy to overlook the lessons this puppy would have gained if being reared by its mother. The chances are, if we are rearing a single pup, that we have great empathy and love for the pup. This love grows exponentially as the puppy struggles and wins its fight for survival. In these circumstances it is easy to see why we would 'spoil' the puppy, as its every whim and desire is tended to. However this may well cause this pup to develop confidence beyond its normal parameters as it receives little or no 'canine correction'.

As they reach adulthood these dogs can become way beyond anything you might ordinarily expect! Confidence, independence and total self-belief can make such dogs hard to handle. It does not have to be this way however. If boundaries are provided through positive training methods, the pup will learn what is expected of him. It is essential that these puppies attend puppy classes, in order that they can learn some general rules from other puppies in a controlled environment. They will learn clear canine/human boundaries at this formative stage before things get out of hand.

HEALTH ISSUES

Umbilical infection

Keep a close eye on the cords over the first week. Ideally they will dry out over a 24-hour period, but if they remain spongy or soft there may be an umbilical infection which can spread rapidly through the body. The bitch may pass this to her puppy whilst cleaning him in the first hours or days.

Fading puppy syndrome

Sadly, some puppies will fail to thrive. Some puppies appear fine at first and then deteriorate, some clearly struggle from the start. If all is not well, a sickly puppy may sleep with their head and neck stretched out as if the body is tense. They begin to refuse to nurse from the bitch, crawling away from their littermates, moaning in distress. Some exhibit wobbling of the head and neck, bloating of the belly, and become notably dehydrated. Despite antibiotics, fluid support therapy and careful nursing, some of these puppies will not survive. It is often the case that a post mortem would then show congenital abnormalities.

Fading puppy syndrome is not a disease in its own right. It is a term used to describe a collective set of symptoms, which may have a variety of root causes. There may be problems with the puppy's digestive system, or it may have a hereditary condition. It may also be suffering from a bacterial infection which could have stemmed from the bitch's birth canal, or via her licking the navel stump. Fading puppy syndrome is also exhibited by puppies with viral infections e.g. CHV (p. 222), although these are more likely to show after several day's incubation, whereas other causes may give concern immediately after birth.

Veterinary advice should be sought early on for the best possible chance of survival, but determining the cause may prove difficult, and this will inevitably have an impact on the final outcome. Fading puppy syndrome is one of the most distressing situations that a breeder will encounter.

Hind leg dew claws

The 'dew claw' is a vestigial digit (one that has lost most of its original function over the passage of time). Most dog lovers will be aware of dew claws on the front legs of dogs. They are found on the inside of the front leg close to the carpal joint, and they are fully formed joints. The dew claw does not touch the ground when the dog is standing. Therefore it may need some regular trimming, although, as some dew claws come into play when the dog is moving, this is not always necessary. Front dew claws tend to be well tucked against the leg. Many dogs use them to grip objects, such as bones or sticks. They are said to be less likely to get caught during exercise than those which are situated on the inside of the hind leg, just below the tarsal joint. Hind dew claws tend to hang loosely and therefore are prone to getting caught during exercise. For this reason some vets will agree to remove them before the puppy is four days old. However, this is a painful procedure, and is actually illegal in some countries. Many vets argue that removal is unnecessary, as few hind dew claws actually cause serious injury.

Dehydration

Puppies dehydrate rapidly, especially as a result of diarrhoea, which quickly rids the body of vital sugar and salts. The affected puppy will need to ingest correct amounts of salt and sugar in solution to allow the body to uptake the water into the cells of the body and thus rehydrate. Lack of saline in the body also causes stomach pains, so your pup may not only look listless but might also moan in discomfort. Check the puppies' hydration regularly by performing a 'pinch test' on skin at the back of the neck (or along the spine). Hydrated skin will bounce back immediately. If the pup is dehydrated, the skin will only return to normal slowly. Dehydrated puppies might look scruffy, as their coat becomes 'starey' in appearance. Puppies that are dehydrated also produce dark urine, in contrast to the pale yellow urine of a healthy pup.

Rehydration mixes can be bought in sachet form from your vet and can be administered orally in regular small doses. In the worst cases, the puppy will receive saline via a drip until the body is sufficiently rehydrated. Failure to rehydrate leads to the body going into shock. The organs close down and the puppy will surely die.

Recovery packs / Probiotics

Another life saver comes in the form of 'recovery packs' of tinned meats which your vet can supply you with. These provide a highly accessible (digestible) form of protein. After any bout of sickness and diarrhoea in a litter, this is the gentlest food you can give to your puppies until they are well enough to return to their own food. Add water and liquidise it if necessary.

After a period of sickness, especially where the puppies have finished a course of antibiotics, it is useful to give probiotics which encourage good bacteria to form in the gut. (These will unfortunately have been destroyed by antibiotics along with the bad bacteria.) Probiotics can be bought in powdered form from your vet, through pet stores or online. Probiotic cultures are also found in live natural yoghurt.

FIRST LESSONS

Touch

From the moment they are born, your puppies will begin to associate your touch with something pleasant, i.e. food! As you move them into position on their mother's teats, or as you hand rear them, the food–touch association begins. All handling should be done with a firm hold, as newborns wriggle with considerable determination and are easily dropped.

Experiences in life that result in a positive outcome build confidence in young animals and children alike. Small adrenalin rushes in new situations are nature's way of preparing the body for a flight or fight response (p. 89). If the adrenalin rush is followed rapidly with a positive outcome, then the puppy learns that the sensation of panic is nothing to fear in its own right. He therefore develops confidence in his ability to cope with new situations, and in your trustworthiness not to let harm come his way.

When a newborn is picked up and moved to his mother's teat, he learns that panic was unnecessary. Gradually you will pick him up for longer and longer periods, to check his weight, to clean his bottom or umbilical cord, and simply to increase his tolerance to time in your company. He begins to welcome your smell and touch.

He will develop confidence with being held in your arms as you carry him. He will grow to realise that you will always gently place him back onto the floor, and he has no need to try to wriggle and escape. He will need to be confident about being carried, as although carrying puppies around for no reason is ill-advisable, he will obviously need to be carried during vet visits and in public places until fully vaccinated.

Toilet training

As the puppies become increasingly mobile by three to four weeks, it is a good idea to increase the newspaper area. Puppies will choose to defecate on the paper rather than their bed. As you introduce solids, they will need a larger pen area because the puppies will need a wider area of newspaper to soil. Because they are beginning to choose the newspaper, rather than the vet bed, you will find that you can also begin to allow them access to small areas of the house. Providing you place large areas of newspaper down, they will usually choose to attempt to reach this rather than to urinate on the carpet. If you praise each achievement, you will have set a good foundation for the puppy being clean in his new home which will please your buyer enormously.

Playtime

Begin introducing toys at around four weeks. Small rubber balls, rubber rings and knotted rope toys will provide your pups with hours of entertainment. At this stage toys can get

dragged through all manner of mess, so they need to be washable!

Puppies learn a great deal about the world and about each other from their play times. Play biting sessions (p. 95) can become painful and fractious, so a variety of toys is vital to help divert attention and keep them occupied. Keep changing over the toys that you give the litter, to keep their interest high, as they will quickly become bored if left with the same toys every day.

If you watch your 'brood' you will learn much about the individual personalities at the five to eight week stage. This is crucial in helping your potential buyers choose the dog with the right attitude of mind for them and their family.

Having balls to play with encourages their desire to chase and retrieve. 'Toy motivation' is central to puppy training.

During play sessions, remember to introduce many other stimuli at the same time – leave the TV or radio on / leave a hairdryer running out of harm's way / gently bang pots around if you are playing in the kitchen, and be sure to introduce puppy to other family pets. If these situations are introduced at such a young age, they are far less likely to present a problem in later life.

All sounds within your household will prepare your puppies for the outside world, but you may also find it useful to utilise 'stimulus tapes'. These are readily available online and include sounds of thunder, fireworks, gunshot etc. If you put these close to the whelping pen and play them softly, gradually exposing the pups to increased volume over the next few weeks, it can help your pups to desensitise to a whole range of noises.

Co-ordination

Although steep stairways are to be avoided while puppy is growing, it is important that puppies get the opportunity to learn how to negotiate different floorings and obstacles. Many adult dogs have a fear of shiny floors and floorboards or lino. This can be avoided with some early exposure to different surfaces. Give them the opportunity to clamber about generally over gentle slopes and small obstacles, and their co ordination, confidence and courage will develop.

Car travel

In the weeks leading up to the puppies leaving, you might like to expose them to car travel. A short couple of trips, to the end of the road and back, ensures a good first car experience. The first car journey most pups get is when they are driven to their new home, with strange people, new smells, and a body pumped full of adrenalin. Such fear can be avoided (as can travel sickness), if only a bit of forethought took place.

TIME TO LET GO!

As the litter has developed you will have been able to keep your prospective puppy buyers up to date with developments. They will eagerly await news of the sexes and colours available, and as time progresses you will determine which pups are long- or short-coated, if you have a mixed litter. As personalities develop you will be able to help buyers find the right pup for them, and to help begin to mould the puppies' attitude to life through early socialisation and play.

Your work is nearly at a conclusion, although the support you offer after the litter leave will inevitably last a lifetime. You will hopefully be sent endless photographs and emails, and you might board your 'offspring' when the owners are on holiday! You may also find that lifelong friendships have been created.

Below is a checklist of the issues you may want to address before puppy leaves you, and items that you will be expected to have discussed with the new owner before they collect their puppy.

- Have you applied for your KC documentation? You will need to do this in plenty of time.
- Are you planning to microchip or tattoo the puppies?
- Have you discussed with the buyer any endorsements you have placed on the paperwork?
- Decide on what level of puppy insurance cover you will provide, and make necessary contacts beforehand
- Discuss with your buyers well in advance if any of the puppies has a slight defect such as an umbilical hernia
- Arrange a vet check for your litter before you let them leave for their new homes
- Order bags of complete puppy food from your supplier, to hand to each buyer
- Make up your puppy packs – Toys / Treats / Small blanket for each puppy, which you can put with the litter a few hours before the pups go

You will also need to make up a folder containing all paperwork:

KC Documentation

Five generation pedigree

Insurance voucher

Liability contract. This will state all issues pertaining to the sale of the puppy. To include issues such as return/refund and breed endorsements. What is to happen if the owner wishes to sell the pup in the future? Be clear to your buyer about where you stand on these issues, to avoid misunderstandings

Food chart: Proposed times, weights, dos and don'ts

Vaccine/microchip/tattoo certificates as appropriate

Details on puppy's worming regime to date

You might also include a 'care plan' which gives general advice about socialising, puppy classes, toilet training etc.

Contact details / date of sale / receipt for purchase price

It is good practice to call buyers the following day to check on how everything is going. You will find that some people are happy to break the tie quite early on, and others stay in close contact. If your door is always open you will no doubt receive phone calls and photos which will update you and to show what a fabulous life your pups lead. Your job will not be over just because the puppies leave. Being informed of the puppies' development over the years is just as wonderful as seeing them enter the world.

A FINAL THOUGHT

Although the character of your puppy is established genetically to some degree, don't underestimate the influence that a dedicated breeder can have through providing positive early socialisation. These experiences will help to make your puppies 'bombproof'.

Beautiful dogs can be produced by breeders with an eye for conformation. Wondrous working dogs develop their skills through the dedication of their handlers. But experiences in the first eight weeks of life – with a breeder who cares about helping their pups develop huge stability of character – can also make the difference between a good dog and a truly great one.

Breed Associated Conditions

Despite being a relatively new breed, the German Shepherd is immensely popular across the world. Such popularity does however increase the potential for incidences of health complaints, in comparison with those found in numerically smaller breeds.

The concentration on popular bloodlines at key points in the development of the breed also has its part to play, as both good and bad influences have been brought to the fore by line breeding and in-breeding practices. It has been long known that the breed has a high predisposition to certain health issues such as hip dysplasia, but the breed also suffers from a range of other disorders. Diagnostic testing for carriers of certain major conditions is certainly the way forward for the conscientious breeder, as and when they each become available.

ANAL FURUNCULOSIS (AF)

Also known as perianal fistula or perianal sinus, this condition is well known among German Shepherd breeders and owners, and it appears that the breed is the most commonly affected. AF is a painful and progressive disease of the perianal tissues, and is hallmarked by ulcerated tracts which destroy the flesh and muscles, and which are notoriously difficult to control with medication or surgery.

There are still some who believe that the tail conformation of the German Shepherd is a causal factor, but research indicates that affected dogs have an underlying auto-immune disease, often in combination with inflammatory bowel disease, which causes the immune system to mount an uncontrolled inflammatory reaction to the normal bacterial flora of the bowel. In the healthy dog, skin is highly resistant to colonisation by bacteria. However, where skin becomes inflamed in a dog with decreased resistance, there is increased skin permeability which gives opportunist bacteria a chance to take hold. The presence of deep pyoderma found in cases of AF is often associated with staphylococcal infection.

Sufferers will lick and often gnaw at the affected area, causing further localised irritation. Defecation is often made very uncomfortable, and in worst cases impossible. Affected dogs will find it increasingly painful to sit down.

Previously, approaches to treatment have included: surgery to remove the affected tissue; antibiotic and steroid treatments; and freezing of the affected areas (cryosurgery). Where surgery is performed, the anal glands are often removed because of their involvement in the disease process.

More recent developments include the usage of the immune suppressant cyclosporine. Prescribed in high initial doses followed by a prolonged period at a lower dosage, this has produced good results in many patients, although it is pertinent to note that this is an extremely expensive drug. Cyclosporine has been used in combination with ketoconazole which is more economical than cyclosporine alone, but requires ongoing monitoring of liver function and may therefore not be as economical as would first appear. As AF is frequently accompanied by bowel disease, dietary management is very important.

CANINE MYASTHENIA GRAVIS (CMG)

Literally translated as 'grave muscle weakness', canine myasthenia gravis is a neuromuscular disorder. The gap between nerve and muscle is bridged by a chemical messenger known as acetylcholine. This messenger has to attach to a 'receptor' on the muscle, in order for nerve signals to be relayed effectively.

There are two forms of the disease, namely congenital and acquired. *Congenital* CMG may well be hereditary, and the affected dog is born with an absence of receptors. There is no treatment for this form of the condition. *Acquired* CMG is an immune-mediated disease. Antibodies attack acetylcholine receptor sites on the muscle. This results in reduced numbers of nerve signals reaching the muscles, causing muscle weakness. Acquired CMG is more prevalent in the German Shepherd than the congenital form.

CMG is characterised by fluctuating levels of muscle weakness, and this is particularly noticeable at times of exercise. Symptoms may include weakness in all four, or just the hind, legs, but may also affect the muscles of the neck and throat. Your dog's bark may alter in tone, as the vocal cords can be affected. He may find it difficult to hold his head up, have difficulty swallowing and breathing.

Blood tests would be undertaken in order to determine the presence of antibodies directed towards the receptors. This is known as an anti-AChR antibody titre. Also a Tensilon test may be performed. This short acting antidote is injected into the vein. Tensilon prolongs muscle stimulation and affected animals show a dramatic but brief improvement following administration of the drug.

Treatments are based on the administration of a longer acting antidote which increases the transfer of messages from nerve to muscle. Medications include pyridostigmine bromide – given orally – and neostigmine, which is injectable. Immunosuppressant drugs are given should there also be a need to suppress the immune system to stop it attacking the receptors. It is common for sufferers of CMG to also exhibit megaoesophagus, and where aspiration pneumonia is also evident this will need to be treated before any immunosuppressant treatment is prescribed. CMG can often be treated with good success especially if diagnosed early. It can also go into spontaneous remission.

Some patients have CMG associated with thymoma, which is a benign mass in the chest. Removal of the mass will cause regression of the disease.

CHRONIC DEGENERATIVE RADICULOMYELOPATHY (CDRM / DM)

This condition is characterised by increasing weakness in the hindquarters, resulting in dragging of back toes, 'plaiting' of the hind legs and 'swaying', especially when turning around. Distress may be clearly evident in the dog, as he struggles to comprehend why his body does not respond correctly. In the early stages, CDRM is frequently misdiagnosed by owners as the onset of hip dysplasia, but the symptoms differ greatly as the respective illnesses progress.

CDRM is not a painful condition in its own right, as it is a disorder of the nervous system which leads to paralysis – the degeneration in the white matter of the spinal cord and dorsal nerve roots which causes messages from the brain to be interrupted. However, trauma may be also caused to the hips as a secondary factor, perhaps due to the affected dog falling badly, or due to arthritis developing alongside muscle wastage. This would inevitably cause pain and contribute to the management difficulties of this condition.

Early signs include scuffing of the dorsal surface of the toes and wearing down of the nails on the hind feet. Your vet may test your dog by performing a neurological examination including inverting the dog's back feet, or moving the legs away from the midline. Often the dog will simply be unaware that the foot is not where it should be and thus will not respond to correct this and realign his limbs. The dog is likely to become increasingly unable to negotiate quick turns and changes in direction.

Surgery is not indicated or effective. (It should be noted that the spinal cord will continue to degenerate and therefore the condition is likely to show itself again.) In terms of daily management, it has been found that the more positive and unflustered you can be in dealing with occasional wobbles or minor tumbles, the better your dog will cope mentally. If you are visibly distressed and resort to cosseting the dog, his sense of unease will develop. This positive approach is widely agreed on by vets and behaviourists. This is not meant to diminish the serious nature of the complaint in any way, and at a certain point the physical issues will become too difficult for the dog to cope with, regardless of emotional support and encouragement from the owner. At this stage, painful but inevitable decisions will have to be made.

In the meanwhile, there are a range of options to consider, which may make daily living with your CDRM sufferer a great deal more bearable for you both. Ramps, slings and carts are widely used for differing stages of the condition. In particular, the use of wheeled carts to support the affected dog's back end and give mobility once more has a large following of happy customers. It is not suitable for all dogs though, and expert advice is best sought before heading down this route. A DNA test is available for screening breeding stock.

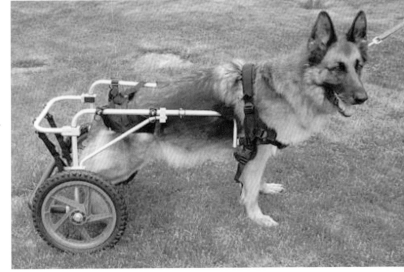

Canine wheelchairs can give CDRM sufferers a new lease of life

247

CRUCIATE LIGAMENT RUPTURE

There are many different ligaments within the stifle (knee) joint. Two of these are the cruciate ligaments, which run inside the knee joint and cross over each other. They lend stability and prevent abnormal movements between the tibia and femur. Known as the cranial (anterior) ligament and the caudal (posterior) ligament, it is the former which is more likely to become damaged. When a rupture occurs, the joint becomes unstable and painful, and the dog will be unable to use the leg correctly. In the most severe cases the leg cannot bear weight even though the dog may still place his toes to the ground, and the joint may be swollen.

Degenerative joint disease (DJD) and obesity usually cause a partial rupture of the cranial cruciate ligament, whereas trauma (such as stumbling or twisting on uneven ground) usually causes a complete rupture. Damage to the medial meniscus often accompanies

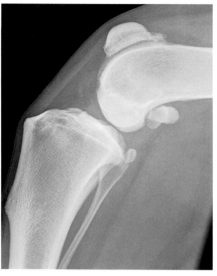

There is an increase of fluid in the joint and arthritic new bone, involving particularly the femur and patella

cruciate ligament rupture. (This is a disc of cartilage which allows the tibia and femur to move smoothly relative to each other.)

Ligament rupture may be partial or total and leads to varying degrees of joint instability. Diagnosis is usually made under anaesthetic and the area is palpated to examine the movement between tibia and femur. Abnormal laxity in the joint is termed a 'positive drawer sign' or cranial tibial thrust. Ligament tears do not show up on radiography, however it is likely that your vet would still perform a radiograph to look for signs of secondary arthritic changes within the joint, which frequently accompany ligament rupture. The cruciate and meniscus cannot self-repair and therefore surgery is usually required.

Correct nutrition will help guard against DJD

CRYPTORCHIDISM

This is a sex-limited condition in that it only occurs in males. Cryptorchidism is the failure of one or both testicles to descend into the scrotum. Unilateral cryptorchidism refers to the situation where one testicle descends normally. The second one fails to do so, but is present in the inguinal canal or in the abdomen. (This is not to be confused with 'monorchidism' where only one testicle actually develops.) Bilateral cryptorchids have both testicles unde-scended, but they are present within the abdomen.

Retained testicles can cause complications, most notably an increased risk of develop-ing testicular cancers, such as Sertoli cell tumours and seminomas, and testicular torsion (a painful condition where the testicle rotates and constricts vital blood supply to the testicle).

Cryptorchidism is a genetic trait and affected dogs should not be bred from. Given the increased risk of cancer or testicular torsion, your vet will invariably suggest that the dog should be neutered.

ELBOW DYSPLASIA

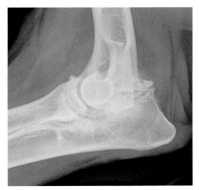

Elbow dysplasia (ED) is a syndrome in which one or more conditions cause the abnormal development of the elbow joint. All are due to disturbed ossification of cartilage as the skeleton develops (osteochondrosis). This includes osteo-chondrosis of the humeral condyle, fragmented medial coronoid process and ununited anconeal process. The cartilage layer between the bones in the joint and surround-ing small ossification centres becomes weak and may fragment. ED occurs in growing dogs, usually between five and seven months of age as this is a period of high growth velocity. Males are affected more often than females. Affected dogs are likely to become lame and are predisposed toward early development of arthritis.

There is a large, triangular bone fragment at the back of the elbow joint, which has separated from the rest of the ulna

When osteochondrosis of the humeral condyle is present, the change of articular cartilage into bone during the development of the joint fails to occur or is delayed. The affected cartilage may form a flap, or break off and calcify; at this stage the condition is known as osteochondritis dessicans (OCD). The fragment floats in the joint causing pain and inflammation. The piece of broken cartilage is termed a 'joint mouse' and is only visible on a radiograph if it has calcified. The diagnosis is usually made by detecting irregularity of the bone surface or secondary arthritis.

Fragmented medial coronoid process is another of the causes of elbow dysplasia. It occurs when a small portion of the coronoid process of the ulna (at the front of the elbow joint) fractures and breaks away, contributing to pain, lameness and joint instability. This is less easily diagnosed as it may not show up on radiography, but again secondary arthritis is typical.

Ununited anconeal process is a condition which arises when the anconeal process (a bony protrusion on the ulna at the back of the elbow) fails to unite with the main part of the ulna. During the puppy's normal development, the anconeal process calcifies until total fusion with the ulna takes place at about 24 weeks of age. If it fails to fuse, it remains as a separate fragment and is termed an ununited anconeal process. As the elbow is a hinge, the ununited anconeal process makes the joint unstable. This also leads to inflammation, arthritis and lameness.

Diagnosis can be made from radiographing the area, when a distinct gap in the bone is seen. Surgery can be performed to fix the anconeal process to the ulna, or more commonly to remove the fragment of bone. Affected dogs should not be bred from as it is likely that this is an inherited disorder. Ununited anconeal process is most commonly seen in the German Shepherd Dog, Basset Hound and Great Dane.

As for hip dysplasia, the British Veterinary Association (BVA), in conjunction with the Kennel Club, runs a radiographic screening scheme for elbow dysplasia. Similar schemes include those offered by the SV, the FCI and OFA (Orthopedic Foundation for Animals).

EPILEPSY

Epilepsy is a brain disorder whose presence is indicated by seizure or 'fit'. Seizures refer to involuntary muscle contractions caused by an electrical storm in the brain. Epilepsy has a wide spectrum of root causes, for example encephalitis, brain tumour, hydrocephalus, brain trauma or poisoning. Where the cause is identifiable, this is termed secondary epilepsy. Where the cause cannot be determined, this is known as idiopathic or primary epilepsy. Many idiopathic epileptics have inherited epilepsy. Inheritance is thought to be polygenic and of a threshold nature, with certain families being clearly implicated. MRI scans and spinal taps are usually required to rule out underlying disease, and if these tests are negative a presumed diagnosis of idiopathic epilepsy is made.

Seizures due to idiopathic epilepsy typically occur first when the dog is between 6 months and 5 years of age. If the cause is a brain tumour the dog is *usually* middle-aged or older when the first seizure occurs. Classified as 'focal' or 'generalised', the seizures range in severity from mild focal muscle twitching to highly disturbing episodes incorporating salivation, foaming at the mouth, rapid eye movement, loss of sensory perception, spasmodic movements, urination and defaecation. Seizures can occur independently or as 'status epilepticus', where the affected dog does not have the opportunity to recover from the last seizure before the next occurs. 'Cluster seizures' are when more than one seizure occurs within 24 hours but the dog recovers completely in between.

Management of the affected dog during a mild seizure would incorporate ensuring that the dog is kept as safe as is possible, and that the owner remains calm and quietly supportive while the fit lasts. Fits are invariably very distressing to witness, and the dog may be aware of some of what is happening, but many dogs appear to have no after effects from a mild episode. Frequently the owner is more troubled than the patient. In more serious cases, the dog may need the administration of rectal diazepam and may exhibit considerable distress following such episodes. Some dogs may bite when in the throes of a seizure, but usually this is a reflex bite rather than aggression; however it is prudent to be mindful of this potential.

Treatment for the dog would depend on the type of epilepsy diagnosed by your vet, and may include anti-convulsant medications such as phenobarbitone and potassium bromide.

EXOCRINE PANCREATIC INSUFFICIENCY (EPI)

The pancreas is associated with hormone production and with the production of various enzymes involved with digestion, especially digestion of fats. Therefore, dogs with EPI have poor pancreatic digestive function, which leads to poorly digested food, especially fat. They might also be slightly more susceptible to diabetes mellitus. EPI is common in the breed, but with developments in terms of accurate diagnostic testing it has become increasingly possible to identify affected dogs robustly such that breeders can eliminate dogs with EPI from their breeding programmes.

Hallmarks of EPI include poor digestion (rancid, voluminous faeces and partially digested food in the faeces), grey-coloured faeces, vomiting and ravenous appetite combined with weight loss since the dogs do not fully absorb the food they are eating. Diagnosis is made through blood testing. Management of this condition combines a low fat diet and pancreatic enzyme preparations (powders, capsules) given to effect. In some cases a diet consisting partially of sheep, pig or ox pancreas might help to compensate. Antibiotics might be beneficial if SIBO is also present (see below).

GASTRIC DILATATION-VOLVULUS, GDV (GASTRIC TORSION)

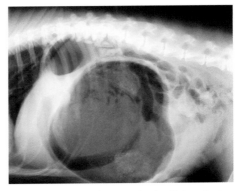

The stomach is massively distended with gas and food, and has twisted so that it lies in an abnormal position

Commonly referred to as 'bloat', this is an extremely serious and frightening condition which should always be treated as a genuine surgical emergency. It can be fatal in a very short period of time. Characterised by the sudden and dramatic accumulation of stomach gases which cause twisting of the stomach, the affected dog will experience great pain and distress. The dog will usually make unsuccessful attempts to vomit and will bring up pools of froth, appearing restless and agitated. He may exhibit weakness and difficulty breathing, and his abdomen will appear distended. It is possible that your dog will shiver spasmodically in pain. He may groan or nibble frantically at his sides. As the gases increase his stomach will distend markedly (dilatation).

Emergency veterinary assistance should be sought, as without treatment the stomach usually will twist (volvulus or torsion). If a twist occurs, blood flow will be restricted to the stomach and spleen, and the dog will certainly die of toxic shock if surgery is not performed immediately. In some instances it is necessary to remove areas of stomach and also the spleen if they have become damaged. Bloat frequently reoccurs, and it is usual that the surgeon would also perform a gastropexy. This will fix the stomach wall to the body wall to prevent twisting in the future.

There are a number of reasons why bloat occurs. These include breed and anatomical predisposition, since large breed dogs and deep-chested breeds (such as the GSD) seem to be predisposed to GDV. Other reasons include over-feeding or scavenging, food being bolted, gulping air whilst drinking ('aerophagia'), and exercising immediately following a meal. Existing inflammatory bowel disease may also be a factor.

It is to be highly advised that GSD owners adopt a preventative routine around feed and exercise. Dogs should not be vigorously exercised within two hours of feeding. Water should be given at room temperature, especially on hot days when dogs may gulp cold water and inhale air at the same time. If your dog is a 'competitive feeder', it is wise to feed other dogs separately to diminish the chances of him bolting his food. Daily rations should be separated into two smaller meals rather than giving one large meal per day.

HAEMOPHILIA A

Haemophilia A is a disorder of the blood, and the condition in the dog is similar to that seen in humans. The disease leads to poor blood clotting. Blood clotting arises as the result of a 'cascade' or chain reaction involving proteins called clotting factors, which are very finely balanced such that blood is neither too thick nor too thin. These clotting factors are numbered using Roman numerals. Haemophilia A is a deficiency in Factor VIII. Depending on the amount of Factor VIII protein present in the blood, the result will range from almost normal to very poor clotting ability with severe spontaneous haemorrhaging.

Prolonged bleeding and also bruising are symptomatic of the disease, as is lameness caused by bleeding into joints and muscles. Something as simple as a bump or knock can lead to a potentially significant haemorrhage, or even the death of the animal.

Haemophilia A is caused by a genetic mutation on the X chromosome, of which females have two and males have one. This means that males can only have either a functioning gene or a faulty gene. Females with a single faulty gene might have normal clotting ability if the second copy of the gene is normal, and will thus be a carrier. Females with two faulty copies of the gene are rare as this requires an affected sire to be mated to a carrier dam. Conscientious breeders eliminate affected sires from their breeding colonies.

Puppies can be screened from an early age. Male puppies have either normal or abnormal Factor VIII levels and are therefore easily identified. This is not the case for carrier bitch puppies, in which only one of the two genes is mutated. It would be optimal to check all breeding stock to prevent as much transmission to future generations as possible. As a minimum, stud dogs should be tested for the condition. The result is easy to interpret and as they might sire many more litters than a breeding bitch could produce, the impact of failing to characterise their Factor VIII status might be greater. Due to schemes across the world, this condition is seen less frequently than in the past, but continued testing by breeders is vital if this improvement is to be maintained.

HIP DYSPLASIA

The word dysplasia stems from the Greek words *dys* (meaning 'disordered' or 'abnormal') and *plassein* (meaning 'to form'). Literally translated, therefore, it means 'abnormal formation'. The term canine hip dysplasia (CHD) refers to a developmental disease which causes the hip joints in affected dogs to grow abnormally. It is a disease which predominantly affects large breed dogs, although all breeds are susceptible, and the German Shepherd is particularly associated with the condition. It is accepted that CHD is an inherited disease caused by multiple genes, with many environmental factors such as age, diet, weight and breed influencing the expression of arthritis.

The hip joint is comprised of the femoral head (the ball located at the top end of the femur or thigh bone) and the acetabulum (the socket within the pelvis). Also present within – and surrounding – the joint are ligaments, muscles, fibrous joint capsule and synovial fluid. The femoral head and acetabulum are coated with smooth cartilage, called articular hyaline cartilage. In a healthy joint, this cartilage will enable the bones to pass over the surface of one another without friction, and the ball will fit snugly into the socket. Hip dysplasia occurs when there is inadequate stability to hold the ball within the socket.

Varying degrees of joint laxity (looseness of the joint) and subluxation (partial dislocation which is a manifestation of joint laxity) cause abnormal forces within the joint. The surface of smooth cartilage gradually becomes eroded. In the most severe cases this erosion allows bone to bone contact. This results in damage and in the formation of uneven areas of new bone growth around the joint, particularly on the acetabulum and femoral neck. The affected dog will experience pain and exhibit lameness as degenerative joint disease progresses. Complete luxation (dislocation) may occur in the most severe cases.

Abnormality can occur for a number of reasons. The inheritance of genetic make-up which leaves the puppy predisposed to developing the condition is of serious consideration to caring breeders. Inheritance is not yet fully understood at this moment in time, as it involves multiple genes, and the expression of arthritis is strongly influenced by the environment.

Excessive or inappropriate exercise may cause arthritis to form earlier than it might have done. Nutrition may be inadequate or inappropriate, with excessive weight gain being a contributing factor. The imbalance of calcium and phosphorous intake during development is cited as a causal factor. Inadequate protein, which subsequently affects production of muscle, is another nutritional factor.

Symptoms vary enormously. Irrespective of the radiographic severity of the condition, one dog may move well, whereas another may show acute signs of discomfort and lameness. Some of the indicators of CHD include early morning stiffness, a swaying hind gait, lameness after exercise, showing difficulty in climbing or descending stairs and 'bunny hopping'.

However these may also be symptomatic of other conditions and therefore practical examination by a vet and radiography are the only way to fully diagnose the condition.

However, radiographs are not only a simple diagnostic tool for dogs that present with clinical signs of CHD. Detailed analysis of radiographs has been undertaken for decades for various schemes available worldwide, which help breeders make assessments of their dogs. Radiographs are evaluated and graded by many different schemes, enabling the conscientious breeder to be well informed regarding the quality of their stock. This information has proven invaluable over the past few decades to breeders and researchers alike, in the tireless battle against this condition.

Radiographic schemes include the BVA/KC scheme, OFA, and the 'a' stamp certification programme offered by the SV. These all rely on a similar approach to

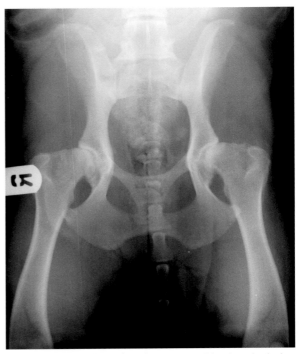

Hip extended view showing severe hip dysplasia in a one-year-old dog.

grading the radiograph, which is based on assessment of arthritis and subluxation of the joints on the 'extended hip view'. The dog is radiographed on his back with the hind legs extended backwards, and this is usually done under sedation or general anaesthesia.

The BVA/KC programme provides a scoring system, with a score being allocated from 0– 53 for each hip. The poorest score is 53:53 which gives a total score of 106. It is clear that such a scheme might reap more comprehensive results were it mandatory for all radiographs to be submitted, and for a level to be set over which breeding cannot take place. It has been offered in the UK since 1965, but half a century later it is still not compulsory for breeding stock to be scored. Even if the breeder is a member of the Kennel Club's 'assured breeder' scheme they can still breed from their dog providing it has been scored – regardless of the result. Submission of radiographs is not compulsory under the BVA/KC scheme. If it is evident from the radiograph that the score will be poor, some breeders fail to submit it to the BVA for scoring and in some instances decide to breed from the dog regardless. The breed mean score (BMS), which is adjusted yearly to show the average score from submitted radiographs, becomes unrepresentative and the gene pool of dogs carrying CHD continues to be affected.

Under the OFA method (established in 1966 in North America), radiographs are graded on a 7-point scale from excellent to severe, but dogs who receive a poor grade (mild, moderate or severe) are not eligible for OFA certification. OFA radiographs are reviewed by a board consisting of three certified radiologists and the average grade is given to the dog. Dogs can only be graded once they reach 2 years of age, however an early screening programme gives breeders an indication of the quality of the hips should they wish to have the dog examined before two years of age. This is known as a preliminary grade. Submission of radiographs for grading is not compulsory.

In Germany, any dog that is radiographed can only be bred from if they receive an 'a' stamp rating: 'Normal', 'fast normal and 'noch zugelassen' are the permissable ratings. If the dog is showing signs of dysplasia recommendation for breeding is withheld. Submission of all radiographs for scoring is compulsory.

The grading of the 'extended hip view' evaluates the construction of the hip joint and any osteoarthritis present at the time of radiography. This view does not give any formal prediction as to the likelihood of the dog developing osteoarthritis in the future. The radiograph taken for the purpose of grading under these schemes is typically done once in a lifetime only.

Although other schemes have paved the way forward over the past few decades, the University of Pennsylvania Hip Improvement Programme (PennHIP) developed by Dr Gail Smith of the University of Pennsylvania, now provides breeders with a wider range of information. The PennHIP programme requires that three individual radiographs are taken under heavy sedation or general anaesthetic, namely the extended hip view, the compression view and the distraction view. The first evaluates the presence of subluxation and osteoarthritis, and the second and third are utilized in a measurement of 'passive hip laxity' which has been shown through multiple scientific studies to be a primary risk factor for the development of hip osteoarthritis. This measurement is called the distraction index (DI) and ranges from 0–1. The closer the DI to 0 the tighter is the hip joint.

 NB 'Active hip laxity' (the amount of laxity when the dog is weight bearing) is not measurable.

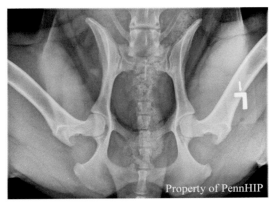

Compression view

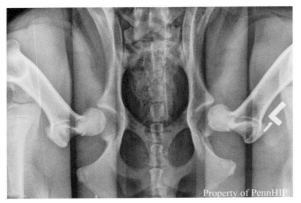

Distraction view

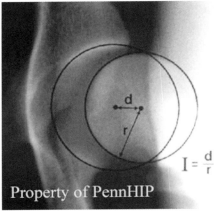

$$I = \frac{d}{r}$$

Calculation

The PennHIP programme differs in many other respects to the various schemes available. It is the only system which measures laxity in the joint. If performed at 16 weeks of age, the information gathered can be correlated with eventual development of arthritis. The BVA/KC and 'a' stamp schemes are performed from one year of age onwards, and two years of age for OFA. Unlike all other programmes, PennHIP can be repeated numerous times. It is not based on a pass or fail system. The scheme not only measures laxity, but results are also given as a 'percentile', showing the animal's DI compared to other members of the same breed.

All PennHIP radiographs have to be taken by a PennHIP qualified radiographer. This too differs from the other schemes, as historically any vet is permitted to take the radiographs for other schemes, and there remains controversy over the quality of extended hip radiographs. (Studies also indicate that the extended hip view drives the head of the femur into the socket, thereby giving a false impression of the tightness of the hip joint.) Until recently, the method of obtaining PennHIP radiographs contravened UK radiation health and safety laws. It is now possible to obtain PennHIP radiographs in the UK as a 'hands-free' technique has been developed. It may be that breeders continue to choose the older methods for some years to come, as the scheme (like all others before it) has its critics as well as firm advocates.

Federation Cynologique Internationale FCI		USA OFA	Germany	Western Australia	NSW and Ontario	U.K. (old)	BVA/KC (new)	NL	S	CH
A	No signs of Hip Dysplasia	Excellent	Normal (a)	A	Normal or	Pass Certificate	0.0 to 4 *Maxim, 3 on one hip*	1	Utmärkt	Frei
		Good		B	Within Normal	Borderline Breeder's Letter	5 to 8 *Maxim, 5 on one hip*	2	U.A.	
B	Transitional Case (Tc)	Fair	Fast Normal (a)		Abnormal or Dysplastic	FAILED	Anything over 8 is the old FAILED	Tc		
		Borderline		C		* Dysplastic *one* hip				
C	Mild	Mild	Leishte Hüftgelenk Dysplastic (a)	D			Each hip rated separately Worst score per hip = 53	Licht Positief (3)	I	I
D	Moderate	Moderate	Mittlere Hüftgelenk Dyspläsie	E			Worst total = 106	Positief (3 1/2)	II	II
E	Severe	Severe	Schwere Hüftgelenk Dyspläsie	F				Postief Optima Forma (5)	III	III
									IV	IV

Copyright FCI

As CHD is degenerative, it will worsen as the affected dog gets older. There is no 'cure' for CHD, but there are a wide range of measures and treatments available which will lessen the pain and inflammation caused by the condition.

It is imperative that the dog be kept at a correct weight for his frame. Affected dogs who are overweight suffer dreadfully, as the extra weight puts further load on already painful joints and hastens the progression of arthritis. Exercise is to be highly recommended. It will need to be steady, gentle and consistent, and must take into account the degree of discomfort already being experienced by the dog. Swimming is a great way of exercising a dog with CHD as it is obviously not weight bearing, and will encourage maintenance of muscle tone.

Supplements may help an affected dog. Glucosamine and chondroitin in particular are felt by many to be beneficial for the CHD patient. They do not cure CHD but they help heal cartilage and lessen discomfort – glucosamine is essential as a building block for cartilage synthesis, and chondroitin lowers the levels of destructive enzymes which accelerate cartilage destruction.

In terms of medication, non-steroidal anti-inflammatory drugs (NSAIDs) are typically prescribed by the vet for patients with CHD.

If surgery proves to be the only way forward, there are various surgical options. Decisions will be made according to the severity of the condition and the developmental stage of the dog or puppy.

MEGAOESOPHAGUS

This literally means dilation of the oesophagus (gullet). The muscles in the oesophagus fail for a variety of reasons, and as a result food and water cannot move by peristaltic contraction through to the stomach. The dog or puppy will regurgitate liquid, food and saliva. Extreme hunger and malnutrition are suffered as a result. There are two distinct forms of the condition:

Congenital megaoesophagus

This form of the condition is generally thought to be due to developmental immaturity in innervation. It is usually identified when the puppies begin to wean on to solids. An affected newborn pup will have exhibited early symptoms such as blowing bubbles of milk through its nose, regurgitating, or exhibiting respiratory difficulties. If the bitch is very attentive and cleans the pup as it regurgitates the breeder may simply be unaware at this stage. Once the litter begins to wean on to solids, the affected pup increasingly finds it difficult to feed, and rapidly loses condition in comparison with littermates. It may not be spotted for a while as littermates will readily eat regurgitated foods and the breeder

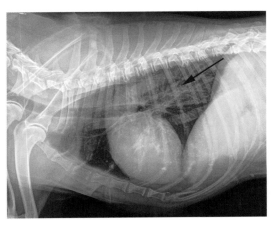

Megaoesophagus
The oesophegus is markedly dilated and air-filled. Patchy opacity (whiteness) superimposed over the heart is due to secondary aspiration pneumonia

may be left in the dark until things have progressed further. Weighing puppies regularly and therefore being aware of weight discrepancies between the littermates, helps prevent this situation. Where the cause is deemed to be idiopathic, there is no 'cure' but it is possible that the condition may improve as the puppy matures.

Another cause of congenital megaoesophagus in the puppy is due to a condition called vascular ring anomaly, the most common type of which is a persistent right aortic arch (PRAA). This is a developmental abnormality which results in the oesophagus becoming restricted and dilated by the abnormal development of the great blood vessels over the heart base. Vascular bundles called the aortic arches usually disappear as a foetus develops, but if they do not, the oesophagus can become trapped between the arch and the heart. The food passage to the stomach will be restricted. Surgery should be performed early, to release a constricting band of tissue which may prevent permanent damage. Prognosis is very much determined by the severity of the oesophageal dilation, and the length of time during which the oesophagus has been enlarged.

Acquired megaoesophagus

Found in the adult dog, this form of the condition may be idiopathic and therefore untreatable. It may also be secondary with factors such as CMG, Addisons disease, or hypothyroidism implicated in some cases. As with the congenital form, symptoms include regurgitation of liquids and solids, and hunger with acute weight loss. Persistent and repeated gurgling in throat and lungs, associated with aspiration of food and liquids may also be present.

If you are clear about the symptoms this will inevitably help veterinary diagnosis. Many people do not realise that the affected dog is regurgitating rather than vomiting. This is a distinctly different process as one is active and expels food which has already reached the stomach, and the other is passive and involuntary, ridding the throat and gullet of undigested foodstuff and saliva which has not reached the stomach. Vomiting involves the rhythmical contraction of abdominal muscles. These actively eject the contents of the stomach. When a dog has megaoesophagus, food cannot pass food from the pharynx (throat) and into the stomach. Food and saliva therefore build up along the gullet, and eventually this is regurgitated in 'balls or sausages' of soft food. The dog will invariably seem to cough up the food.

The presence of megaoesophagus can be identified with X-ray/contrast radiography. Diagnosis of the causes of acquired secondary megaoesophagus may be complex, consisting of blood tests, urinalysis, and an anti-AChR antibody titre to determine if the cause is secondary to another condition such as CMG (see above). Prognosis varies greatly. However, careful management can improve the quality of daily life in many cases. Postural feeding by placing food and water bowls on raised surfaces may be helpful in some cases. The dog will need total calm after a meal and will need to be held with the forequarters elevated for some time after the feed to promote the passage of food to the stomach. There are slings and chairs available for this purpose and some have proven to be effective. The dog will need more frequent, smaller meals and possibly will need these liquidised to some extent. These meals will need to be of high nutritional value.

Secondary complications generally include malnutrition (as essential nutrients do not reach the stomach), and aspiration pneumonia. Aspiration pneumonia is common as the protective laryngeal reflexes (which usually close whilst swallowing takes place), fail to close effectively, and therefore saliva, fluids and small food particles can be inhaled directly into the lungs.

PANOSTEITIS ('PANO')

Literally meaning 'inflammation of all bones', panosteitis is an idiopathic painful bone disease found in young dogs, typically aged 6–18 months. It affects large and giant breeds, and is well documented in the German Shepherd. Characterised by intense and sudden lameness, not accountable for through trauma, it can also be accompanied by fever, tonsillitis and elevated white blood cell counts. It is thought generally to have a genetic component, but may also have a nutritional basis, or even a viral causal factor. Other possible factors are auto-immune problems, and the influence of canine distemper vaccine.

An affected dog exhibits lameness which shifts from leg to leg, and he may appear depressed and off his food. Your vet will discuss all symptoms with you, and will perform deep palpation of the long bones on the affected limb which will give rise to discomfort on direct bone pressure. He will want to determine if other issues are involved, as panosteitis can occur in isolation or in conjunction with other juvenile orthopaedic diseases. X-ray results will show subtle and localised changes in bone density in the centre of the bones.

Periods of the most intense pain typically last for 2–5 months and many dogs recover spontaneously. Non-steroidal anti-inflammatory drugs (NSAIDs) and painkillers are typically prescribed although it is important to note that these mask the condition rather than cure it.

The condition is self limiting and therefore continued lameness in the adult dog is of a very low incidence.

PITUITARY DWARFISM

Although dwarfism can be seen in other breeds, it is most commonly the result of deliberate, selective breeding. Dwarfism of the long bones is the result of selective breeding which produces shorter and shorter legs whilst keeping other features normal (e.g. the Basset Hound). This is known as disproportionate dwarfism or chondrodystrophy. Selective breeding in order to produce whole generations of 'proportional' miniatures results in another example of dwarfism (e.g. the Miniature Pinscher).

Neither of the above should be confused with pituitary dwarfism where miniature examples of the breed are produced by dogs of normal size and proportion. This is a condition seen most commonly in the German Shepherd but which exists in other breeds such as the Weimaraner, Karelian Bear Dog and Spitz breeds. The word 'pituitary' relates to the pituitary gland in the brain (hypophysis), which regulates certain hormones including growth hormone. Pituitary dwarfism is an inherited abnormality, which affects the function of the pituitary gland. The gene can be carried by successive generations, and remains unexpressed until one carrier is mated to another. If a pup only inherits one of the possible two abnormal genes, he will become a carrier, and will be physically normal. If he inherits an abnormal gene from each of his parents he will develop pituitary dwarfism.

A fully grown pituitary dwarf may only reach the size of a three month old puppy. Many sufferers have a persistence of a soft puppy coat, dry skin conditions and areas of alopecia. Where hair loss is suffered it can vary in its intensity and lead to a 'Chinese crested' appearance. Many dwarfs are fox-like, with wide set ears and a more pointed nose. It is likely that some affected foetuses die in the uterus, or suffer from fading puppy syndrome. Those which do survive may not only suffer from the physical defects mentioned, but may also suffer renal failure, underactive thyroid, cryptorchidism and light sensitivity.

Although the physical traits may appear conclusive, full diagnosis is made from blood tests which reveal hormone deficiencies attributable to a defective pituitary function. There is no cure for pituitary dwarfism. Treatment with porcine growth hormone is expensive and produces varying results in terms of controlling complications arising from the condition. The dog will still retain his short stature.

Most dwarfs are not long lived, but if they are lucky enough to be with an owner who will provide them with hormone treatments, they can enjoy happy and active lives, although the long-term prognosis is guarded. A DNA test is available for screening breeding stock.

PYODERMA

The pyoderma is a painful skin complaint, characterised by acute inflammation of the affected site, with wet, raw and oozing areas causing great discomfort. The affected sites can spread at a fierce pace. Pyodermas are classified according to the depth of the infection (surface, superficial or deep), and are likely to be secondary to other issues such as fleas, allergies, skin trauma or hormonal imbalances. Affected dogs may well possess a genetic predisposition to immune deficiencies which allow the development of infection by the bacteria. *Staphylococcus*, *E coli* and *Proteus* species are typical causal factors.

Treatment is likely to involve a prolonged course of antibiotics, and sensitive nursing of the affected area. Medicated shampoos and a possible change of diet may complement antibiotic therapy. However, pyodermas can be frustrating to treat as they are often non-responsive to medication and nursing, and frequently relapse. Determining the underlying cause is crucial to successful treatment. So too are extended periods of antibiotic therapy after the lesion appears to be resolved. Care is needed throughout treatment, to prevent the dog from self-inflicting trauma at the affected area.

SMALL INTESTINAL BACTERIAL OVERGROWTH (SIBO)

This disorder is caused by the excessive multiplication of bacteria in the small intestine, and usually manifests as persistent diarrhoea with loss of weight and body condition. The bacteria compete with the dog for nutrients, and can cause irritability of the small intestine. Appetite is often severely reduced and irritation of the large bowel may also be present. There is usually a build-up of excessive gases from inappropriate bacterial fermentation.

In affected dogs, the gut flora changes to predominantly anaerobic bacteria. In the German Shepherd, SIBO is thought to be related to immune defence issues, notably a deficiency in gut surface immunoglobulin A.

Blood, breath hydrogen and faecal testing can be suggestive of SIBO. Other factors such as internal parasites, obstruction and EPI should be ruled out through less invasive testing at an earlier stage in the investigation. Duodenal juice cultures, sampled by endoscopy, can be the ultimate test following a series of less invasive tests and dietary trials.

Long courses of antibiotics such as oxytetracycline or metronidozole might be recommended by your vet. A highly digestible diet will also be beneficial.

Part Seven
The Legacy

• Tributes to a Noble Breed •

'Pride'

Tributes to a Noble Breed

At the end of this journey, I hope that I can be forgiven for indulging in a little tribute. The German Shepherd clearly inspires us to care for him in a deep and committed way, but it is not always an easy task as his needs can be complex. So what drives our devotion? What are the qualities we see in him, and what is it that we feel he offers us during his time by our side? Here is a small range of stories which provide illustrations to the virtues of this unique breed. There are undoubtedly thousands of stories such as these, because the German Shepherd has so very much to offer.

DILLIGENCE

'Pride' is a working police dog with West Midlands' police force. He was bred by them as part of their internal breeding programme. In March 2009, Pride and his handler PC Adrian Sheargold were called to participate in the search for an 18-year-old-girl who had gone missing. Her disappearance was totally out of character and she was classified as a high risk missing person. A large music factory was the last place that the girl had been seen, and was searched extensively by officers to no avail. Although there was no evidence to suggest that the missing girl was at this location, an intuitive response by an officer led to Pride and PC Sheargold subsequently being called to search the premises further. At the time both the officer and dog were only six months out of training, and their relationship was still very much at a formative stage.

During a detailed and extensive search, Pride indicated in an unusual manner a number of times, and eventually located a hidden compartment in a crawl space beneath the building. The compartment was behind a wall panel, not visible to the naked eye. Pride repeatedly touched the panel with his nose, and he also scratched and barked at the wall to alert his handler. His instincts were correct. The missing girl had been hidden by her captor in a tiny space behind the panel, handcuffed, gagged and terrified, for 48 hours. She had not been given any water or food, throughout her horrendous ordeal. Pride's earlier indications revealed clothing and a mobile phone on closer inspection, hidden in a roof space. Further investigation revealed the presence of a ransom note and a coffin within the building.

It was felt by all who were involved in the search that Pride and PC Sheargold's persistence and team work had proven vital, and had it not been for them, the girl would not have been found alive.

Above: Trakr, 1996
Right: Trakr and James at Ground Zero
© TeamTrakr Foundation

VALOUR

On 11 September 2001, the world witnessed the unfolding of events which would shake us to our very core. The 9/11 attacks will stand as one of the most horrific and disturbing acts of terrorism that the world has ever seen. In the aftermath of those attacks, amidst inconceivable conditions and horrors, the emergency services strove hour after hour, day after day, in the search for survivors.

Amidst the teams of search and rescue dogs, a German Shepherd named 'Trakr' worked tirelessly alongside his trusted handler James Symington, as they searched for survivors beneath the twisted rubble of the twin towers. Trakr's work rate was relentless. In an environment which is beyond all comprehension, he was required to walk across hot steel beams, as fires raged in pits many hundreds of feet below. Amidst the dense, acrid smoke, he braved perilous footing, and crawled through narrow tunnels of crumbling debris.

Never once did Trakr show fear, reluctance or a moment's hesitation. James says of his beloved dog: *'He simply forged ahead because of his remarkable valor and ability to sense the desperation around him.'* Trakr located many victims and he also located the last survivor who was buried beneath the rubble.

A tenacious worker, Trakr had already attained hero status during the 1990s, both as a police dog and as a search and rescue dog. His skill and determination in finding people and property were well renowned. Trakr was also well loved as a wonderful community service volunteer, being closely involved in charity work, and visiting children's schools, hospitals and organisations. He loved nothing better than having his belly rubbed and bringing a smile to the faces of the many disabled children he met. He was always instinctively gentle and brought great happiness wherever he went.

Following the 9/11 attacks, Trakr subsequently became an international hero. He was presented with a humanity service award by Dr Jane Goodall, United Nations 'Messenger of Peace', and he has been featured in books and magazines dedicated to the 9/11 attacks.

This very special dog lived with his devoted human companions, James Symington and his wife Angeline. In 2009 Trakr passed away peacefully at home at the age of 16, but his remarkable story did not leave this earth with his passing. He was named the 'World's most clone-worthy dog', before his death, and his DNA was used to clone five puppies. All of these puppies – Trustt, Prodigy, Solace, Valor and Dejavu – are now charged with carrying on Trakr's extraordinary legacy, under the watchful and loving eye of his lifelong handler and the Team Trakr Foundation.

'Cassie'

PATIENCE AND KINDNESS

Heroism comes in many forms. The huge acts of courage, and exhaustive lengths that the Shepherd will go to in order to reach his goal often lend themselves to awards and notoriety, although these are never asked for. But it is equally important never to forget those who go quietly about their daily lives, bringing love and pleasure to those who face difficulties in life. 'Cassie' is one such dog. She is to all who know her, an angel in canine form.

Undemanding, graceful and always ready to give affection, Cassie is a beautiful, black, long coated Shepherd, owned by Mrs Jillie Wheeler. Jillie became profoundly deaf following the death of her husband, and Cassie became 'her rock'. It was Jillie's love for her gentle dog, and the affection which was returned, which inspired Jillie to start fund raising. At the tender age of four months Cassie's fund-raising career began at a charity event where people were more than happy to make a donation in return for a cuddle with this delightful puppy.

Jillie and Cassie therefore began raising money with a 'Pay for a pat' box, whereby people could pay to stroke Cassie. Given her beauty, calmness and her extremely gentle nature, she and Jillie soon were raising large sums of money for those in need. Over £26,000 was raised for the Isle of Wight Earl Mountbatten Hospice, over £7,000 has been raised for Friends of the Animals, Battersea Dogs Home and the PDSA, and they have also raised £13,000 for a minibus for the Saturday Club for Deaf Children. To date, their efforts have accumulated over £45,000.

Cassie is also a registered Pets as Therapy (PAT) dog, and regularly visits local nursing homes to offer comfort and encouragement to elderly residents, and to aid in the recovery of stroke patients. The role of the PAT dog is an extraordinary one, and Cassie performs this role with quiet grace and affection.

In 2010 Cassie and Jillie were presented with the Isle of Wight Fundraising Award, and were presented with a Community Champion Award with a citation which reads:

'In recognition of the time you give to improve the quality of life for others'.

We are indebted to Cassie, and others like her, for the comfort and solace they bring to those in need.

The gentlest of dogs

PC Powell and 'Magnum'

COMMITMENT AND DETERMINATION

'Magnum' was PC Geoff Powell's first police dog. They were licensed in 1987 and the young Shepherd showed from the first day that he was a natural police dog, strong of character, keen, responsive and quick to learn. The course's trainer remarked that he was sure Magnum had 'read the manual'!

He was a big, black and gold long coat, with attitude and courage to burn. He and PC Powell formed a formidable and respected team in the years that they were together, both on the streets of Cambridgeshire and in terms of trials successes. Above all else, Magnum's great love was tracking. He routinely achieved long and complex tracks, in the 'golden days', before the helicopter, heat-seeking equipment, and the age of the mobile phone changed the regularity and success rates of this natural canine skill.

Magnum and PC Powell are admirably remembered for an arrest they made in 1992. In pursuit of a burglar, Magnum tracked across the Cambridgeshire countryside on a dark winter's night across dykes, ditches, and fields. The track criss-crossed a motorway and a lock on the river Nene, and wound its way through a long, pitch black railway tunnel. The suspect zig-zagged across the countryside in a vain attempt to throw Magnum from the scent. For four long hours, the pair tracked the burglar through the night until he was finally apprehended, complete with stolen jewellery.

Magnum and PC Powell were awarded a commendation and their Force's 'Dog Handler of the Year' award. They also were given the first 'Pride of Peterborough' award, and a citation from Eukanuba. The track was logged at the time as just over 11 miles and it is thought to be the longest ever successful track by a police dog and its handler in the UK.

What makes this achievement all the more remarkable and poignant was that Magnum was found to be lame the following day, and an injury was suspected. However, he had never wavered from the task. It was subsequently discovered that his lameness was not caused through injury. Tragically, this beautiful and gifted police dog was suffering from advanced bone cancer, and he had to be put to sleep shortly after.

Gamin and Officer Godefroid

LOYALTY

During the late 1950s tracker dogs were being used by the Algerian military to locate enemy troops that had managed to outwit security systems. One of the dogs utilised for this purpose was 'Gamin', the German Shepherd. Based at the military kennels at Beni-Messous, Algeria, Gamin was a remarkable working dog, but his days in service seemed numbered as he was immensely difficult to handle. A final attempt to pair him with a handler was made, and Officer Gilbert Godefroid formed a tight bond with the complex and hostile dog.

In late March 1958, a patrol of the 4th Hussars ran into a troop of around 200 men who had broken through the electrified fencing on the border with Tunisia. The troop escaped towards the scrubland. As reinforcements arrived and began searching the area, Officer Godefroid and Gamin were requested to assist.

In the early morning light, Gamin began to track without hesitation, leading his handler and the unit into the hills. Four hours later, they were still in full pursuit, despite the exhaustion of the regiment. Reinforcements arrived from the 1st Parachute Regiment, and the dog and handler continued to lead the way. After five hours of intense searching, they finally came across the troops in dense scrubland. Some thirty metres ahead of their own soldiers, Officer Godefroid was mortally wounded, and Gamin was badly injured with gunshot wounds.

Gamin dragged himself to his handler's side, licked his face and lay across his body. While the fighting ensued he never left his handler's side. He had led the regiment into battle, and they successfully eliminated the threat posed by the invading troops.

After the fighting was over, Gamin continued to guard the officer's body. It took six men with a tent sheet to overcome Gamin's protests, and he was taken back to camp for treatment for his wounds. He had been shot in the chest and the head, but nothing was going to prevent this loyal dog from remaining loyal to his master.

Gamin was awarded a police medal during a ceremony which honoured the memory of Officer Godefroid. Following the death of his handler, Gamin sadly lost his enthusiasm for work, and was granted a peaceful retirement at the Gramat police central kennels. He was to be given 'dutiful care until the day he dies'. Sadly Gamin passed away – some say of a broken heart – only two weeks after his arrival. His ashes are kept at Gramat, and a monument has been erected to his memory.

'Timber'

LOVE

'Timber' was a long coated, blue sable Shepherd, who spent many years beside me at a children's home, where I worked as the Assistant Manager. I lived-in for much of the time, and was fortunate to be given special permission to have Timber with me. Most of the children that our staff team looked after had suffered unspeakable trauma, and found it desperately painful to make connections with adults as a direct consequence. Timber helped bridge that gap. His steady, gentle approach to each child in turmoil was consistent and measured, and he made a difference which would be impossible to explain in words. He offered unconditional love and kindness in abundance to those children who craved affection, but who simply could not bear to receive this from another human being. Whilst they learned how to build trust in adults again, Timber's presence was invaluable beyond measure.

At times, a child's inner chaos would boil to the surface with aggression and distress. Timber remained the same calm presence, always ready to lie down nearby, where he could be hugged or cried upon. He also brought fun and games to daily life in the home, and the children were fascinated by his unquestioned obedience to them all. His love of playing hide and seek with the residents was legendary, and if ever he was missing, you could guarantee that he was with a youngster who was having a bad day, offering quiet and undemanding company. He was adored by every child that he ever encountered.

"Somewhere in a different world, my friend now walks ... steady on velvet paws.
A tender-hearted gentleman, whose warm and honest eyes would hold my gaze:

Never with threat.
Never with defiance.
But with wisdom, and serenity, and implicit trust.

Out on the breeze, he dances with effortless grace and untamed power,
And I am lost to think that he alone, loved my every move.

Or perhaps he's somewhere close by?
But I'm deprived to touch his noble head,
Or to see his smiling, gentle face as he bounds to greet me.

Walk by my side, dearest friend.
Stay close while I walk this earth without you,
And be there to greet me, when my time here is done."

I have been fortunate in spending an almost unbroken fifty years with German Shepherds in my life, and have witnessed endless love for this wonderful breed.

Over the years, I have become aware of how complex the breed is in its requirements, both physically and mentally. I am not a 'breed specialist', but a lifetime spent with the Shepherd has now combined with my love of writing, and I hope that the lengths which I have gone to in order to collate a wide range of information, will enable this book to achieve its aims. (It has been produced in part, with a hope that year by year, donations can be made to various canine causes. See www.thegsd-apassionforlife.co.uk)

Writing about the care of the dog is fraught with particular difficulties, as everyone involved in the dog world has their own opinion about each issue! I have attempted to offer a balanced approach, so that the reader can make important decisions for themselves about the care of their beloved canine companion. I have been extraordinarily lucky in terms of the level of expertise afforded to me for this project. Knowledge and time have been offered with great generosity of spirit.

Research into all areas of canine care will continue to develop as the years progress, and 'fashions' will come and go. But one thing will never alter: we will continue to be in awe of a dog that assists some of our most vulnerable members of society, yet whose temperament and intelligence is also channelled into acts of immeasurable courage. He has become a symbol of all that is strong and honest – an unequalled working dog and our truest friend.

I hope you will feel that I have done him justice.

Kate Powell

Index